PSYCHOLOGY AND THE

PROMETHEAN WILL

Psychology and the Promethean Will

A Constructive Study of the Acute Common Problem of Education, Medicine and Religion

By

William H. Sheldon, Ph.D., M.D.
Formerly Assistant Professor of Psychology in the University of Chicago

HARPER & BROTHERS PUBLISHERS

NEW YORK AND LONDON

PSYCHOLOGY AND THE PROMETHEAN WILL

D-W

CONTENTS

PREFACE

THIS book as a whole is an introduction to a point of view in psychological medicine. In short here are some fragments of the literary trail of a psychologist bent upon devoting the art and techniques of the psychological profession primarily to sustaining what seems to be the *essential* function of both the priest or minister, and the educator, namely the prevention of the tragedy of the divided soul. There appears to be eternal conflict in human life between two elemental wishes; a wish to harness and restrain, and a wish freely to express the direct desires of the biological self. When the former wish is pathologically dominant a condition of *repression* is said to exist. This has been widely written about in the popular and unpopular literature of the day. But when the latter wish is pathologically dominant the far more dangerous condition of *overstimulation* occurs. Against this evil we have not been so effectively warned, although the condition is outstandingly characteristic of our generation throughout all Western society. Where overstimulation occurs the soul is sooner or later destroyed, and the very brain then dies back to a fraction of its activity span. Under such circumstances men must fall back for their glorious adventure upon war, upon possessiveness, upon sexuality, and upon the lust to dominate each other.

Historically there are two essentially different methods by which ameliorative minds have sought to prevent the tragedy of the divided soul. One is the theological and philosophical method of seeking to embrace and comprehend the rational significance of the outer universe as a whole. The other is the clinical or face to face method of searching the inner self for the key to a pattern of emotional integrity and oneness of purpose. This is the method of the confessional, and more recently the method of medical psychology. Each method has been practised, and abused, both in the name of religion and in the name of psychology. Each is extremely dangerous in the hands of unchastened and unmellow priests, who abound in psychology and medicine as well as in religion. Yet in the hands of wise and inspired men, whatever labels are worn, these two approaches to human conflict remain pregnant with hope, and each is vital or complemental to the other. It has therefore seemed wise to devote this introductory volume largely to the task of clearing the relationship between these two human attempts to meet what may be the only really important problem in the affairs of men.

I cannot too often or too vigorously emphasize that the term *religion* is used throughout in a psychological, not in a theological sense. Theologies like nations, are born, live for a time, and die away; yet religious consciousness remains as native to human life as sexual consciousness or hunger consciousness. Emotional awareness of relationships in the universe which lie beyond the clear knowledge of the present point in time, constitutes religious consciousness. From the point of view of sustained happiness this is by far the most vital and significant area of awareness, but we have lacked even the rudiments of an intellectually respectable psychology attuned to the contemplation of this side of the mind. We are afraid of this area of thought. The whole Western world has recoiled in mortal fear from the contemplation of its own soul, as once it recoiled from sexual reality, and as remoter ancestors unquestionably must have recoiled from the thought of hunger and from the contemplation of their own possible starvation. Yet as one who fears to fall when crossing a stream, tends to grow dizzy and loses his balance, so our mortal fear concerning the most vital element of consciousness leads inevitably to the catastrophe of its loss.

This repressed fear of loss of the soul I have sometimes called the *animectomy complex* in good-natured appreciation of the Freudians' utterly delightful *castration complex, Oedipus complex* and the like. The implication reflects well the essential difference between the Freudian position and my own, which is in this respect close to Jung's psychological outlook. I think that the roots of much emotional bafflement go back to sexual frustration; and also to social and to economic frustration. All of these three elemental philosophic materialisms carry wisdom, and I am sure that there have been many periods in human history when one or the other of them carried the central or most pertinent lesson of the age. Yet I think that the truly crucial problem of today does not lie in any of them, but in the fourth area or fourth panel of human consciousness; namely, in that area pertaining to purposive orientation in time. In short, however involved and perplexing our economic, political and sexual affairs may on the surface appear to be, I am convinced that the really acute *educational* problem of the day lies far deeper than these matters reach.

Psychologists have up to the present been of little help in the matter. Psychology, purporting to become the scientific study of human consciousness, has perhaps naturally manifested the animectomy complex more painfully than any other profession. For years psychologists have shouted down the soul with an intensity which recalls the puritan shouting down his sexual consciousness. But now we begin to feel the imperative need of a psychology which can face this fourth area of the mind. This we need even more than we need economic, political and sexual wisdom. It is with the description of the foundations of such a psychology that this study is concerned.

The leisure for writing this book has been made available to the writer through The National Council On Religion In Higher Education. For helpful and critical suggestions there is an especial debt to Dr. Jung of Zürich, and to Mr. Gerald Heard of London. The personal debt is very great to Mr.

and Mrs. Leonard Elmhirst of Dartington, England, where the book was written.

W. H. S.

437 West 59th Street
New York City
January 1, 1936

Chapter One

INTRODUCTION.
THE COMMON PROBLEM

"What is needed is continuous education which lasts all through life."

—CHARLES W. ELIOT

Chapter One

INTRODUCTION. THE COMMON PROBLEM

1. THE DYING BACK OF THE BRAIN

WILLIAM JAMES used to suggest that even the maturest minds may not yet have developed a tenth of the functional possibilities of the great human forebrain, and later psychologists[1] have shown that *if once the habit and the desire are established*, expanding horizons and the eager pursuit of knowledge may as readily characterize the later as the earlier decades of a life. Yet mental growth is still so rare in the later decades that a matured intellect remains for most people an abnormal conception. The days of youth teem with fragments of living knowledge; with dawning philosophies; morning dreams; plans. But the human mind at forty is commonly vulgar, smug, deadened, and wastes its hours. Everywhere adult brains seem to resemble blighted trees that have died in the upper branches, but yet cling to a struggling green wisp of life about the lower trunk.[2]

There are a few who go on toward full mental growth. At twenty these cannot ordinarily be distinguished from other young men and women, except that they are perhaps a little more shy, less certain of themselves, and often seem young and underdeveloped for their age. Even at twenty-five no safe prediction can be made; but usually at thirty-five it can be gathered from half a dozen sentences that here is a mind still

[1] Notably E. L. Thorndike in his *Adult Learning*.

[2] There is not yet any demonstrable anatomical evidence of this kind of degenerative process in the brain. The microscope has not revealed differences between a well-used and an ill-used brain, but that some sort of retrogressive change does go on in relatively inactive cortical cells can hardly be doubted. The atrophy of disuse is readily enough demonstrated in other bodily tissues.

growing. Interests are expanding, the philosophy is tentative and sensitive, there is an eagerness for new knowledge, there are visions, dreams, impersonal enthusiasms. Personalities showing these qualities at thirty-five generally continue their growth throughout the second half of life, not infrequently gathering headway and strength even in the final decade. For such individuals a year in the fifties or sixties is worth in intrinsic feeling value far more than a year of youth, when conflicting life desires were still altogether at loggerheads and the future was a jagged welter of hopes and fears. These few live more for the second than for the first half of life. They are happier and stronger in old age than in youth. Their lives suggest the uneasy intuition that where youth is a disproportionately happy period, life is perhaps a great failure.

Why only so few reach full human consciousness, while thousands of apparently normal personalities all around them abruptly stop growing and go to seed in the second, third, or fourth decade, is beginning to loom as the most important question in human affairs. The observant student of life watches a launching into the world of wave upon wave of young human beings, each in a little flare of heroic parental sacrifice; he follows the childhood years as emerging minds take hold of the world with eager exhilaration; sees the mental flame burn brightly through early youth; feels it flicker a little at about the time of college; and then at last he must stand by helplessly while the young mind struggles in little tragic fits and starts as if caught in the grip of an unseen suffocating force, only to die back in the end to the dull smudge of a coal that did not catch.

The brain seems to develop functionally only to a point just beyond the maintenance of an existence, then hesitates a little, and appears to settle back to a level. It is as if a strong runner were to start a race at his best speed, but upon looking about and finding that all the other runners seem crippled or sick, or carry heavy burdens, hesitates for a little and then drops back to the common pace, only to find after a time that now he too can only crawl. One mind develops where many merely adapt to circumstance. This is the tragedy of the waste of brain.

2. THE VOICE OF PROMETHEUS

Yet somewhere in the deeper strata of human awareness a voice persists which continually whispers, "No, this is not good enough, there is somewhere something better." At moments there comes to perhaps every human being a well-nigh painful sense of the nearness of richer and broader human happiness. We deeply feel that some relentless, invisible, yet not quite insurmountable barrier bars the way to an inexpressibly better life. The clearness and vividness of this sense of the better possibility must vary within extremely wide limits in different minds; in some it is a passing, momentary, rare and quite unimportant mood; in some it never breaks through at all to full consciousness. But in a few minds it becomes a dominant mood, and a friend I once knew used to refer to this mood as the hour of the splendid urge. Another always calls it the voice of Prometheus, and minds in which it is dominant he calls Promethean minds.

It is the voice of Prometheus that so often dies away during early middle age, and this book is in a sense the soliloquy of a psychologist who has found the study of the Promethean voice a supremely alluring hobby. It is an interest which leads far afield, to the exploration of many walks of life in strange corners of human society, for the dominantly Promethean personality is rare, and is often difficult to recognize. An especially arduous element in such an interest lies in the fact that it carries one unavoidably across three distinct though closely related fields of systematic human inquiry, namely the fields of psychology, religion, and medicine. For the dying away of the Promethean voice presents a problem too difficult for any one of these three professions ever to handle alone. If this problem is to be met, it will be met by minds capable of coördinating psychological, religious, and medical energies.

Psychology is concerned with developing insight into the nature of the mind; religion has to do with steering the mind's development, wisely or unwisely, along particular patterned channels; and the study of medicine necessarily must underlie both psychology and religion, for without the background of an intimate and clinical familiarity with the personality as a whole, in its basic physical problems and fears and hopes, psychology and religion tend to become but dissociated, superficial conceits.

He who would seek to know the Promethean vision must learn to think in the grooves and patterns of these three traditional disciplines through which Promethean men and women have tried to meddle with human destiny, thereby to surmount the barrier which seems to block fulfillment of the ancient dream of joining the gods. Yet this alone is not enough. The seeker of Prometheus must also learn to live widely in the world with human heart and searching eyes. He must know the eddies and the back currents of life; must feel it all, and love it, if he would throw light upon the Promethean wish, and upon the conflict with the antithesis of that wish which causes the dying back of the brain. Only when rich, warm, and eager personalities shall as psychologists find the will to mold their intellects in a long and patient discipline, will psychology emerge from academic isolation on the one hand, and from therapeutic cultism on the other. It will take a psychology wise both in academic abstraction and in the earthy experience of life to save the aging human personality from its fatal false love of the things of youth. Yet only such a psychology can prevent the dying back of the brain.

Chapter Two

THE PSYCHOLOGICAL MEANING OF CONFLICT

The dying back of the brain is but one response to human unhappiness, and the first cause of unhappiness lies always in an inadequate philosophy of conflict. It is not conflict itself, however, but failure of the mind to make peace with the principle of conflict, that leads to frustration and to the wish for war. In building a philosophy of conflict it is well to avoid the dangerous and misleading concept, "the unconscious." Conflict occurs not in the unconscious, but in all of the dimensions of consciousness.

Chapter Two

THE PSYCHOLOGICAL MEANING OF CONFLICT

3. HAPPINESS AND THE NATURE OF WAR

HAPPINESS is essentially a state of going somewhere, wholeheartedly, one-directionally, without regret or reservation. Under the stress of prolonged internal or external conflict, men have periodically resorted to extreme measures in order to create conditions favorable to a state of one-directional movement. Deep in the remoter layers of human consciousness, as every observant psychologist knows, there remains for this reason a dear love of war. For in the passion of one intense purpose all of the conflicts of a life can be swept away like clouds before the wind. Then even in heroic ecstasy I cannot be absurd, or be laughed at. It is safe and pleasant at last to be caught serious. All *right* creatures are straining together in the same direction. The faces to the right and the left, in front and behind, all carry a noble common purpose. And back at the seat of life, at home, every fiber of every heart is straining to a common end.

I am *right*, and with this thought there surges through my whole being the mystic certainty of the oneness and the meaning of life. The very muscles of biting tingle with it; it suffuses down the spine, out across the shoulders, and through all of my body. I am master of my whole self and of all those conflicting, earth-binding instinctive desires that have hampered and mocked and bullied my soul, and have robbed me of my rightful place among the gods—master at last of the mortal lusts and fears that would have kept me dust. In war I am lifted to a higher plane, and I feel the heroic ecstasy that is the heritage of the brave. Even in mortal agony I breathe through the nostrils of the eternal hero, and all perspectives are romance-tinted. Pain can be laughed at and death is only an incident.

War is not essentially a rational problem. Whoever would abolish it must go deeper than the penetration of argument and conscious resolution. It is caused by hate, but it cannot be cured by resolving to love. It is caused by greed and the lust for temporal power, but it cannot be cured by inflating the dollar or by rationalizing economics. It is caused by group arrogance, but it cannot be cured by the League of Nations. It is caused by the pressure of overbreeding in the lower levels of all populations, but it cannot be cured by birth control. It is caused by the mutual intolerance of conflicting theologies, yet theologies like war itself are but expressions of the wish to escape from doubt and conflict. Whoever would abolish war must learn to deal with inner and with outer conflict concurrently. To do this he must master a psychological outlook and an application of it which will steer his own mind between the Scylla of *error*, which is prematurely resolved conflict, and the Charybdis of *frustration*, which is conflict frozen against itself.

There are cheaper ways than war by which human beings find the experience of one-directional movement. Children know how to do it in a hundred ways, for their younger imaginations are not blunted and broken upon the hard rocks of unaccepted reality. Their emotion is more free from immediate conflict, and therefore their imagination is creative, within the limits of its lesser intellectual span. Fully adult minds know how to do it in a thousand ways, for their richer and more extensive imaginations have met and made peace with reality. They have not only reclaimed the creative imagination of childhood, but have married it to understanding and have chastened it with reality. Such minds are free. In the later decades of life they grow to a power and a delight which may altogether transcend the more physically conditioned ecstasies of youth. They avoid the common snares which reduce most human minds to the war-susceptible level, and having had the courage to grow up, they become the true giants of the earth. For them the second half of life is not only the better half, but it is also the happier half. In old age they love children, but they do not spend the declining decades in unrequited love for the child within themselves. Whoever would abolish war must go to school, and must wander with searching eyes out into the world, until he learns how it is that fully adult minds come into being, and why they are so few. He then will have taken the most important step toward becoming a psychologist.

Happiness may be defined as a condition of moving successfully toward a difficult or receding objective. The secret of planning a happy life lies in the selection of a general objective which will extend the potentialities of a personality to their fullest, yet never recede so far into the western horizon as to lie beyond the reach of reasonably imagined ultimate fulfillment. For any healthy person with available educational opportunities, such a goal lies within the reach of imagination in the concept of fully adult understanding, that is to say, in the completest possible human understanding of life. But *understanding* is built necessitously upon *feeling.* It rises from feeling as a tree rises from the earth, and when feeling and knowing become far separated in consciousness, both tend to wither and atrophy, and the mind settles back, like a dying fire. The forces at work in human life which tend to dissociate these two cardinal elements of consciousness collectively constitute the cause of the functional withering of brains. Their roots lie, not in conflict itself, but rather in false human conceptions of the nature of conflict, and in unnecessary fear of it. It must therefore be the first function of psychology, as I use that term, to allay these vague, irrational fears, especially in a time when the world is socially crowded and hence full of both internal and external conflict.

4. CONFLICT, AND "THE UNCONSCIOUS"

One morning not long ago, on a university campus, the concrete walk seemed quite deserted except for a brisk-tailed gray squirrel, and one of those ginger-walking, expensive-looking co-eds that may often be seen on college campuses. The co-ed and the squirrel had met face to face under an oak tree and each had stopped to survey the other inquiringly; the one frisking his tail and the other making funny little baby talk mouth noises, each in a half friendly, half suspicious attitude. After a brief period of preliminary overture, the co-ed reached into her pocket and pulled out a peanut, holding it out very tentatively toward the squirrel. The latter frisked his tail emphatically and advanced in little hops to within about a yard of the co-ed. From a hundred feet away it could now be observed that both principals were in a state of some nervous tension. Suddenly the squirrel in a great surge of courage leaped half way across the intervening distance, but just as he seemed within striking distance of his objective, both he and the co-ed appeared to lose courage simultaneously. The co-ed made a funny noise as if stung by a bee, at the same instant leaping backward, while the squirrel whirled in mid-air and dashed a dozen feet to the rear, chattering as if he thought the devil was after him. Both soon pulled themselves together however, and the game began all over again, the co-ed making baby noises and wiggling the peanut, while the squirrel made short, jerky little dashes forward and backward, and wiggled his tail. But whenever the distance between them became less than a yard, both grew very nervous, and began little incipient movements of sudden retreat. This alternation of the dominance of incompatible desires might have gone on indefinitely had not the co-ed finally, by accident or intent, dropped the peanut, whereupon both peanut and squirrel disappeared like a flash into the tree.

Such a homely scene illustrates some of the essential characteristics of conflict, and opens the way to a preliminary definition. *Conflict may be defined as a state in which an individual is impelled toward two or more incompatible objectives, between which he has been unable to effect a whole-minded choice.* This is a simple statement, yet not very full of meaning as it stands, and it may pay to look for a moment in perspective down into the biological mechanisms of life to see if these will not put more meaning into the idea of conflict.

We live in a universe which maintains its integrity and character through the nice balancing of opposed forces. In a physical and chemical sense, and in a biological sense, conflict is simply opposition of forces, and is everywhere manifest in all things. Energy as we know it appears to be always the manifestation of a movement from some disequilibration or imperfect opposition of forces, toward equilibration or perfectly balanced opposition. This "principle of the opposites" is illustrated clearly in the physiological foundations of life, and those well informed or uninterested in biology may skip and forgive a brief digression into that field.

In the human body the skeletal muscles are arranged in opposed groups or systems so that all movement involves not only the activation of the contracting group, but the simultaneous inhibition or relaxation of the opposing group. In the central nervous system the higher centers of the forebrain exercise a general inhibitory control over the lower nerve centers, and if the influence of the brain is suddenly removed from the lower centers, as in the case of a decerebrate animal, the whole skeletal musculature goes at once into sharp general contraction. With the higher centers intact the muscular system may be compared to a great steel trap which is set, and in balance; but with these centers cut off, it is as if the trap were sprung and now tightly contracted against itself, incapable of further action. This is the phenomenon seen in post-mortem rigidity, when the skeletal muscles contract strongly after death and remain so until their available fuel supply is used up. The higher centers have the function of holding in equilibrium the antagonistic energy potentials which, when so controlled, give the organism the power of *tentative* behavior, which is the foundation of mind.

Besides the central nervous system, which is composed of the brain and spinal cord together with their peripheral connections, there is in the human body another, simpler, and biologically more vital series of nerve centers. These constitute the *autonomic nervous* system, which is really a system of motor relays connecting and associating the *visceral* structures of the body with the central nervous system. That is, it has to do with the innervation of the digestive, circulatory, respiratory, reproductive, eliminative, and glandular structures. Structurally it is a series of nerve centers lying outside and for the most part ventral to the axis of the spinal cord. There are three fairly distinct divisions: an upper, *cranial* segment, a lower, *sacral* segment, and a more extensive intermediate section called the *thoracico-lumbar* segment. The cranial and sacral segments carry essentially the same general function and are usually referred to as the cranio-sacral or C-S element. The thoracico-lumbar segment, which as a unit carries an opposed function, may be called the T-L element.

The sharp functional antagonism that exists between these two elements of the autonomic nervous system gives the clearest picture that we have, of the physiological basis of conflict. In general, every internal organ has a double autonomic innervation, receiving fibers from each of the two autonomic elements. Thus the T-L relaxes the digestive musculature and constricts the blood vessels of the digestive system; the C-S stimulates the digestive muscles and generally augments the tone of the whole system. The

T-L inhibits or paralyzes sexual and eliminative activities; the C-S stimulates and heightens them. The T-L accelerates the heart; the C-S (vagus nerve) slows it, or quiets it. The T-L dilates the pupil of the eye; the C-S constricts it.

The C-S mechanism is seen to be concerned with reactions which are essentially expansive, expressive, biologically positive, pleasant. It augments appetite, digestive and sexual, and prepares the organism for seeking, expansive behavior which leads directly to its biological fulfillment, both individual and racial. The T-L mechanism brings about activity of a very different nature. Its impulses halt the digestive and sexual machinery by paralyzing its muscles and constricting its blood supply, thus shunting the main flow of blood to the skeletal muscles, to the brain, and to the skin, where the long-distance sense organs are. In short the T-L element prepares the body for emergency and defense. The dominant feeling tone of C-S activity is pleasant and expansive, while that of T-L activity is unpleasant and contractual and produces the emotional patterns of alarm, anger, fear, or desperation.

It is apparently the function of the C-S element to promote direct, immediate biological fulfillment—positive movement toward a goal; and the T-L element promotes a conserving, protective, defensive counter-movement which prevents the organism from self-destruction in the headlong pursuit of its goals. Without this balancing function, human life would presumably dash itself to pieces against its world as a moth against a light. Yet in this basic antagonism between expressive and inhibitory behavior lies the ultimate source of the great perplexities of human consciousness, and new religions or new psychologies can generally be shown to constitute at bottom a compensatory pendulum swing of emphasis from one to the other of these two basic attitudes.[1]

[1] Thus the cardinal virtues of the original Christianity were inhibitory, self-disciplinary virtues: poverty, chastity, and obedience. These virtues are clearly enough reactionary from the Dionysian or Bacchanalian spirit

The physiological importance of the basic antithesis grows more evident if it is borne in mind that these nerve centers directly controlling the vital organs represent the oldest, most universal portion of the nervous system. It is probable that what neurologists call the central nervous system really constitutes an evolved appendage growth, elaborated from older structures which very likely resembled the present autonomic structures.[2] Giving rise as it does to all of what we now consider the higher functions of life, the forebrain must have developed in the first place as a subsidiary "organ of alternative selection" in the service of the two basic and antagonistic tissue needs which are now seen most clearly down at the simpler autonomic level.

Neuro-physiology then lends two fairly definite analogies, at least, in the way of stuff from which to try to visualize a conception of human conflict. These are (1) the idea of a very fundamental antithesis which seems to lie at the bottom of all human motivation, and is represented in the whole bodily structure; and (2) the idea of inhibition as a function which higher, complex brain centers exercise over lower, less complex neural arcs. For those who love to think in terms of form and structure rather than in words, these two elementary biological facts provide a certain framework for visualizing conflict in two dimensions; a right and left dimension with a positive and negative pole,[3] and an up and down dimension with flexion and extension reflexes at the

---

of self-expressiveness which dominated the pre-Christian Roman period and had in turn constituted a reaction from older, distinctly disciplinary religious practices. Similarly in modern times, it is not difficult to perceive the reactionary nature of the new Freudian religion of self-expressiveness, with its intense hatred of the Christian cardinal virtues.

[2] For a fruitful and thought-provoking elaboration of this hypothesis, see E. J. Kempf's monograph, *The Autonomic Nervous System and the Personality.*

[3] That is, a pole of seeking, expansive behavior, and an opposite pole of contractual, avoidance behavior.

bottom and the relative and the absolute at the top.[4] The depth dimension and the time dimension are still needed to render conflict a comprehensible, concomitant function of natural conscious life. The time dimension we shall consider in later chapters,[5] but concerning the depth dimension some preliminary contemplation will perhaps be worth while.

Psychoanalysts speak of finding conflict in the *unconscious*, and several systems of procedure have been elaborated by which patients are assisted to recall and bring up to the light of clear consciousness events and desires long since apparently forgotten and buried deep in the past. There are quite a number of these devices in use. Here half a dozen may be briefly mentioned.

(1) The method of systematic discussion of the *readily available conscious associational content* of a mind. The value of this procedure lies in the plan of it, and in the wisdom and maturity and insight of the consultant. All of the other devices may be considered as merely aids and special supports to this general inquiry into a personality. (2) In some instances at least it is possible to use the material of *dreams* as a starting point from which to reconstruct a picture of the underlying desires and of the conflicting trends of a personality in clearer perspective than would be possible with only the material of full consciousness. The same purpose has been served (3) by using a series of words as controlled stimuli as in the *word association tests* of Jung; and

[4] At the bottom, simple reflex activity, mediated through the spinal cord; at the top, the highest reaches of conceptual thought, involving the full play of the forebrain.

[5] In the sense that religion is concerned with maintaining orientation in time, the religious function may be defined epigrammatically as the *time-conditioning* element of consciousness. A particular religion or religious belief is, I should say, simply a response of the human mind to its realization of the time dimension of conflict. A religion is then only as good or bad as the mind which formulated it, and the *function* of religion becomes a legitimate branch of social psychology.

(4) through analysis of the material of *phantasies and day dreams.*

(5) It is a very common observation that when a person who has long been away returns to visit the place of his childhood, he is often astonished to find how familiar things seem, and how readily names, faces, and anecdotes come back to memory. On the day before returning he perhaps could not have recalled the names of half a dozen inhabitants, but upon seeing these formerly familiar faces the names flash again into consciousness. Thus by *returning with a patient to the actual scene of his early childhood* I have in my own practice frequently found it possible to pick up very essential clues to the underlying motivation of a perplexed mind. (6) *Aesthetic preferences* in music, in art, in the world of nature, in voices, various personal tastes, and especially an analysis of the selection of friends—all of these are at times extremely useful devices for quickly reaching the deeper levels of consciousness.

The last five are methods of penetrating into those characteristics of a mind which do not come readily into the conscious focus. They are devices for going *deeper* into a mind. But in *naming* these deeper areas it is well to remember that there is nothing in human life so dangerous as words. At any given moment in history there are always a few especially dangerous, rampant, magic words. Words are like shifting rocks in the channel of thought, and a whole civilization can founder and wreck itself on one of them. Such a magic word is the term *the unconscious,* and it must be approached with great caution. The most careful students of psychology do not find it necessary to use this term at all, for they believe that the phenomena to which it refers can be more accurately described in terms which avoid the dichotomy which the term implies. There has emerged a popular notion of the unconscious as a sort of "other mind" or place where forgotten things are stored and get into mysterious relations with each other, even evolving a detailed code language or symbolism of their own, whereby they succeed in emerging into consciousness again, on masquerade. In all this there is a certain amount of truth, and a vast amount of dangerous psycho-religious cultism.

At a given moment the clear conscious content of a mind is comparable to a point of light in a great surrounding darkness. It is as if consciousness were a finely focused searchlight, sweeping continually across the night landscape; but it is a landscape with which a person has been somewhat acquainted in days of the past, and as the light stops for an instant upon some object or face or even upon a blade of grass, the darkness falls back a little and the thing is seen as in a familiar setting, related to other things, some of which can also be seen, certain ones clearly and certain ones only in vague suggestive outline. At times the darkness falls back abruptly quite a long way, and the mind seems to sweep rapidly across a wide sector of related things. These times are moments of insight, of inspiration, or of sudden apprehension of meaning. Frequently some little constellation of recalled experience flashes through the focus, and there is the vague feeling of having felt this, or seen it before, though the wider setting cannot be summoned. Clearly it is this wider setting as a whole, this system of conscious associations which have existed, and many of which will exist again in the stream of consciousness, that is referred to as the unconscious. There is no doubt of its importance in psychology. The question is simply one of how best to describe it.

The meaningfulness of the idea of the unconscious rests upon the extent to which a person has been able to think his way through to a *perspective* concerning these phenomena of relatively remote awareness which collectively have been referred to by that term. Whatever else may be true of consciousness it is normally a system, a oneness and not a twoness. It consists of a relative clearness and unclearness, with no separating absolute differential. There are meanings of which we become sharply and repetitively aware; and there are vague, distant, dim, deep-lying meanings which come into consciousness rarely, or perhaps never have reached the clear awareness focus at all. There are intermediate associations of every degree of clearness and frequency. Further, there are tremendous differences in individual minds. Some persons are relatively very familiar with their own deeper levels of consciousness, that is, they are systematically introspective; while others live chiefly at the surface, as it were, and are dominantly occupied with external relationships, a fact which led Jung and his followers to set up as a working hypothesis a dichotomy of *introvert* and *extravert* types.

By using the term *the* unconscious we force ourselves into the position of referring to much that goes on in a mind as unconscious consciousness, a logical absurdity which has caused many psychologists to shy off altogether from studying the deeper levels of the mind, and to label such a study charlatan or "unscientific." Thus when a student in psychology at a famous English university asked his instructor to explain what is meant by the unconscious, he was told not to worry about it; that since it is not a scientifically valid concept, it has no importance. This instructor was reacting to the danger of the magic word by avoiding altogether one of the most essential of psychological concepts.

Yet there was a certain wisdom in his academic cautiousness. It is indeed a crime against human understanding to use a term which obscures meaning if there is any possible way of expressing the thought in less equivocal language, though the medical profession and many psychiatrists claim exemption from this important moral law on the ground that patients do not always know what is good for them, and on the further ground that there is an element of suggestion in medical therapy. Therefore prescriptions in bad Latin are better than prescriptions in good English, and the worse the handwriting the better the prescription. It is from minds trained in this sort of outlook, and unchastened by psychological discipline in accurate, reverent handling of the tools of thought, that such words as *the unconscious, libido, ego, id, superego, Oedipus complex,* and the like have crept into the common language channels. Translated and reduced to a becomingly humble simplicity, all of these terms refer to simple psychological concepts, some of them to useful ones. But in the mouths of unchastened persons they become dangerous magic words, and their usefulness, if any at all, rests upon uncritical suggestibility on the part of the patient. Lovers of simplicity and truth do not hide their light of wisdom behind mystery-deepening terms.

One of the profoundest wisdoms that human beings can learn lies in a reverence for words. Our fathers used to teach children a healthy respect for loaded guns. We, the children, must teach a deep respect for loaded words. The deeper, remoter levels of consciousness may be adequately described and clinically studied without using such a term as the unconscious to refer to what is actually an element of consciousness. It is more meaningful and far less presumptuous and misleading to refer simply to the deeper, remote levels, or if one prefers, to the depth dimension, of consciousness. It is too easy to found dangerous theologies upon the concept of an absolute unconscious.

The Goal of Education Must Be Toleration, Not Resolution of Conflict

Conflict is a natural concomitant of mental life, occurring like consciousness itself *in a depth dimension,* not "in the unconscious." It is universal, inescapable, and the function of the student of mind must be to comprehend and control, rather than to try to eliminate it. Human conflict is only a special instance of universal equilibration or opposition of forces in the world. It is through harnessing this equilibration process, that is, through *tentative* mental problem solving and through intellectual toleration of conflict, that the mind is able to maintain its balance at a point far removed from the safe earth. In nature all forces tend to move toward a state of rest, and the forces which contribute to human consciousness are probably no exception in the end; yet the life course of a mind at its best may be visioned as a flare of energy which rises to a height and widens a little the outer horizon of human consciousness, as the brightening reflection from a fire widens the circle of clear vision into the night.

Conflict is infinitely deeper and more universal than human consciousness. Only in a mentality wholly omniscient and wholly omnipotent could conflict come to an end. But in such a consciousness the dynamic process of life as we know it would also be at an end; for thought, having emerged entirely from the problems producing it, would of its own inertia cease to take place. With all of the problems dead there could be no further stimulation to consciousness.

The maturest minds are mature not because they have eliminated conflict but because they have elevated it to intellectual levels. At these higher levels conflict becomes tolerance, suspended judgment, the back and forth play of ideas. It becomes intellectual *play*, and hence a source of mental delight. But at deeper levels of consciousness conflict seems to mean not the play of ideas but a heavier, slower, and more turgid trending of energies. It is when opposing tendencies of a personality settle into this deeper, loggerheads opposition in the remoter levels of consciousness that conflict changes over to pathology, and in the end to the phenomena of frustration. The human problem of conflict does not lie in resolution, but in comprehension and toleration of it.

In the earlier history of the human mind, conflict was chiefly externalized, arising more from clash with the will of other animals and with what men personified as the diverse wills of the elements, than from the clash of socially conditioned wishes. Now in the face of enormous biological and psychological increase in human population, consciousness has of necessity become progressively more dominated by problems of social inter-relation. Transportation and communication devices have so contracted the world that *psychologically* population has increased perhaps many hundredfold within two or three generations. Thus the present acute pathological manifestations of conflict become in a certain practical sense suddenly emerging perplexities of human life. Unmistakably we are swamping our children, and for that matter ourselves, with overstimulation. This throws a terrific strain upon the orientational influences[6] of society, for to maintain an orientation in the face of overstimulation is like trying to remember a half-learned poem in the midst of a bombardment. Yet the essential problems of civilization[7] are clearly orientational problems, and therefore a psychology

[6] By orientational influences I mean those influences which are concerned mainly with the *direction of development* of human thought and hope; in short with formulating the conscious purposes of life. This is really a matter of maintaining orientation in time (see p. 37). Theoretically the religious institutions control this most vital of all human mental functions. In the long run the idea of religion and the idea of orientation doubtless are pretty nearly synonymous. Yet religion is a human function and human minds are fallible. There are consequently times when the *institutions* of religion run amuck as it were, lose the trail, and are left behind. We are living in such a period now, and consequently the function of orientation has gone over diffusely into lay educational, into psychological, and even into psychiatric channels, not to mention hundreds of cults and isms of many sorts. We must avoid being caught in the quibble as to whether or not this function should still be called religious, and must proceed instead to develop a psychology adequate to carry the function.

[7] From the standpoint of the immediate needs of individuals one might agree with Marx and with modern communists that economic needs come before orientational ones; or with Adler that the urge to social power may be paramount in the motivational hierarchy; or even perhaps with Freud that sexuality is the deepest and most pervasive motive. But the first need of *civilization* is that of a cohesive or coördinative principle strong enough to overshadow and redirect these elemental human desires arising from individual biological need.

effectively pertinent to the modern need, that is to say, an effective *social* psychology, must lay its primary emphasis upon the orientational rather than upon the sexual, economic, or social-dominance cravings of human beings.

Civilization may be defined in one sense as the intellectualization of conflict, and there is a certain quality of buoyancy and toleration of uncertainty that marks the truly civilized character. Yet the quest for certainty at low levels of human understanding everywhere blocks the development of this quality. The human mind is still a thing of very poor toleration of doubt. In past generations individuals who have overcome the grovelling love of certainty, and have flowered in a magnificent expansion of speculative uncertainty, have almost invariably done so under the hatred and persecution of religious institutions. But the traditional intolerance of religion for critical thought, and that of critical thinkers for religion, may be only special instances of the intolerance of immature human beings for conflict. In order to grow up the human mind must lift its conflicts to the level of play. Mature minds project their conflicts both inwardly and outwardly, and in place of the petty systole and diastole of personal fears and wishes that worry most men into an early dying-back of the brain, they find immortality both in the outer stars and in the reminiscent insight of their own introspection. These people achieve happiness without resorting to war.

Chapter Three

THE ESSENTIAL MEANING OF RELIGION

Feeling and knowing constitute the elemental qualities of consciousness, and when these two are well harmonized in a mind the will, or dynamic expressive aspect of the personality, is effective and one-directional. Such a personality is happy. But through inept human response to conflict, feeling and intellect tend to become dissociated or separated in individual minds. The will is then split against itself and loses rapport with outer reality, which is represented in consciousness by the intellectual element. One of the first and most vital concerns of man is the maintenance of integration between feeling and intellect. It is a need fully as imperative to human happiness as the need for food, and to meet this need is the true psychological function of religion, as I believe the term should be used. The theological structures built up in the process are incidental. There is a secondary function of religion, which is the prevention of cruelty in the world. In the long run religion and the applicational aspects of psychology seem to constitute a common human effort, which is probably an expression of the elemental orientational motive in human consciousness.

Chapter Three

THE ESSENTIAL MEANING OF RELIGION

5. THE FIRST, OR DEEPEST MEANING OF THE TERM

THE term religion ought to be used with the utmost caution. So many men call their work religious when their actual objectives seem directly antagonistic to the growth of wisdom and understanding, that many clear thinkers prefer to try to build the essential meaning of this term into another word. It is the old problem of the wine and the bottles. But as we grow on into life, that which seemed new often turns out to be old, and what seemed old sometimes proves so very old that it is neither old nor new but both. Things are continually being forgotten and rediscovered. In one sense religion is an outworn and discredited concept, but in another it may carry a partially forgotten significance of the most vital and elemental importance to human happiness. On the chance that much truth may lie in this second alternative, it seems worth while to examine the concept.

Man is engaged in a continual struggle against the disproportionate gravitation of his interests back to his hereditary, biological needs. He is forever caught at some point in an eternal conflict between the urgency of immediate elemental desires—food, comfort, and sex—and the mental stirring of remoter, ideationally or ideally represented values. It is upon these relatively remoter values that social life is founded, and social life in turn gives rise to the opportunity for further development of intellect. Thus a gracious circle is established, and the mind grows from a double support, like the span of a bridge. One end rest of the span is discipline, first socially administered, and later self-administered; while at the other end is the progressive expansion of consciousness. If the two supports are well balanced the mental bridge may rise to a great height.

Ideally in this expansion of intellect, if feeling is not in some manner shunted off and left behind, the sympathies and emotions become likewise broadened in their scope and are projected out from the self until in the end there emerges a new *feeling of the unity* of outer life, and an emotional identification with it, which is perhaps not very different from the first sense of unity a child realizes when he comes to feel, long before he understands, the coördinate relationship that exists between the various parts of his body. This feeling of the unity and meaningfulness of life constitutes a sort of mental substratum which is quite as necessary and vital to the emergence of that sense of one-directional movement which is human happiness, as is physical well-being itself. Psychoanalysis has revealed clearly enough that the elemental feeling of unity in a mind is simply a state of compatibility between the inner wish and the outer symbol, that is, between the conscious elements *feeling* and *knowing*.

The first function of education ought certainly to be that of carrying the feeling element of consciousness, along with intellectual growth, to the full maturing or ripening of a personality. Yet this is precisely what education is failing to accomplish. The motivational end of the job is not keeping pace with the intellectual end. Something of the utmost importance is being omitted.

This neglected function is that of the maintenance of harmony and mutual acceptability between the inner and the outer world of awareness; between the world of human feeling and desire, and the world of objective, intellectual presentation. The maintenance of such a harmony in the human mind is unquestionably one elemental need or motive which has given rise to religion. Specific religions seem generally to have erred by distorting or suppressing the intellectual, in favor of the wish function,[1] yet the basic psychological function of religion has probably remained constant. *Religion has to do primarily with the integration of feeling and intellect.*

It is the loss of the sense of *feeling for things* somewhere along the way, that has come to constitute the vital tragedy of modern life. Such a loss takes the whole principle of cohesiveness—the sense of unity—out of a mind, and leaves only diffusive, little fragmentary constellations of value. The mind that cannot *feel* what it *knows* becomes like a body with no skeleton. When there is no order or principle to the arrangement of the mental bones, the concept of *character* fades and vanishes. The integrity of such a personality can be maintained only by going all the way back to the most elemental instinctive values and rebuilding on them. In order to reëstablish rapport with feeling, the individual must revert to the instinctive foundations of his consciousness and start over again, possibly under guidance of a psychoanalyst. *Psychoanalysis is then indeed nothing more mysterious than a highly specialized technique for dealing radically with desperate religious problems.*

[1] At this point we need not digress to discuss the particular rationalizations or concept systems which have emerged through the exercise of this suppression function. The gods came into the history of human affairs and followed their evolutionary course, because they were wanted and needed, not because their existence was logical or likely. They came because of the strength of the wish function in human life, and the essential meaning of religion will always lie deeper than any theological concept can reach. Theologies must be viewed as products, not as primary elements, of the religious function of the human mind. Our great need is to penetrate to a simple comprehension of this deeper function, and in the light of such a need it becomes vitally important to avoid the common mistake of defining religion in terms of particular beliefs, or in terms of a relation to God. God is an important concept in most religious minds, but He is in no sense *primary* or elemental to religion, as I believe the term must be used psychologically. Intense atheists are also intensely religious.

6. THE SECONDARY IMPLICATION

Once a child lived near the seashore, and grew to love all the living things of the sea. Among them was the great blue claw crab, who dwelt in the deep pools where tidewater reached the salt marshes. He was a formidable creature in a small boy's order of things, greatly to be respected and even more wonderful and mysterious than his little cousins the fiddler crabs, who lived in holes in the sand. He was wary and slow to make friends, but if once you won his confidence he would come to you to be fed, and he would almost, but not quite, let you touch him. His great pincers would snap a heeded warning whenever you put your hand too close. He was the noble, powerful, independent, and self-sufficient lord of the pool.

But when he shed his beautiful armored shell, he would lie very quietly for many days at the bottom of the pool, a soft, defenseless, tender creature. Then he was a soft-shelled crab. When in this defenseless condition, he was a delicacy greatly prized for the table, and this never sat well with a child's belief in the natural justice of things, but there came a shock to this child consciousness from which I believe he never fully recovered, when he grew aware of the manner in which many human beings customarily treat the blue claw when they catch him in this condition. *They boil him alive.*

It is said that he tastes a little better that way. I do not know whether the child to whom I refer was unusually tender-minded, imaginative, or merely loyal to his friends; but the horror of this callous and unimaginative thing sat upon his soul more poignantly than could in later years the burning of Bruno, the killing of men in war, or even the torturing and murdering of neurotic women by our own New England ancestors. And I believe that every human child to a greater or less degree experiences a similar shock upon becoming for the first time fully conscious that there are human beings in the world who *hurt* or *kill*, with unnecessary cruelty,[2] *that there are minds so unimaginative or so stunted and deadened that they can cause pain to a living creature without at the same time feeling a sharp reflection of pain in their own consciousness.*

The religious mind is a tender mind.[3] Basically it is a *feeling* mind. It is a mind that can carry the emotional im-

[2] There is so much cruelty in the world, and it appears so early in children, that superficial observers of life often speak of cruelty as instinctive and inevitable. This may be so, but it *may* be only imitation of bad habit. The capacity of children to imitate the moods and attitudes of adults is nearly incredible. Furthermore, the tremendous differences in children with respect to cruelty, and especially the differences between boys and girls, is strongly against the instinct hypothesis. It is also significant that Buddhist children do not characteristically show any signs whatever of cruelty. We are forced to the very strong presumption that cruelty, like other vulgarities in the human personality, is merely a bad habit, though an extremely difficult one to eradicate.

[3] In the light of the persecutions and cruelties so often carried on *in the name* of religion, this seems indeed a paradoxical statement. It brings out clearly the difference between what I have called the overt, and the psychological interpretation of history. Overtly, cruelty and ruthlessness have been associated with everything that man has done, whether in the name of trade, patriotism, love, or religion. From the historical purview, rapacity and violence always present the more striking and conspicuous elements of a situation or event. As history is recorded, even in "religious" writings, it seems a dreary panorama of selfishness and hate. Yet the fact stares us in the face that in spots, at least, civilization has actually moved *away from* selfishness and hate. The psychologist knows that there has been a counter-balancing element in human consciousness, which has wielded a stronger influence in the long run than have the self-loving forces in human nature, just as he knows that the soft parts of the fossil trilobite were actually more significant than the hard parts that left the record. I am of course not concerned with trying to prove that this force which drives man toward social cohesion and toward the love of experience transcending the direct assuaging of selfish desire, is *religion*; for I write not as a religionist, but as a psychologist. That there is a tender and feeling element in human nature, however, must be taken as a fact. That it can be more usefully harnessed and encouraged and educationally transmitted by identifying it with the concept religion, and that indeed it has always been one of the essential implications of religion, is only a hypothesis.

agination of a child into adult life. If you ever hear of a person frying a living animal alive, you must know that this is not a religious person, as I should want to use the term, however he may wear his collar. In some manner the human mind has become hurried, and in growing up loses the sense of feeling for things, at all of its levels. Men can kill, even each other, and fall back for their orientation upon some infantile ritual or stereotyped word formula which has so completely lost its feeling value, i.e., its real value, that what actually happens is complete dissociation of consciousness from reality.

This is why religion is a medical and psychiatric, as well as a psychological problem. And it is why the vast majority of human beings all about us are *themselves* in the position of the soft-shelled crab. In losing the sense of feeling for things they have lost their whole defense against discouragement. They have lost emotional integrity, their heart of a child, their significant identification with life. They have yielded up what we call the soul, this sense of feeling at home in the universe, and they are thereby rendered defenseless against the multiplying distractions and illusions of an overstimulated human world.

In one very important secondary sense religion carries the function of prevention of cruelty in the world. This can be achieved, of course, only by starting where cruelty is most common and most careless, yet where the watchful eye of the child sees it eternally in all its nakedness; namely in adult attitudes toward the lesser creatures of the earth who, not closely resembling the human form, cannot arouse kindness and sympathy in a human imagination which itself has all its life been deadened and coarsened by careless example.

The ordinary adult has little realization of the tremendous alertness and imitativeness of the very young child. If the adult has in his consciousness warm kindliness for the living and moving things of the *little* world about, the child mind will reflect it more accurately than any mirror, and will express it at times far more effectively than the adult himself. If there is dull unawareness, or worse, overt cruelty on the part of the adult in these tremendously vital matters, the child has been harmed from a religious point of view, as deeply as by any overt crime that could have been committed against it. *For in one of its elemental aspects the human soul may be defined as the capacity for imagining pain,*[4] *and whatever stunts this capacity stunts the whole personality.* The mother who would see in her child the dawning growth of a soul would do well to take a cue from the Buddhistic faith, and found the early child consciousness upon a sincere and pervading kindness to living things.

The fear of loneliness exercises a strong influence in discouraging young adult minds from growing up. They fear to grow up, as a child fears the dark, and they cringe back, away from the implications of a wider consciousness, because it seems to mean isolation from life and warmth. This could not be, except where adult senses had long been deadened to a world of matchless life that can support the human soul in warmth and delight, even at the loneliest heights of intellectual maturity. There is no loneliness for him who is at home in the heart of the forest, and the friends he finds there are psychologically immortal. They are always the same, and they can defeat loneliness as nothing human will ever defeat it. But friends such as these must be met and won in childhood.

7. RELIGION AS ORIENTATION

Psychologists well know that the deepest element of human happiness is embodied in the idea of movement toward something; movement in the "right" direction, and all

[4] In its other elemental aspect the soul is the capacity for imagining delight, or ecstasy. See p. 117.

of the devices of therapeutic psychiatry are really only shoves and pushes and suggestions intended to help a mind find its own particular right direction of movement. Continued observation of this basic dynamic nature of happiness, especially in clinical psychological practice, leads almost inevitably to the conclusion that deeper and more fundamental than sexuality, deeper than the craving for social power, deeper even than the desire for possessions, there is a still more generalized and more universal craving in the human make-up. *It is the craving for knowledge of the right direction—for orientation.*

This craving is not quite so obvious as the other patterns of human desire, because it is more general, deeper, and the positive and negative feeling tones it engenders are not locally felt, hence come less often to a specific attention focus. Yet every system of philosophy, whether called religious or not, is at bottom a human attempt to satisfy the craving to be pointed in the right direction, and I am afraid that all educational and psychotherapeutic systems which fail to recognize this deepest *orientational* nature of the restlessness and uncertainty of the unhappy educated mind, are destined to play but a transitory and palliative rôle in the history of thought.

At an intellectual level, Dewey has emphasized the significance of the craving for orientation in his *Quest for Certainty*; yet it is not primarily an intellectual problem. It is necessary, if one would reach the root of it, to go much deeper than conscious thought, deeper, I think, even than human life. Human observers of the world of other life have always been forcibly impressed by the remarkable ability of all the so-called lower animals to find their way about in the *spatial* world. "Instinct," it has been called. But that only passes the problem along for someone else to explain. Do homing pigeons and migrating birds find their way because of an instinct of direction; and the bee, why is his bee line always so straight from point to point, in the deepest forest? There is a basic principle in scientific thinking called the Law of Parsimony, which demands that the simplest possible explanation of an event always be invoked before remoter, more general explanations are allowed. One or two systematic observations of bees and pigeons well illustrate the importance of this often disregarded principle of thought.

In Chicago a number of homing pigeons were hatched and reared in a small box-like coop in a backyard, in such a manner that they were prevented from seeing the outer environment. One was released, a few blocks from his home. It was the first time he had seen the world beyond the inside of his coop. He did not find his way back, but flew about aimlessly and was later recovered in a half-starved condition. Others were similarly released at nearby points, but none found the way back to the coop. One was set free in the next yard, and he seemed as bewildered and lost as the others, finally roosting at a point farther from his coop than that at which he had started. However, some of these same birds, when later released *from their roost* and allowed to explore at their own will, showed no lack of ability to find their way back, and after several weeks of freedom a number of them were taken to a point fifty miles away and released. They came straight home.

This well-known experiment demonstrates simply that pigeons have to *learn* their way home. They have no instinct *which shows them the way*, but there is something much more general and fundamental in their mental make-up, which predisposes them to become almost incredibly accurate topographers. They put the human mind to shame as accurate observers and rememberers of the geographic relations in their environment. This deeper principle is perhaps in pigeons too a craving for orientation, but in their lives it plays a far more immediate and compelling rôle than in the life of man, and they are preoccupied with spatial, rather than with remoter, temporal orientation.

Bees are famous forest pathfinders. I once took ten newly matured workers from a Wisconsin hive, marked each with a spot of white ink on his thorax, and released them all in the woods about a mile from their hive. None returned to his own home. Later a dish of honey was set in a sunny place in the woods about a mile from these hives. Soon a bee appeared and after some maneuvering, took a load and started to leave. But he was detained, marked with a red spot, and taken in a darkened jar to a point several hundred yards from the honey, where he was released. He rose into the air, circled about as bees always do when leaving a "find," and disappeared. A companion remained to watch at the point where the bee was released, while I stationed myself at the place where the honey was. The bee returned *to the place where he had been released*, and alighted on an empty saucer that had been left there to fool him. This experiment was repeated several times. The bees did not always come back to the point of release, but not one of them found the way back to the honey again. In the meantime a number of other bees found the honey, were marked with a black spot and released. These returned again and again, apparently bringing other bees with them.

Bees too have to *learn* their way about, but they also are amazingly accurate topographers. Presumably they do not think about these matters, saying to themselves, "Now I must remember this blazed oak and keep it in line with that dead pine." Possibly they do it in their "subconscious," bending some deep inner attention to orientation because of a necessitous compulsion that drives them to note spatial relations; some urge not altogether different from the drive that leads to mating behavior, to nest building, to eating. If anyone desires to call this underlying compulsion instinct, and is certain that he can always make it clear what he means, then the term may be justifiable, but it is a dangerous word. It encourages students in the delusion of having said something when really they have only made a verbal noise.

It is neither descriptive nor accurate to leave this matter simply with the statement that birds and bees have an instinct of direction. There is something more fundamental here that we have not fathomed, a profound craving that is too universal, too deep, to be dismissed by a biological term. These lesser brains have some sort of inner compulsion to maintain orientation, and they use their minds, what honest minds they have, to the utmost in the service of this desire. Even the ameba, who has no brain at all, readily learns certain spatial relationships. At least he learns to avoid some quarters as threatening harm, and to seek others as offering good. And plants know where the sun is.

It may well be that the same compulsion for orientation lies inherent at the foundation of human consciousness, overlaid as it is with later, more specific urges, and enormously modified and complicated by the growth of the forebrain, by the development of abstract thought, and by the emergence of the concept *time*.

Religion is often identified with the idea of orientation, but that kind of conscious feeling which has been vaguely called *the religious instinct* does not come into existence, I suppose, until the forebrain has become sufficiently elaborated to give rise to the thought of *time* as well as of space. Just when this happens I do not know. It is universal in the human race; it seems certainly present in anthropoids;[5] the close observer of dogs continually reports evidence of it; and I should not be surprised to know, if ever there should be a way of knowing, that it does not end abruptly in a particular species, but tapers off into a shadowy vestige far down in the span of consciousness. Whether there is in the squir-

[5] For fairly ample evidence, see Koehler's interesting book, *The Mentality of Apes.*

rel's mind during his busy autumn afternoon of collecting, some faint suggestion of consciousness of the future—something resembling those dim time-conscious stirrings in the human mind which we call the dream of God—I do not know, though I should very much like to know. I can imagine that wild animals in captivity dream of other places and of other *times*, perhaps in a hoped-for future.

When man discovered time, he discovered a new world. It was then that he actually emerged from the grip of instinct into the consciousness of conflict and hence into a world of choice, or free will. The idea of living altogether by a conscious plan and of modifying the normal responses of life in the light of the ideational influence of an expected tomorrow seems to us uniquely human, though the general concept of time probably is not. It is this continual modification of the normal or natural response in the light of a remembered past and an expected future that is the great achievement of the human mind. In the world of time, to every possible response in life there comes to be not only an alternative, but a whole hierarchy of them; a whole new *dimension* of them. Psychologically, time may be somewhat meaningfully defined as the dimension[6] of alternatives. The consciousness of time and the consciousness of conflict are inseparable. That is, time as an idea and conflict as a problem are one. *Conflict is the reflection of the dimension of time, in a consciousness which has emerged from a spatial into a time-spatial universe.*

Perhaps it would be better *in the long run* to do this other, alternative thing. This is the universal formula of conflict, and of all in human life that gives us the impression of being *essentially* different from other animals of the earth. Out

[6] Thus time is the dynamic dimension, or movement dimension of consciousness, and in the sense that movement always involves the selection of a direction, there is always present the element of choosing between alternatives. Wherever consciousness of time exists, there also is to be found the time dimension of conflict.

of it grows the concept of causation, or controlled sequence in the universe, hence the possibility of interference with sequences, and finally the idea of varying sequences in accordance with conscious wishes. This is *will.* Where will is exercised the resulting behavior is purposeful, and the symbolized, i.e., intellectually represented future event in the sequence is *a purpose.* Since the most fundamental of human tissue needs are stimuli-to-be-moved-toward and stimuli-to-be-moved-away-from, it is not surprising to find a positive and negative pole in every human conscious system of purpose. When thought of in perspective and abstracted, this positive-negative antithesis becomes the opposed principles of good and evil, and in every purposeful act or thought there must be a balancing of these two principles; though from an individual's point of view one seems usually to dominate over the other.

Practically, religion always has to do with the definition of good and evil, and with the effort to bring the human mind to desire a maximum of the former and a minimum of the latter. This is the problem of ethics. Psychologically it is the problem of orientation in time. The essential thing about it, whether it be called ethics, religion, or merely orientation, is simply that it remains a problem of understanding the nature of conflict, and its happy outcome rests upon the ability of minds to carry and tolerate conflict at progressively higher, more intellectualized levels.

8. THE REAL FUNCTION OF RELIGION LIES IN THE TOLERATION OF CONFLICT

In its most essential meaning religion becomes that influence in human life which is concerned with bringing feeling support to the development of the thought process.[7] In each

[7] Or, as Professor McDougall once put it, in a conversation with me, religion is concerned with bringing about functional integration between the affective and the cognitive elements of mind. In McDougall's psychological system there is a third element, the conative, or striving element,

of the great religions there is personified and illustrated in some picturesque manner the will to withdraw some of the intensity of feeling from the biological self, and to focus this emotional feeling upon a cohesive system of ideas which *as a system* transcend it. The self is thus transfigured and ennobled, and the mind is pointed. It is in a state of readiness to grow. Yet, even so, it does not always grow toward wisdom, *for wisdom implies simultaneous triumph over both conflict and error. Religions traditionally have prematurely allayed the pain of conflict by selling the soul over to the remoter evil of error. Yet we know that error can be conquered ultimately only through the toleration of conflict, and that the key to such a toleration must lie in some satisfactory balancing of the subjective functions of feeling with the objective functions of intellect.*

Historically there has never been for long such a balancing, though there have been pendulum swings back and forth between the extreme objective, and the extreme subjective interpretation of life, and much of the advancement of human understanding seems to have been accomplished on the wing, as it were, during these great transitional periods. We have been living in a period of rapid shift of worship from the subjective toward the objective bias. It has been a period of great expansion of intellect, but we now approach the end of it, and have begun to grope, a little hysterically, for some power that can balance and modify the extreme consequences of the present trend.

It was once hoped that such a power might lie in psychology, but psychologists as a group have thrown their weight far over toward the leaning side of the boat, and it

---

and there are as many kinds of elemental conation as there are fundamental instincts. Using McDougall's language, we might meaningfully define religion as a human conative effort toward the ecstasy of both feeling and knowing the mystery of life at the same instant. McDougall's conative, striving element is represented in my system of thought by the fundamental urge to maintain orientation, first in space and then in time.

begins to look as if this balancing function may after all rest entirely upon religious shoulders. Psychologists in following the star of the physical sciences seem temporarily to have forgotten where the earth is. Yet in the long run psychology must concern itself with subjective, *mental* phenomena, as well as with objective, concrete phenomena.

The underlying method of human defense against the pain of profound conflict is that of establishing in the conscious system a positive and negative pole of values, conceived in such a manner that the sense of moving toward a goal can be maintained and emotionally felt, even in the face of unfavorable, warring circumstances, three of which at least have so far proved stubbornly resistant to objective amelioration. These three are death; unequal social privilege; and the persistent, almost humorous recalcitrancy of sexual desire.

There is no available defense against these circumstances, except an internal mental hierarchy of values strongly enough held together to overshadow the instinctive desires and to bring them into harmony with conscious purposes that transcend them. In the presence of such an internal hierarchy, mental control may safely be taken over by the higher intellectual functions of the brain, but in order that it shall be an efficacious and a safe control, there must somehow be maintained a close associational alliance between these intellectual functions and the deeper functions of feeling. Without such an integration with deep feeling, there is only the rational aspect of mind, and without the latter there is only a sentiment. Neither, alone, has vitality or self-sustaining quality.

In order to achieve an integration of thought and feeling which will produce happiness, it is therefore clear that the religious mind must always be prepared to face a compromise. *If religion would maintain a creative marriage between the feeling and intellectual qualities of mind, it must tolerate a certain weakening of both. Religion weakens feeling by at-*

taching it to abstracted, rather than to direct sensory elements of consciousness; and it in turn weakens the rational function by trammelling and limiting it with the heavy drag of feeling.

A human defense against conflict is made possible only through a compromising alliance between the rational and the feeling functions. And I think that it is in this compromise that both the eternal weakness and the eternal strength of the religious mind lie. It is a weakness because highly rational minds and strongly feeling minds must always somewhat resent the influence of each other, and accordingly both will be found ever in rebellion against the influences of contemporary religion. The religious mind always has the least educated element of society, and the best educated element, pitted against it as against a common enemy. They form a queer sort of alliance, these polar enemies of religion, and if you look closely at a communist parade or at one of those Sunday afternoon "atheist" meetings that occur on big city commons, you can always make out a sprinkling of both elements. The furtive face of the hater of civilization and the pale brow of the scholar will both be there. Religion finds few friends among the best intellects, and none among the worst. That is the price it pays for the compromise it makes.

Yet in this compromise there is a great strength, for although religion loses the support of the upper intellectual extreme, it stands to escape the great weakness of it, which is its tendency to self-destruction. A highly rational mind sometimes removes itself so far from the earth that it forgets the purpose of life, and not infrequently may be found hard put to it to advance a rational reason for living at all.

The dominantly intellectual personality tends to become centrifugal, and removes itself far from the earth, thus straining the ties binding it to the nourishing centers that support its will to live. Only the presence of a great intermediate connecting body of personalities who have accepted the compromise of life makes possible its support, for these form a kind of sustaining trunk that brings it life and protects it from exploitation by less civilized social elements. Even so, the intellectual personality tends to die off[8] rather than to reproduce itself at high altitudes, and so its contributions to the human good are in the end expensively bought. It takes a good deal of human sweat and suffering down at the lower levels of the mental pyramid to support the few really developed intellects that are to be found at the peak. This support of the higher refinements of the rational function, one of the truly great achievements of human society, seems to be a by-product of the compromise that religion brings about, however much individual religionists and individual intellectuals may hate each other. The real function of religion seems always to lie in the toleration of conflict.

9. THE TWO GREAT RELIGIOUS PITFALLS

The necessity of the eternal compromise brings into relief two practical difficulties that the religious mind seems never to have satisfactorily met. (1) Since the element of good and evil is general, and cannot be confined to one kind of purposeful behavior, the problem of religion must likewise be general, and it can never be confined to one sphere of life activity. Yet the religious mind, concerned as it always is with conflict and with the deepest of human controversy, repeatedly commits the fatal blunder of *becoming involved in particular conflicts*; and then religion is automatically identified with a controversy. The religious mind is continually caught in controversy as flies are caught on sticky paper. It becomes identified with a pattern of government, and we hear of the *divine right of kings*, or that God is with *us*; with economic

[8] We still read with compassion of the poor Harvard graduate, who is destined to beget only seven-tenths of an offspring.

patterns, and money lenders are chased from the temple, while for later generations Christ becomes the first *Rotarian*; with sexual morality, and someone discovers that religion is *sexual* sublimation. Not long ago an American Y.M.C.A. director told me that he considered the main function of religion to be that of developing *healthy bodies*. Religion had become a branch of the university athletic department! In such manner religion loses its usefulness and is shunted off into inconsequential temporal conflict. By becoming entangled in the silly business of prohibition, the Protestant religious mind in America made itself particularly ineffective at a time when civilization most needed its support.

(2) The problem of orientation in time leads inevitably to the thought of a time perspective which extends beyond the span of individual biological life, and the human mind long ago postulated the concept of a great unknown which lies beyond, and all around us. This perfectly natural idea paves the way to the second great religious pitfall. Ideas concerning the unknown are peculiarly difficult to refute, and hence should be advanced with very great caution. Yet in the name of religion premature emotional support can be brought to virtually any plausible system of such ideas that may lie within the range of imaginative possibility. In this manner conflict in the time dimension is *prematurely resolved*, and living human problems are put to unnatural death.

There is always great temptation to settle the question of the nature of the unknown, for to do so offers a quick means of control over the moral behavior of population masses who themselves seemingly could never be taught to carry conflict or to tolerate uncertainty. Religious people persistently take this bait, convincing themselves and others that here is at last the *right* answer to the mystery of what lies beyond the span of human life, and here is the true solution to moral perplexity. So religion becomes identified with the presumption of supernatural insight into the unknown, and under the pressure of popular encouragement, claims special knowledge of what is not yet knowledge. In other words the religious mind yields to a cheap temptation and turns intellectually dishonest. On this basis it then attempts to found a moral system and to build human character!

Religion becomes identified with frequent and easy recourse to the authority of the absolute, and so cuts itself off from integration with intellectually respectable minds. It puts itself upon far too familiar terms with its God,[9] and the penalty is degeneration of its God. It is, then, not impossible to understand why a man like Freud should give his book on religion the expressive title, *The Future of an Illusion*. Having lived all his life entirely outside the influence of the better type of religious mind, he is, we may suppose, only reporting what he has seen.

Perhaps no real help in the great social perplexities can ever be looked for from *institutionalized* religion until this pretentious claim to special knowledge of the unknown has been replaced generally by a more chastened and humble point of view. Such a chastened outlook has long, perhaps always, been characteristic of individual religious minds throughout society, but as yet the Church as a body, even in its liberal Protestant branches, teaches a theology which runs so far ahead of the humility to which it lays claim, that its influence is dropping year by year to lower and lower intellectual levels. This difficulty presents a dilemma which cannot be ignored. If we are to continue to regard religion as in any significant sense related to the activities of the Church, churchmen as well as philosophers must come to regard the toleration rather than the resolution of doubt as the objective of religious education.

[9] Mussolini and Hitler, aware of the danger in familiarity, forbid that their names be used in familiar conversation at all.

10. RELIGION AND PSYCHOLOGY

The concept of the widening span of time grows as mind grows, and religion is in one sense man's endeavor to keep up with his idea of time, or at least to keep his spirits up to it. Religion has for the time being failed in this function of spiritual expansion, perhaps mainly because it has been too closely occupied with outer matters and too little concerned with what actually has been going on in minds. It is perhaps because of this distorted outer focus that nearly all recent contributions to psychology, and hence ultimately to religion itself, have been coming through medicine and biological science rather than through religious thinking. Psychoanalysis, for example, is certainly far more a religious than a medical problem.[10] Yet the most important contributions to it have been made by medical minds, and most of the individuals now practising it are rather emphatically anti-religious. Traditionally the priest was the man to whom people turned when their minds were caught in perplexity, but priests in general have now nearly lost this function. Yet in the long run view of matters, the problem of religious orientation and the problem of conflict are one, and it is the man who is concerned with religion who is in the end most directly and significantly concerned with conflict in individual minds.

I think it is therefore a fair statement that psychology and religion together actually carry the common general function of integrating feeling with intellect, however far it may become necessary for psychology to separate herself for the time being from institutions which *in the name* of religion ignore this function. Such is the thesis of this chapter. *A good psychological mind is simply one which possesses insight into itself and into other minds; and religion is the applica-*

[10] In the sense that the application of psychological techniques to the development and guidance of normal and superior minds is probably more important, in the long run, than therapy or the mere prevention of gross mental pathology.

tion of such insight to the conflicts which are causing the greatest blockage of the general development of minds. Yet except for a little individual therapy here and there, both religion and psychology are playing essentially futile rôles during an interesting and perhaps important period of human history. This seems rather a shame, for among the two professional groups many naturally fine minds are numbered.

The central problem of any culture always becomes finally a matter of determining how far it dare encourage minds to grow, and every individual is at some point torn between the splendid urge to go on toward understanding, and the craving to go back to safety. Great numbers are caught tragically in this conflict. In a time of religious chaos many of them in their quest for orientation throw themselves upon the psychologist who, if he is successful, either helps them to rebuild an orientation, or to clear away the wreckage of a lost one; either to go on toward spiritual wholeness, or to scramble back to a lower and more instinctive level of life. Thus through the years I have come to feel that professional work in psychology and psychotherapy can be only a rather superficial palliation of the more fundamental orientational problem of religion until religionists at large shall become equipped to make use of the best available intellectual and technical resources for dealing with conflict; more particularly and more immediately with the conflict in their own minds.

The goodness or badness of a religion or of a psychology is always to be measured in terms of the effect which it exerts upon personalities coming under its influence. If a personality moves conspicuously in the direction of emotional and intellectual maturity, finally combining kindness with understanding, the religious or psychological influence has been of the first water. If however, a personality is seen to stop developing at a point short of its best possibilities, certainly it does not have a good religion in a psychological sense, or a good psychology in a religious sense.

Cheap religions lie in wait on all sides, offering escape from uncertainty in exchange for a soul. *A cheap religion is any orientational system which offers self-satisfaction with the achievement of less than an individual's best intellectual and emotional development.* Such a religion may be embraced in the flush of a great hope or as an escape from bafflement and frustration. It is an escape channel, or leakage channel, through which energy which could have been harnessed to produce a higher maturing of the personality, is allowed to drain off and to escape at relatively low achievement levels.

In the fact that exactly the same psychology can hardly be adequate for two different personalities, there is a consideration which should give pause to the religious mind. For neither can the same religion apply perfectly to two different individuals. What is one man's meat is sometimes another's poison, and what is an adequate religious outlook for one individual, with his particular native equipment, may be only an escape channel for another person, or for the same person at a later period of life. Thus the spirit of giving has ennobled many a mind and has *started* many a personality on the road to growing up; yet to be generous is by no means to have made the best of the possibilities of a well-endowed brain. A generous person may for half a lifetime have shirked his moral obligation to come to a sympathetic understanding of the economic system under which he lives; how it works; its history; where it pinches; what are the psychological implications of charity in a society; and what is the relation of war and reproduction and nationalism and Christianity to poverty. When minds equipped by heredity and by opportunity for great richness of development, permit themselves to be satisfied with being generous, this is a sign of the failure both of religion and of psychology in their world.

Similarly personal love is sometimes a profoundly ennobling experience. Yet there are millions who live essentially mean, self-centered, unripened lives while basking under the presumption of righteousness because they have expanded the self *just a little*, to include one or two other similarly undeveloped selves. They *love* someone, thus striking the highest note they will ever strike, and in the end their souls will be as slightly expanded fleas upon the dogs of heaven. Personal love is often an entering wedge to a great development and expansion of the personality; it sometimes acts as a beginning of things on a new and broader plane; but far more often it becomes instead merely the end of things; a final little gasp of achievement, ushering in a life of selfishness for two or three instead of for one.

Likewise patriotism, the love of one's country, offers the same key to a nobler life. But where the relation between feeling and understanding, between religion and psychology, is weak this too becomes only the reënforcement of a selfishness, a menace to the welfare of man, and a cause of war. The same is true of loyalties of every description; of loyalty to one's church, to one's lodge, to one's college, one's race, one's political party, one's ancestral tradition. Loyalties are only the seeds of a process of growth which when carried to its full expansion may lead to maturity of mind and greatness of soul; but when these seeds fall upon uncultivated and unchastened ground they produce only the tangled weeds of conflict and suspicion and organized hate. A man who loves his own family too well is but one small step nearer maturity than he who loves himself too well. These are psychological problems, and they are religious problems.

It grows clear that we cannot speak very meaningfully of the function of religion or of psychology except in terms of each other. Together they have the function of the development of personality, though neither alone quite expresses that idea, even after much explanatory or apologetic qualification. If personality development were subject to some standard ideal pattern, so that a formula could be applied with the same result to different individuals, then religion might get along very well without psychology. Such is far from the case; it requires shrewd psychological judgment, based upon insight into the inner life of many minds, to prescribe the wisest religious loyalties for a given personality. And conversely if minds could live for any length of time at levels remote from the warmth of loyalties and emotionally felt purposes, then psychology could do very well without a supportive religion; but as things are, such a hope leads only to jazz and to the inflation of sex and money, that is to say, to some temporary widening of well-worn escape channels.

The great problem of modern life is not *primarily* economic planning, nor deflation of money and sex and national arrogance, nor even the cutting down of noise and speed and bewilderment. I do not believe that the greatest *immediate* problems center around war and the wise control of reproduction, however vital these matters must be to future human happiness, *but it may be that there is a most important need in human life, and that this is the shrewd reconsideration of the relation between religion and the psychologies.* In the end it may be only the development of a wider human feeling-awareness that counts, and neither the religion nor the psychology that we now know is contributing very much to such a development. Yet if even a few highly religious minds can be trained to become also able psychological minds, it may be that they can gauge the temper of modern orientational needs, and can lay educational foundations for building integrative harmony between the inner world of dreams and the outer world of intellect. The most vital of all the "business" of modern life may be that at present infinitesimal part of it which is embodied in an effort to develop in naturally religious minds the best possible degree of psychological insight.

As a race we have been far too much concerned with the outer structure of things; have done far too much manipulating of the rules of the game; too much gross, overt, social bustling about things, and in the great business of educating one another "for citizenship" have overlooked the fact that the final destiny of citizenship cannot be other than building human minds and developing personality to its highest consciousness. We have gone in for enormous quantity production, and now in America alone there are something like two hundred thousands of tons of human brains walking about in various stages of decay and disuse. It is good material, but it is not being utilized to a hundredth of its optimum happiness. So far as I am aware the best and possibly the only way to bring about any extensive salvaging of this staggering waste of brain is to find a way of diverting the enlightened attention of the religious institutions to its development.

Yet in turn, probably nothing can save religion except for ministers to become the kind of psychologists that psychologists themselves have not yet become. If this can be accomplished it may then be that civilization will gently move across from the era of the economic interpretation of history to the era of the psychological comprehension of conflict.

Chapter Four

CHARACTER, AND THE WASTER MIND

It is the main purpose of this book to shape in broad lines the framework of a psychology adequate to carry the orientational functions in perspective with the other branches of social thought. To this specific project we turn in Chapter Six. But in attacking orientational problems, man is really trying to make peace with the deepest conflicts, with the most central cleavages in his consciousness. These are the great religious conflicts of life. To designate and describe these primary conflicts should then be the first objective of a psychology aiming to include in its purview the religious panel of consciousness. This is the task essayed in Chapter Four.

Summary: It seems clear that a central conflict can be made out; that it centers around a very fundamental divergence between a time-conditioned *or* character-phyllic *trend, and a* waster *or* character-phobic *trend in human personality. But there is a vitally important secondary or cross cleavage which splits the character-phyllic mind against itself, weakens it, and hampers it in its struggle against the waster. This secondary conflict lies in the struggle between radical idealism and conservative idealism. It is the Promethean conflict, the conflict in the religious mind, the struggle between the prophet and the priest.*

Chapter Four

CHARACTER, AND THE WASTER MIND

11. THE MEANING OF CHARACTER

THE term *personality* is commonly used in two rather different and quite distinguishable senses. It refers, (a) to the whole general pattern of a person, to all of his traits—physical, emotional, intellectual, social, and aesthetic—taken as a whole; or (b) to the overt social impression that the person typically creates. Thus in the latter and more common usage of the word, we say that such a one has a striking personality, or a lovable, or truculent, or gentle personality. But when it is said that a person has *character*, something more definite and descriptive is implied. This term refers not to the whole make-up, nor to an impression, but to a pattern of implied internal structure.

Character in its psychological sense refers to the end result which emerges from the interplay of two factors in a personality; namely, the hierarchy of *conscious values* or *purposes* that has been built up in the course of a life, and the extent to which this intellectual structure is warmed and enlivened by *feeling support* from below. The end result may be described as a degree of trustworthiness, dependability, nobility, moral integrity, or the like. A person high in these qualities has strength of character. Two elements are always to be carried in mind when character is mentioned; the pattern of ideals, and the extent to which this is a *felt*, as distinguished from a merely intellectual pattern. In fine, *character is the extent to which a mind is purposively cemented together and can resist disintegrative influences.*

In the sense that mind refers to general conscious process, character is a completely teleological word, implying the presence of purpose or direction in the process. A man of strong character is a man of strong purpose, who is pointed in a straight direction. That is to say, he is clear in his orientation, and is on his way toward a goal. The mind has come into focus and has got its bearings, and the personality is therefore pointed. Character is the quality of moving toward an objective. If happiness is a condition of moving successfully toward a difficult objective,[1] character is the first prerequisite to happiness. It is the vehicle of enduring happiness.

The satisfaction of the deep, general craving for orientation in the time dimension is probably in the long run as vital to the happiness of an animal carrying the huge human forebrain, as the satisfaction of hunger. Character is the extent to which a mind has succeeded in establishing and reenforcing its pattern of orientation. It is as necessary to enduring happiness that the thinking personality should include such a supportive pattern or frame, as that the physiological personality should include a skeleton.

At the level of physiological mechanics character is arrangement of structure, and at the mental level it is the existence of a clear hierarchy of relative values. Some appreciation of the possible significance of mental character in the human future may be provoked by contemplating the span of time that has been involved in the development of the physical character of the body. Compared to the patterned awarenesses that constitute consciousness, these physical structures and coördinations are immeasurably old, and they represent an immeasurably greater span of trial and error. Mental character is relatively young in the world, and perhaps it is not so much to be marveled at that man has so little of it, that he lacks perfect orientation in time, as that he has achieved so much. The development of mental orientation is as clearly a trial and error process as the development of a leg, and

[1] See p. 11.

the human intellect, being a product of the struggle for existence, as Mr. H. G. Wells once said, is no more necessarily a truth-finding apparatus than the snout of a pig.

Nor is it altogether strange that in the face of many uncertainties character has now and again faltered, and that man has dreamed too longingly of outside help from the gods; even has frequently persuaded himself when driven to sheer desperation by pain and suffering and by his own ineptitudes, to see revealed signs assuring him of salvation. Inscriptions in stone, voices from bushes, the rediscovered writings of ancestors, the psychoanalytically revealed wisdom of the unconscious; these all carry easy suggestions of the lost word. Even in modern times individuals find in delusion a short cut to wholeness. The cry is still raised that the magic formula has been found, and always there are unhappy thousands eager to ring the echo of the cry. The temptation to find character by slipping back to a less independent and less intellectual level is always lurking hard by, and any new religion, however cheap, gives a sense of character for a little time. The human mind is forever lured by an easy way; by some short cut; some salvation by faith alone, which is salvation by dissociation of the intellect. Yet to try to achieve character through mere intensity of the wish is like solving a puzzle by throwing half of it away. There are always the two variables of feeling and intellect in the concept of character, and if the level is found by throwing one of them away, the character achieved in the end can be at best only a pitiful little character.

Character can never be defined in terms of particular beliefs. We are made to fail and only from many belief-failures can we ever weave the net that will hold the white bird of Truth. Particular beliefs are but the steps in the rock, cut by the intellectual vanguard, by which the mind at large slowly advances, and most beliefs are in time seen to be but divagations; sometimes retrogressions, retreats, escapes.

Likewise character is not a particular *morality*. The relation of a morality to character is like the relation of a crutch to walking. When you cannot walk without it, the crutch is well nigh indispensable. I should expect a son in the flush of his youth to feel a certain contempt for moralities, and for people who carry them conspicuously. For a conspicuous morality is an advertisement of weakness, and of lack of the kind of responsibility that will lead to the growth of mature understanding. Yet later in life I should expect to see this same son grow mellow, and look with sympathy and understanding upon those weaker ones who have found it necessary to carry a morality on their faces and in their conversation.

I am using the term conspicuous morality here in the sense of professed virtue. To profess a virtue bespeaks a deep sense of weakness, as any psychologist will readily explain.[2] Where character is conspicuously professed, most people feel intuitively that here is a personality that cannot really be trusted. Its inner structure, the *true* character, is not in order, and that is why it must depend for virtue (strength) upon an outer scaffolding, and upon the continual reassurance which kind people always give to those who are weak and professedly righteous. In the normal development of a mind, morality needs to merge over into character and quietly disappear, as knowledge disappears into wisdom and into the toleration of doubt.

Children are given many helps, or crutches, for stimulation and encouragement of their social adaptation. These little moralities they sometimes display proudly and thereby gain merited praise. They are praised for *being good*. This kind of morality is like the first teeth of character, though violent objections are raised even against this in certain psycho-

[2] Nietzsche has Zarathustra say, "Hold thy virtue too high for the familiarity of names: and if thou must speak thereof, be not ashamed to stammer." *Thus Spake Zarathustra*. Everyman's Library Edition, p. 28.

analytic quarters.[3] But as a personality grows up into adult life, we expect it to have established a character of its own, to have assumed responsibility in the ordinary elemental social relations, and thereby to have opened the way for the emergence into its world of the still new and daring dream of freedom. Freedom is possible only in a society which has generally replaced the milk teeth of *morality* with the sterner tissue of *moral and intellectual responsibility*.

Morality is character only for those who are too young or too undeveloped to have character. The realization of this has gone abroad and has brought sore perplexity to mankind, for there are millions who in the wake of the great emancipation from morality have thrown it eagerly away, but having neglected first to develop character, now lack even a crutch to lean on. It has indeed become so shameful a thing in well-educated circles to be called moral that men and women travel to heroic extremes to escape the danger of such a charge. This is the underlying motivation behind much of the blasé flavor of modern life. Better to pretend to a relish for ill-conceived beverages; better to assume a great interest in vulgar aesthetic drivel; better to keep up an insipid social function far into the hours of the morning, than to risk the suspicion of a taint of morality. It is really

[3] According to the Freudian doctrine, children necessarily recapitulate various stages of savagery and of ruthless and destructive behavior. All this should be *expressed* and tolerated, even encouraged, for if it is *repressed* it will be retained in the *unconscious* and will reappear later in more dangerous guise. Hence the Freudian anti-moral educational doctrine of expressiveness. The real flaw in this psychology lies in the fact that it overlooks the tremendous power of early habit formation and places far too great an emphasis upon instinctive predetermination of human character. Actually, children lay the foundations of character in the first years of life, and if allowed to be little savages during this period, that is essentially what they are likely to remain. The Freudian answer to this is that these negative instincts, if expressed in childhood, are thereby got rid of, and disappear. If this were carried out to its logical conclusion, we should have to *inhibit every good or generous impulse* in the child, on the ground that if allowed expression, it would be lost, like a spent dollar.

a predicament to live in a world where you haven't character and are not allowed morality. This is the predicament of possibly the majority of young minds, and of many who are not so young any more. Yet the attempt to eliminate morality from education is like trying to cure lameness by prohibiting the manufacture of crutches. There is an outer sign of health in it, but as Dean Inge has said, when Satan captures a position he seldom bothers to change the flag.

Man to be happy must have either morality or character. Mind is biologically an evolved appendage for moving in time, but mind has grown so amazingly complex and unwieldy that without the mental skeleton of character, we run grave danger of suffering the fate of the great saurians who from unwieldable overdevelopments of their own—physical ones in their case—have gone down to extinction before us. They presumably lacked character, in the sense of self control.

Character is a quality of personality. It is the degree of consistency and system and internal integrity that a personality has achieved. Religion is in a practical sense the application of techniques for the development of character.[4] Religion and character bear much the same relation to each other as do architecture and its products. Character is the product, or better, the ideal goal of religion, but where there is extensive failure to achieve character in a culture, religion tends to drop back to the function of the promulgation of a morality. This is a lower order of function, and it achieves feeling-thought coördination at lower levels, but where character has failed it becomes a vital necessity. In this manner, through human weakness, religion continually becomes entangled with morality.

I do not mean to imply any sharp threshold between character and morality. The one grades over imperceptibly into

[4] Dr. Harry Emerson Fosdick sometimes defines religion as reverence for character, or reverence for personality.

the other, like the mature into the immature. Character is a high, responsible level of dependability. Morality is dependability with the qualification of implied outside pressure, such as that of a system of real or postulated rewards and punishments. The personality controlled by morality is simply one not quite trustworthy to make its own elementary decisions, not sufficiently mature for social responsibility. The moral question is, can the person be trusted to *behave* in an approved manner under particular circumstances? The character question is, what are the purposes that dominate this person; where is he going; toward what is he pointing; is he on the way to a mature mind, and is he going to get out on the growing point of some branch of learning, or of some application of learning? Has he noble aspirations; has he the splendid urge; is he going to develop a great feeling-identity with life—a great soul? In his mind a time-dimensional mind? Character is the positive aspect of personality, and it is character in this sense which must become the focus and objective of religious teaching if the vast institutionalized resources of religion are to play an effective rôle in the coming struggle between the time-conditioned and the waster trends.

12. THE EMERGENCE OF THE WASTER MIND

The real significance and danger in the popular movement against morality does not actually lie in the scope of morality at all, but in its bearing on the much larger problem of character. If the true meaning of character centers around the conception of a life outlook characterized by a certain poignant awareness of the dimension of time, and consequently by a chastened, or reminiscent, or wistful quality of consciousness, then there has come into prominence during the decades of the new century a fairly clear type of mental pattern which is the fundamental antithesis of the idea of character. It seems to be the precipitation of a long accumulating resentment of those chastening influences of civilized life which lead to character. As a concept it may be called *the waster mind.*

The dominant characteristic of it is a rampant impatience with the idea, and with all of the implications, of inhibition. To the waster, all inhibition is *repression.*[5] And with a gesture of impatience he would resolve conflict at large simply by dropping back to a more untrammelled expressive level. The waster loves to *do* things, to wield power over things, to use up things fast, to be as a king or a god. *He is hearty, big, expansive, fast, and a lover of that which is farthest removed from sentiment and conservation. He is in all things the antithesis of the chastened mind.* The waster is particularly prominent in America, for there is something in the combined influence of vast resources and democracy that seems to have tacitly encouraged his development. In a democracy, one man is as good as another, and that *may* mean that all men should aspire to the rôle of king; that is, to the irresponsibility and wastefulness that weak and undeveloped minds enviously associate with being a king.

The clear antithesis between the waster and the man of character is to be seen in their respective attitudes toward the inflation of money. The lover of character continually desires to hold money at a fixed standard, and thereby to neutralize it, to deëmphasize it, and to make it excessively difficult to get rich, or to escape from debts.

The waster wants lots of money and wants to get it fast, in one generation if possible, and he is ready to sell over the future and to betray the past to get it. It is the present, his own point in time, that dominates his thought. Of the past and the future he is relatively unaware. He lives intensely *at a point* in the time dimension, and digs in there vigorously, like a sheep tick. His mind does not move in the time

[5] For discussion of the meaning of this, and of certain other common psychoanalytic terms, see Appendix, Section 4.

dimension. If the waster has incurred debts he sees no harm in repudiating them by debasing his money. He seeks short range adaptation at the expense of long range adaptation, success at the expense of character. He wants "prosperity," which means to him speed, fast turnover, quick using up of things, and easy money. He has no affection for *things*; no economic chastity; he is a builder and a destroyer. The same temper may be seen in his attitude toward sex. He wants to use it, express it, get the most out of it, inflate it, and make a great objective of it. He is in these things an open enemy of character. Above all else he hates "principles."

The real enemies of character are not to be found among atheists or critics of religion or non-conformists, but they are the lusty, noise-loving expressivists, who believe in living for the present, in having their fling, and who say, "Let's have no more long faces; no inhibitions and no wet blankets at our party." They are the good livers, unchastened, unreverent souls. Popularly they have become associated with the term extravert, though it would be more meaningful to call them the feebly inhibited.[6] They live at the surface of awareness and are dissociated from their own deeper consciousness. They have moved sharply away from the principle of reminiscent contemplation, and have gravitated far over toward the principle of sensuality, thus sharply dissociating the conscious focus from the deeper levels. Wasters perforce seek overstimulation, love city life, and have a profound horror of the inferiority complex. Their god is Expression, and their spiritual counsellors are sometimes the psychoanalysts. Flushed with sudden release from Christian inhibitions, they are resolved to smash away all that was ever associated with the spiritual, or religious, or reminiscent, or chastened mental outlook, and their exultant ecstasy finds its channels of expression in the material processes

[6] Professor Davenport's term.

of manipulating things, of social domination, and of sexual conquest.

It may be that the waster trend is in some intimate way associated with the reckless profligacy with which nature insured the business of reproduction back in the days before the forebrain came into existence. The sexual overproduction still continues even though human beings have now developed the forebrain with its potential function of forethought. *It may be that the waster mind is merely a pathological intensification and spreading of this sexual energy, and that for the waster, Freud's general motivational hypothesis is sound.*

These truly unchastened individuals are happy opportunists. At the moment they may actually constitute the happiest element in society, for they are moving toward something definite, and they are wholly devoted to the life that they lead.[7] They will remain happy so long as they are able to keep the pace and are never brought to a reckoning with their own deeper consciousness. To the waster, life is a race between death and the necessity for self-contemplation. For him enforced solitude is more fearful than any pain. But as life is now ordered in America and in Europe, the earth is mainly his until the pendulum swings and the time-dimensional mind again becomes dominant. You can hear waster tom-toms and radios and automobile horns and overstimulated voices far into the summer night.

But these naturally unchastened ones are not to be confused with the vast army of baffled souls who in a generation of educational chaos have never found themselves at all, who have no orientation and no hope of one, but go frantically up and down the country trying piteously to imitate the conspicuously happy wasters. An observant person can distinguish the true waster from his unhappy imitators at a

[7] The philosophy of ultra-materialism offers, for a short time, from the standpoint of the healthy, youthful male, a very nearly ideal religious orientation. The objectives are definite, direct, attainable, and concrete.

glance, for the waster is true to himself. The true waster is *really* that way.

He is hearty and expressive and loud; he does not have to strain in his rôle. He buys an automobile four times too big for him and overstuffs and overdresses his women, not to keep up with somebody else, but because he really likes things that way. He wants above all else to be a waster. And he is well loved, for he is generous, bountiful, and never does anything mean, or humble, or conservative.

The waster never stints. Read sometime a sketch of the life of Al Capone, of whom the Chicago coppers used to say, "He's a regular guy." Study his face. It is an open face, and it eloquently and truthfully expresses his nature. This is usually true of wasters. They are almost invariably generous, and they usually have lovable, "open" faces. They are easily distinguished from the misguided, bewildered, pale young adults who collect in hundreds of thousands in American and European cities, pouring out nightly from the theaters and clubs and entertainment places like great droves of seeking, troubled sheep.

These poor exploited creatures are like babes in the woods, completely lost and frustrated. With any sort of intellectually acceptable religious education, most of them could have developed happy and useful minds. They could have been far happier and much nobler than their grandparents were, for they have the materials lying about for infinitely greater achievement, and they have greater freedom for systematic, creative thought. But compared to their grandparents they are actually miserable, degenerate creatures, living cramped, scrambled and half-smothered lives. Politically, economically, and sexually they are freer than men have ever been before, but orientationally they are in chaos.

In a society whose orientational influences have collapsed at the higher educational levels, these undirected souls emerge in a vast procession from high schools and colleges and turn in numb bewilderment to the cheap commercial exploitation of "amusements" which enterprising opportunists readily provide. It is because of the easy exploitability of such swarming thousands, who have been a little exposed to education, that wasters prosper so well and set up their vicious circle. Al Capone did not become a great commercial and political power in Chicago through the intentional support of his own kind, but through the herding and flocking and drinking of callow, hip-flask souls who, having been shorn by education of their morality, stood naked and characterless before the wind.

The waster ideal was adopted in the colleges in the nineteen twenties as a sort of vogue and a symbol of youthful high health. It prospered and grew mightily and soon made its presence felt in high places. It did not want education in the sense of an influence toward intellectual maturation, nor did it want the wisdom of the past and the reminiscent speculation of the present. It wanted only that which would contribute to its material prosperity, only facts and techniques, and not too many of these. Thus campus after campus was "taken," and many of the colleges that a generation ago were valiantly freeing themselves from the control of fundamentalists are today floundering in the power of the waster, inflating mind.

Many sensitive young persons, under the influence of the waster vogue and of the popular horror of the inferiority complex, become persuaded in college years that they must balance their weaknesses and marry an opposite. They therefore fall in love with a waster, and it is like the marriage of a finely bred setter dog with a barking collie. If there is the strength and courage to go on through to divorce, the complaint is usually mental cruelty. The real complaint is inadequacy of early orientational education. There was a muddled character, and hence no insight, no trustworthy intuition.

America has grown an enormous crop of waster minds, and has established countless nursery schools, children's clinics, and child aid societies dedicated to creating children in their image. We are to have "normal," socialized, extraverted children—children who can be happy in crowds, though they will never be able to tell a robin from a woodpecker, a butterfly from a moth, or a wise and kind face from a vulgar one. We now have this great increasing horde of unchastened individuals, and we cannot go on indefinitely inflating dollars in order to keep them happy and active and to give them something to chase. Dollars simply won't hold out. It may be that for a generation or two the thing can be kept going by the rise to power of some medical dictator who can find a way to inflate the sex experience and so to expand the sexual business into a prolonged jubilee. Yet that too would in the end pall and grow wearying, like the other games of youth. Sooner or later, a waster civilization must always fall back upon war for excitement.

These hordes of undeveloped brains that have been to college and are bachelors of philosophy, yet have really found rapport with life only in external relations and in the direct gratification of cravings, present an educational problem far more baffling than appears on the surface. For officially and from the point of view of the young, these people are educated, and what *they* are is what it is going to be like to be educated. They are for youth the best available reflection of the future. Yet for most of them education has proved but an insulation against thought, and by their college degrees they are doubly fortified against the world of mind and time.

The waster has created havoc in education, yet he is tolerant of education to a degree, for he can see some practical use in it. It may lead indirectly to a better job. *But what pray, is the use of religion?* What *are* these religious people after? Why *must* they concern themselves with other people's affairs, and why are they forever talking about the future and the past? Why can't they learn to live in the present and enjoy life? The trouble with them one and all, the waster says, is simply that they need to be taken on a good party. D. H. Lawrence had the right idea: if their beloved Jesus had just been taken on one or two good parties, all the little Jesuses ever since would have been more human. That is what is the matter with all moralists, reformers, preachers, uplifters, wowsers, medicine men and righteous Reginalds. They need a good party now and then—need to get it all expressed.

13. THE SUPPRESSION OF THE WEAKER SIDE

In the face of Christian history during the centuries of the greatest power of the Church, it behooves the religious mind to pause and consider that hidden in this resentment of all things religious is the partial awareness of a great truth. In the past, the human mind has never proved itself much more wise or kind, or far-seeing, in the name of religion, than in the name of anything else. It has resolved its conflicts wherever possible by the suppression of the weaker side of consciousness. This is what the waster is doing now. He is continually trying to get away from himself, to drown out and destroy the feebler element in his own mind, which for him is the sense of time, or conscience, or the "superego," according to your language preference.

At the height of Christian power people were doing essentially the same thing, though it was couched in different concepts. A theology had been postulated which involved the rationalization of the most elemental human wish concerning time.[8] Once such a theology had been made dominant in consciousness, to tolerate doubt became automatically the deepest sin, and the professed doubter was a criminal for whom no punishment could be too severe. It is possible that in our own immediate future the waster mind may

[8] The wish for transcendence over time. By deducing the idea of individual immortality, man reduced death and time to the position of mere incidental phenomena in his life—so long as he could keep doubt away.

achieve so strong a position that it too will undertake to suppress institutionally the other part of its consciousness,[9] which always lies just below the threshold, ready to confound. And then there will be a jolly hunting and torturing of theists as bloody and as soul-satisfying to the righteous as was ever the burning of atheists.

If that comes to pass, it will be the same people, the same *kind* of people, who do the persecuting, and the same ones will be persecuted, as was the case under Christian religious dictatorship, and has always been the case. It is the questioner and doubter, the one who voices and champions the repressed side of consciousness, who is always persecuted. When either side of his nature definitely gets the upper hand, man hates and hunts the chastened, self-aware one who sees the thing in perspective; who is aware of his own mind at its deeper levels, and so is tolerant of the weak side, and can intellectualize and carry the problem of the opposites. It is always the sure one, who has repressed one side and so cannot see deeper than the surface of his own mind, who reaches out and agglutinates with other sure ones, thereby deriving strength from numbers, and destroying by force where he cannot understand.

It makes little difference what is the name of the cause under which men undertake to eliminate heresy from the world; the same drama continually reënacts itself. It is always the smug and the sure and the undeveloped who in self-righteousness destroy the chastened mind, whether in the garb of bishop, baron, bolshevik, or rationalist. The inability of the undeveloped mind to tolerate and intellectualize conflict constitutes the deepest bafflement of civilization.

[9] There is of course no such person as a "pure" waster. Everyone is partly waster and partly character-phyllic. We all have impatient moments and reverent moments. The problem of types in psychology is really a problem of the dominance of expressive and inhibitory patterns, or habits. Yet the problem remains real enough. Personalities do become dominantly waster, dominantly Promethean, etc.

In the light of its importance all other problems of life pale and fade to insignificance. It is possible that the only really significant thing that man is now doing lies in the extension of his understanding of conflict. If this is so, then the deepest tragedy of human life lies in the irrelevancy of psychologists.

Until there emerges somewhere in the world a strong social cohesive force whose function will be to protect and support the matured mind against the less matured mind, it may remain as pitifully futile and idealistic to urge men to know themselves, to intellectualize conflict, to grow minds, as to ask them to love their neighbors. To do these things is still nearly fatal, even for those who are economically secure, for it means isolation from their own kind, and these isolated ones are hated by waster and reactionary, by communist and fascist alike. *In the past religion has bound minds together effectively only at low levels of intellect. It is a vital question whether men can find a way of using religion as a cohesive and protective force in binding together minds determined to intellectualize conflict, and so to achieve a common purpose at high levels of self-understanding.* It is really the question of whether or not coördination can be effected between psychological and religious training. Unless distinct headway is made toward such a coördination, both psychologists and ministers of the near future will remain as futile as in the near past.

A religious movement is always the crystallizing of a system of ideas which for a long time have been playing near the surface in many minds. It is barely possible that this idea of uniting the functions of psychology and religion has already grown close enough to the awareness threshold in thousands of religious minds to serve as a matrix about which a true religious movement may come into being. Such a movement seems likely to be the only alternative to the settling back of Western culture into the truculent little national arrogances and militarisms that have for so long characterized its history.[10]

For ages the best and most sensitive minds have been caught and destroyed in the pendulum swing of power back and forth between the intellectually obsessed *realist* and the wish-obsessed *idealist*. Character has thus been continually cut off at the top of its development. No power can change this situation except a power which can *teach*, rather than merely preach, such insight into the deeper levels of individual consciousness that well-educated minds will everywhere be restrained by forces *within themselves*, both from the school-boyish folly of "rationalism" and from the insanity of emotionally charged theologies. No such power yet lies in academic or medical psychology, nor is it to be found anywhere in the formal teaching of religion. The burden of our speculation is concerned with whether or not it can be created through combining and focusing the wisdom of these three human ameliorative influences. Can an influence be brought to bear which will prevent the mind from continually dying back and destroying itself by suppressing its weaker side?

This, I think, is the crux of the religious problem. Traditionally religion has always been used as a force for the suppression of the weaker side of the mind. If it can be turned to the counter-purpose of maintaining the mental balance *by supporting the weaker side against the stronger side*, we may thereby tap an immense unsuspected reservoir of creative im-

[10] This "Decline of the West" has now been predicted in a great volume of widely read pessimistic literature. Certainly Spengler, and so far as I know all of the sanguine prophets of futility, overlook the tremendous potential power in religious movements. If a religious movement should come into being, which is at the same time a psychological movement carrying techniques for preventing the dying-back of the brain in early middle age, there is no predicting how far it may go. I suspect that human inner life can be changed as rapidly and as radically by such a religious movement, as outer conditions have been changed within the memory of some of us.

pulse, and of security for the aspirational element of civilization.

14. THE CHARACTER CONFLICT AND THE PROMETHEAN CONFLICT. THE DEEPEST HUMAN STRUGGLE

The mind can hold together at high levels of understanding only by building an extension of consciousness into the time dimension. It is not possible for long to tolerate the full awareness of the meaning of death except in terms of a point of view in which the span of human life bears somewhat the same relation to the span of the envisioned objectives of life, as a conception of three dimensional static existence might bear to the idea of movement through time. This time dimension is about what character means to human consciousness.

The time-heeding element of the mind is forever engaged in a struggle with the time-oblivious element for conscious dominance. It is the war between high-level dominance and low-level dominance; between mind and instinct; between a chastened, or reverent psychology and an impatiently expressivistic, waster psychology. *This struggle for character is the central conflict of life. It is the deepest cleavage that splits the human mind, and the profoundest manifestation of the eternal struggle of the opposites in the panorama of consciousness.* Because it centers so clearly about the concept of character I have long called this most basic conflict the *character conflict*.

Superimposed upon the character conflict, there is in nearly every religious mind the persistent awareness of another, nearer, and more immediately vital general conflict, and the haunting sense of a mortifying and unnecessary ineffectiveness, which *just barely* seems to stop us from entering into a fairer world. In the psychological analysis of religious minds I have again and again come across a disturbing "feeling of the almost." It is as if the human mind stood upon some misty threshold and could almost but not quite see across into a way of life infinitely closer and warmer than the Christian heaven; an actual world of present life, barred from realization now only by the lack of quite the courage to say, *I will.*

This feeling of the almost is so common and so widely known, that often there is vexation and shame in the mood, as if the individual had stood at this threshold many times before, and always had failed, yet knew that he need not fail. A former patient has described the mood to me in a letter. "I often feel it when it is late and I am tired. I seem to stand in some important position in the world, at the head of an army or on the bridge of a great ship. There is urgency of action, and I must act. I must do something of very pressing importance in the face of a crisis. I am on the verge of acting, and it is as though I could not move. I am not paralyzed, as in the car track dream; it is more that I am caught in some internal struggle, and the forces in me are at loggerheads against themselves. I know what to do, that is very clear, and I know that the moment I do it I shall be free. All about me seems charged with readiness, nay eagerness, to declare the greatness of my deed. And then it all rises up inside me and I am vexed and irritated and unhappy with myself. I am sure there is some vexing internal conflict which I ought to control, but somehow cannot quite control."

This is a deeply religious man. He is a minister and in ordinary life he is jolly and full of wit. He is quite clearly conscious of himself. He is not caught in the character conflict, but he has written a remarkably suggestive indication of the presence of another general human conflict which is of the greatest importance in understanding the religious mind. There is a factor in human consciousness *which splits the character-loving mind against itself*, and continually renders it unable to cope with its own weaknesses, though in numerical strength it necessarily greatly outnumbers the waster mind (for if this were not so, civilization would fly at once into chaos). This factor I have come to call the *Promethean conflict*.

Chapter Five

THE PROMETHEAN CONFLICT

The Promethean conflict splits the character-phyllic mind against itself and cripples it in its warfare against the waster trend. The Promethean element of consciousness is the forward straining dream of a better world. When dominant, this element gives rise to radical idealism. The Epimethean or backward straining element is the wish for safety and for the security of righteousness. Epimetheanism is conservative idealism. The dominantly Epimethean personality is as intensely religious, as noble and selfless, and as character-phyllic as the Promethean, or even more so. In minds unable to intellectualize conflict there is continual struggle between Prometheus and Epimetheus, often resulting in the end in general frustration or in a passionate giving over to waster impulses. Promethean dominance is of course extremely dangerous, and is very much rarer than Epimethean dominance. Through Epimethean hatred and suppression of Prometheus, the latter is often driven to a false identification with the waster, and hence is sometimes crucified with thieves. Prometheus is the prophet, Epimetheus the priest.

Chapter Five

THE PROMETHEAN CONFLICT

15. PROMETHEUS AND EPIMETHEUS

THE late William Jennings Bryan feared and disliked the mind of Clarence Darrow far more than he could have feared an opportunist or a ruthless exploiter of natural resources, more than he ever feared any waster. Yet these two are classic examples of two radically different kinds of character-loving minds. They were great-hearted leaders of rival camps of idealism, as they glared across at each other in that famous trial at Dayton, and were much alike inside, except for one seemingly minor difference. They had resolved the Promethean conflict at opposite poles.

In Greek mythology[1] the Titan Iapetus wedded the fair Clymene, an ocean nymph, the daughter of Oceanus. These two became the parents of four immortal sons, Atlas, Menetius, Prometheus (Forethought), and Epimetheus (Afterthought). Prometheus and Epimetheus molded an image of clay similar to the form of the gods, Eros breathed into its nostrils the spirit of life, and Pallas endowed it with a soul, whereupon man lived, and moved, and looked out upon his new domain.

Prometheus gazed upon man and his heart was filled with a great compassion for his handiwork. He longed to express his deep paternal affection with a noble gift unshared by any of the other creatures of the earth; some gift that would bring man nearer to the immortal gods. He begged Jupiter to permit him to bestow the gift of fire, but Jupiter refused, and after long conflict in his own mind Prometheus resolved to

[1] Following Guerber's interpretation in *Myths of Greece and Rome*, pp. 14-17.

obtain this gift for man in spite of the will of the gods. Therefore on a dark night he entered the abode of the gods on Olympus, quietly hid a lighted brand in his bosom, returned to earth, and presented the stolen treasure to man. But soon from his throne on the peak of Mount Olympus Jupiter saw a strange light upon the earth, and thus discovering the theft, his wrath knew no bounds. He seized Prometheus and bound him fast to a rock in the Caucasian Mountains, where he summoned a great vulture to feast day by day upon the unfortunate offender's liver, "the tearing of which from his side by the bird's cruel beak and talons caused the sufferer intense anguish. All day long the vulture gorged himself; but during the cool night while the bird slept, Prometheus' suffering abated, and the liver grew again, thus prolonging the torture. . . ."

> Thy godlike crime was to be kind
> To render with thy precepts less
> The sum of human wretchedness,
> And strengthen man with his own mind.
>
> —BYRON.

Wherever mythology is known some form of the Promethean legend appears. Prometheus is the bringer of new light, the restless penetrator of the future who, heedless of his own world of present comfort, eternally yearns to discover new knowledge. In so doing he eternally endures the resentment of the other side of the mind, projected as the righteous hatred of the gods, who have always seemed a little unreasonable about the tree of knowledge. "And the Lord God commanded [the] man saying, Of every tree in the garden thou mayest freely eat: But of the tree of the knowledge of good and evil, thou shalt not eat of it; for in the day that thou eatest thereof thou shalt surely die. . . . Now the serpent was more subtil than any beast of the field . . . and the serpent said unto the woman, Ye shall not surely die; for God doth know that in the day ye eat thereof then your eyes shall be opened, and ye shall be as the gods, knowing good and evil. . . . And the Lord God said unto the [Promethean] serpent, Because thou hast done this, thou art cursed above all cattle, and above every beast of the field; upon thy belly shalt thou go, and dust thou shalt eat all the days of thy life. And I will put *enmity* between thee and the woman, and between thy seed and her seed. . . ."

The Promethean wish to penetrate the unknown is actually the keystone upon which the Christian explanation of sin and unhappiness rests. Prometheus carries the torch of inquiry to the outermost reaches of thought and to the inner recesses of the soul. He is the inventive genius of the human mind, but he is thereby always tempting the patience of morality, and so becomes the object of intense suppression. More serious for his own welfare, he is made the victim of spurious imitation, and thieves often claim identity with him. He is therefore fortunate when he escapes crucifixion with thieves, and it is only the rare Promethean who lives to see the triumph of his own vision.

Epimetheus is the follower of the right, the adapter to the present, and the worshipper of the wisdom that is. He is the supporter of the will of the gods, and the counter-balance of the restless Promethean urge. His values are the values of the right way. Thus Spitteler has him say to the angel of worldly affairs, ". . . Pray give me a conscience that I may learn '-tion' and '-ness' and everything that is just."[2] This unswerving morality is soon rewarded. "And so it came to pass, as Epimetheus rose up, that he felt his stature was increased and his courage more steadfast; he was at one with all his being, and his whole feeling was sound and mightily at

[2] Carl Spitteler, *Prometheus and Epimetheus*. Translated from the German into English by J. F. Muirhead and published by Jarrold's, London, 1931, p. 24. Muirhead retains in his translation the German "heits" and "keits" in place of "-tion" and "-ness," which appears in a translated quotation from the same source by Dr. Jung in his *Psychological Types*.

ease."[3] In the formula of -tions and -nesses, carried by his conscience, Epimetheus has a sure shield against both the misanthropies of man and the jealousies of the gods. He is "in." He is one of the blessed, however Prometheus may scorn him and taunt him with having bartered his soul for salva-tion and righteous-ness.

Epimetheus is afterthought, the spirit that carries the sacred tradition. He is less heroic but not less noble than his brother Prometheus, for he is the cement of the social order. Without him there would be no human world, and the habit of civilization would vanish in a flash to chaotic fragments. Epimetheus personifies what James must have been thinking about when he referred to habit as the great flywheel of society. Prometheus is the inner flame of desire for a *better* world; the will to aspire to the stature of the gods; the spirit of the splendid urge. These two aspects of the human mind are not quite expressed by the terms conservatism and radicalism, for there are many conservative people who are not Epimethean, and many radicals who are far from Promethean.

Conservatism often is mere selfishness, and radicalism often is mere negativism; yet Prometheus *is* radical, and Epimetheus *is* conservative. The meaning lies deeper than these terms reach. Both Prometheus and Epimetheus are noble. Both are responsible, time-dimensional characters. Both are, in the widest sense, highly religious, and each stands in antithesis to the waster. Yet each perpetually mistakes the other for the waster, and human tragedy follows, for then the religious mind makes war against itself.

When Prometheus is dominant in a mind it stands alone, often against the world, always against its immediate world. The Epimethean mind means wholeness, support and reassurance; but always reassurance in an approved rightness,

[3] Spitteler, *ibid.*, p. 24. This passage as quoted is from Dr. Jung's translation, appearing in *Psychological Types*, p. 213.

not in a patent selfishness. *A religion* is invariably Epimethean, but its founder is often far over toward the Promethean extreme. Christ, of course, is Prometheus, the noble sufferer for mankind, but the later hosts of his followers and believers are predominantly Epimethean. Prometheus is never a follower; he is the bringer of *new* light. A religion is heavily Promethean in its youth, but it soon grows Epimethean or it dies. Prometheus only launches ideas into the world; he does not carry them beyond the critical period of their pragmatic evaluation. In a sense Prometheus is the spirit of youth, but only of the youth of ideas, for in human life physical youth is actually a period of predominant Epimethean thought. This may be true only because of our slow and heavy education, and because of the need in a disoriented world for devoting so much youthful energy to the matter of social and sexual statuses and to earning a living.

There are then two sharply divergent paths, between which the responsible, time-conscious mind becomes confused and loses its way. There is a high road and a low road, a dangerous and a safe road. The Promethean way is along the high road; it is the wish of man to be a god, to transcend, to awaken to an undreamed splendor, to follow the splendid urge. The Epimethean road leads through the valleys of safety and certainty.

The religious mind generally resolves the conflict after a time by becoming essentially Epimethean, but the Promethean urge still lies not far below the threshold of consciousness, and there are few sincerely religious persons who are not haunted by it all their lives, in phantasy, in revery, or in dreams. This, I think, is the origin of the persistent "feeling of the almost" that is so dominant in religious minds. The recurrent splendid impulse to do something of vital use in the world is the Promethean wish, and the sense of helplessness, or paralysis, or insignificance and futility in the face of this great life desire is the price the Epimethean religious mind must pay for the compromise it has made. The Epimethean sells his soul for -tion and -ness, but he is still in conflict below the surface. The Promethean wish is *almost* conscious.

16. THE PROMETHEAN, THE EPIMETHEAN, AND THE WASTER

The waster does not know the Promethean conflict, for he is free from inhibitory morality and has no sacred, burning inner impulse to lead him into suffering for the sake of mankind. His impulses are dominantly outer impulses. Therefore he is free to express his wishes and antipathies in essentially wholeminded channels. His one noble antipathy is directed against the religious mind, which he sincerely and perhaps truthfully stigmatizes as the meddling mind, the reformer mind, the righteous or moral mind. Since most religious personalities are dominantly Epimethean, it is practically the Epimethean character that the waster hates, and between these two there is waged a bitter, eternal warfare. The Promethean is necessarily rare, both because no society can support very many of him and remain cohesive, and because he is almost inevitably self-eliminative, rarely enjoying comfort and recognition and rarely reproducing his kind. Further, because of his aloofness from the world of adaptation, he is almost never recognized for his true nature, but is most often classed among "thieves and radicals."

The Epimethean typically knows the Promethean only as one different from himself, and so confuses him with the waster enemy. It was Epimetheans who crucified Christ and burned Bruno. Similarly the waster knows Prometheus not, and therefore scorns him as an Epimethean, or moralist. Following the great revolution of the nineteen twenties in America, in which the wasters wrested the upper hand from the Epimetheans, Prometheus was put to the sword (pen) with hearty gusto. He is continually caught between these two deadly hostile elements and suffers the cross-fire of both. Moreover, there are waster minds cunning enough to hide behind him, and to quote him with just sufficient misinterpretation to meet their own objectives. For illustrative purposes, morality and fundamentalism are Epimethean; experimentation is Promethean[4]; and inflation is the waster mind rampant.

The religious mind is hampered in its warfare against the waster by this eternal inner struggle between the Promethean impulse and the tightening mold of precipitated, Epimethean thought. It need struggle far harder against the hardening of its own traditions and institutions than against the waster. Without *some* of this Epimethean hardening of the mold of habit, mind could never have become cohesive, and civilization could not have existed. Yet without the counter-balancing Promethean wish man could never have aspired to a consciousness transcending his own instincts.[5] So far as we

[4] That is, the inspired application of experimental method; the will to discover new knowledge. There are of course whole armies of men and women calling themselves experimental scientists, who, far from being Promethean, are merely job holders.

[5] Here as everywhere is the eternal problem of the opposites—the *enantiodroma* of human life, as Jung likes to call it. We seem to ride to higher consciousness on a very slender track, and any force which throws a mind off balance appears to be fatal to it. Wisdom can be achieved only through *carrying* these deep-lying human conflicts into high levels of intellect. To *resolve* them is fatal. This is what I mean by the urgent necessity of intellectualizing conflict, a necessity which constitutes the Gordian knot of religion. Yet there is more to it than that. In order to be able to tolerate suspended judgment concerning these deep-lying, ultimate alternatives, it is necessary to establish clear decision in minor, mundane matters, and to reduce much that otherwise produces social and intellectual stalemate, to the automaticity of habit. It is the problem of establishing a hierarchy of discriminative insight into the relative importance of things. Character refers to decision and predictability in immediate, personal matters, but also to a dependable elasticity and toleration of conflict farther out at the periphery of consciousness. Without the former quality, the latter is unachievable. It is only by coördinating and disciplining elementary functions that we free the mind to meet wider problems with

know, no animal that has gone before upon the earth has travelled so far, but all have frozen in somewhere along the route, victims of an external or internal shell of their own precipitation that gently closed about them and locked them in forever; victims of some hardening of the pattern, causing the suffocation and death of their Prometheus. They *resolved* the Promethean conflict, and in so doing inevitably destroyed their soul. To *resolve* deep-lying conflict is death to the soul. To intellectualize it and to carry it at higher levels is life abundant.

Prometheus, the will to understand, struggles forever to break, or stretch, or bend the shell of mental habit, and by this eternal struggling man has climbed far from the solid earth. In better moments we feel this to be a climb along some invisible magic ladder that must lead at last to the abode of the gods. In these better moments the Promethean spirit waxes and the human heart is light, but time and time again we crash. It is then that men say, "Look at Greece, look at Rome, look at Russia. Let Prometheus be chained for yet a while." The Christians burned Bruno, but it was not Bruno they hated and feared. It was the Prometheus in their own hearts that they tried to destroy. Had they entirely succeeded they would have destroyed the human soul.

The most trenchant problem of religion is to learn its own mind, and to distinguish between the Prometheus in its inner consciousness, and the apparent enemy without. A mind

---

elasticity. Without such discipline, every temptation of the day can throw a mind off center, creating chaos and frustration.

The centipede was happy quite,
Until the toad in fun
Said, "Pray which leg comes after which
When you begin to run?"
This wrought his mind to such a pitch
He lay distracted in a ditch,
Uncertain how to run.

which has made internal peace with the Promethean conflict, uniting its own Prometheus and Epimetheus in a functional brotherhood, can resist any waster influence that ever flourished upon the earth. It is only when one of these elements is crippled by the premature resolution of the Promethean conflict that the dogs run away with the game.

Forethought and afterthought, when brought into adequate integration with each other, constitute a well-balanced religious mind. Together they are an orientation in the time dimension, and of all the suggested criteria for the recognition of fully adult intelligence, I know none so revealing or so valid as evidence of an adequate understanding of the Promethean conflict and of the history of the play of it in one's own consciousness of the past. A man who has insight into the manifestations of "conservatism" and of "radicalism" which have characterized his own intellectual and social history; who sees these in relation to each other and in relation to his consciousness as a whole, is almost certainly one who can be trusted to teach the young, to keep happy, and to confound all wasters.

The physiology of the Promethean personality may some day be understood, though probably not until after its psychology has been mastered. It is certainly related emotionally to the child mind. Only persons capable of a childlike focusing and concentrating of feeling, are capable of the great sacrifice of the Promethean way of life. The Promethean seems to have carried the heart of a child into adult life. His sacrifice lies in estrangement and dissociation from other generous, feeling minds, as he moves farther out on the intellectual gradient, closer to the gods, and away from the sympathetic understanding of his brother, Afterthought.

The Promethean conflict is the strife which takes place in the human mind between the yearning for understanding, and the nearer, more immediate pull of those living affections and desires which are conditioned upon the good will and the support of fellow beings; desires for the happiness of loved ones; for the alleviation of pain and disappointment in minds that cannot understand the inner dream; and for the warm reassurance of mundane honors. This conflict is the rock upon which the religious mind founders and is split against itself.

In the same sense that it is possible for a mind so inclined to find sexuality at the foundation of all conflict and to define all explanatory concepts in such a way as to support this supposition, it would likewise be easy to so stretch the meaning of the Promethean conflict as to read into it the origin of all human perplexity. Such a point of view could be used to explain the religious mind, though it would actually fail completely to grasp the motivation of the waster mind, just as the Freudian sexuality formula or the Adlerian social dominance formula really apply intelligibly to the waster mind, but completely miss the motivation of the religious mind.[6]

In spite of the great sacrifice, the *fully* Promethean personality is happy, and he may indeed be the most intensively happy of people. The legends concerning Christ paint him as so happy that he was able to maintain orientation even in the face of mortal agony. On the cross he complains apparently less of pain than of the momentary loss of the vision: "My God; my God; why hast Thou forsaken me?"

The lives of true Prometheans strongly suggest that great happiness may lie in intense suffering, if only the mind can be kept clearly pointed.[7] Likewise the clearly Epimethean personality is happy. He is probably the only *common* exponent of solid human happiness on the earth, for so long as he keeps clear of the Promethean conflict and remains sure of

[6] In general men can see only what they can feel. Freud has throughout his life *felt* intensely anti-religious.

[7] An intensely focused mind seems able to gather and redirect the energy released by pain, turning it to ecstasy. Is masochism, then, essentially an attention phenomenon? And the sexual inversions?

his -tions and -nesses, he is impregnable. On the other hand the waster is seldom prolongedly happy, for his happiness is conditioned upon both the perpetual renewal of his own appetites and the inexhaustibility of materials upon which to exercise them. He lives for the first half of life, and like Peter Pan could find prolonged happiness only in perpetual youth. After the flush of youth is gone, either his appetite or his materials are forever giving out, and the waster then pays for the upper euphorial range of his cycle with recurrent periods of profound depression and frustration. His life is an alternation of extremes. In mental pathology he tends to become the *manic-depressive* of the psychiatrists, while the time-dimensional mind in pathology tends overwhelmingly toward the other general psychiatric category of *schizophrenia* and *psychasthenia.*[8]

In practical psychology not many individuals are found who are clear examples of any of these three extreme patterns. We meet only trends. Yet the trend with reference to the character conflict becomes almost necessarily rather definite by the time middle life is reached. Most personalities settle during the thirties, if not earlier, into a permanent temperamental identification with either the expressivistic waster outlook, or with the time-contemplating point of view. But

[8] This is true, at least, of religious minds that have come to my professional attention. I have the impression that the "hysterical," or expressive neuroses are quite rare among the sort of people I have been describing as religious; and that when religious minds develop symptoms of strain, they are generally depressed, often psychasthenic symptoms. Statistical data are nearly worthless here because of the lack of any standard definition of "religious." Identification with the ministry is certainly not a valid criterion. I have known ministers and priests who seemed as far from the broader religious outlook as professional politicians sometimes are from the international outlook, or professional prostitutes from a wise sexual philosophy. But such data as I have may be presented for what they are worth. In a series of thirty-six cases of neurotic complaint among ministers and theological students, I have only three records showing expressive, manic, or euphorial symptoms. The predominant trend is toward psychasthenia, chronic fatigue, self-abasement, and anxiety.

there remain a few individuals who seem unable to achieve even this fundamental orientation, and these oscillate back and forth between profoundly antagonistic loyalties until they become the most bewildered and unhappy creatures of the earth.

Where such a condition of disorientation prevails into middle life, the character conflict may break over into overt behavior in all of the classic symptoms of neurosis. When the deeper levels of the personality tend toward the waster side, the symptoms are typically hysterical[9]; when the deeper levels tend toward self-control, the symptoms are typically psychasthenia, depression, chronic fatigue, and the anxiety neuroses. From the point of view of the clinician who treats the neuroses of middle life, this central conflict is far and away the most essential cause of human disorientation, and nothing can be of greater importance to the patient than an accurate diagnosis of it; for such persons can often be reeducated with astonishing results. They can be turned either way. A good religious mind can generally turn them toward the dominant development of time orientation, or an antireligious psychoanalyst can make of them happy wasters.

But from the point of view of the student of religion it is the secondary Promethean conflict that presents the most trenchant problem, and in the adequacy with which this conflict is recognized and handled there probably rests the answer to the question of the survival of the religious mind in its present cultural continuum. Socially responsible groups need perhaps above all else to be taught an insight into the manner in which the character-phyllic mind struggles against itself and permits its vital energies to leak away.

For practical purposes this may mean that the most urgent primary objective of religious education should be to reach the Epimethean mind and bring it to an awareness of its own repressed Promethean desire. If this is the case, then

[9] That is, expressive, wild, uncontrolled.

clearly one of the most fruitful investments of religious energies of the future will lie in the further development of psychoanalytic techniques and in the application of them to religious purposes. The great army of Epimethean minds represents a gigantic potential energy, certainly enough to overpower the waster trend in human life almost overnight; but it is energy that is locked and unavailable, like the energy of a very hard anthracite coal. There is insufficient free Promethean fire to kindle the religious mind to effective action.

Meanwhile the few Prometheans who do become articulate, more often find themselves identified with some remote and impossible radicalism, some premature socialism or communism or objectivism,[10] than with their natural Epimethean brotherhood. The Promethean fire and courage that could give the religious mind all that it needs to take unquestioned leadership in the world of human affairs, is either repressed entirely, or fired off at long, ineffectual range. Here is the acute psychological problem of religion: to reach the Epimethean mind with educational techniques and to divert some of the latter's energy toward better coördination with its more volatile and adventurous Promethean inner self.

Typically a religious person reacts far more violently to the Promethean than to any other influence. It is almost a valid test for religion to ask a man what he thinks of some prominent Promethean contemporary. The response of the religious mind is likely to carry an emotional color, and is more often negative than positive. In this active fear of the Promethean, there is the fear of disturbing a balance. It is like the fear of looking up when crossing a stream on a nar-

[10] This well-known tendency of Prometheans to throw their energies into futile protest movements and to identify themselves with the early verbal skirmishings of extreme left-wing threats, constitutes one of the most poignant tragedies of human life. It is so patently a railing and struggling of sensitive idealism against fraternal dullness and smuggery. It is the impetuous gesture of the grown-up sensitive child who, starved of understanding and affection, dreams of heroic, spectacular sacrifice.

row and uncertain bridge. Out of such fear the embattled Epimethean attacks his own recessive Prometheanism in the persons of those who express it dominantly. That the Christians put thousands of Prometheans to violent death in good religious faith, condemns religious effort only in the sense that bad cooking condemns the desire to eat.

17. THE SACRIFICE AND RESURRECTION OF PROMETHEUS

Gerald Heard points out in his book, *The Social Substance of Religion,* that man seems always to have regarded himself as *at present not happy,* though sure that he has been happy in the past, and will be so again in the future. The present is like a valley between two higher, happier areas of ground. This feeling I have continually found in consultation work with religious individuals. Some vague shadow of the story of the garden of Eden and of the promise of redemption floats in the semiconscious periphery of every religious mind. At conscious levels it becomes the wish to go back to the good days of the past, or to build for the good days of the future, according to temperament. The Freudians too have found this tendency in human minds, but it becomes for them only a yearning back to the womb.

It may be this persistent, vague sense of dissatisfaction and conflict with the present civilization that has given rise through time to the many Promethean and Epimethean legends of folklore. Forethought is the leader of the way out of the present unhappiness into a brighter future. Afterthought points the way to recover the pleasant past. Where these two wishes have grown into balance at a good intellectual level, the whole personality points toward a nobler future, yet strives to reach it through cherishing and cultivating the wisdom and the happiness of the past.

The kind of future then imagined is simply one which preserves and extends what has been loved in the past, while eliminating as much as possible of what has been painful.

It is a future not too remotely different from the past as seen through a golden haze of individual and collective memory. To imagine it does not strain the intellect.

But man tends to grow restive under the strain of his central conflict, which is the eternal struggle with the waster element of his nature, and hitting upon the idea of super-reward and super-punishment as a bold stroke toward settling this struggle forever, he postulated a fixed supernatural heaven and hell. This is an idea which will work only if the mind is prepared to accept a *discontinuum* of natural sequence, which automatically contradicts and discredits the function of intellect. That is, it will work only if Prometheus is cut off altogether from consciousness. The supernatural idea as a moral control demanded the sacrifice of *natural* intellect in return for an automatic morality. This was the supreme sacrifice; man darkened the light of his own intellect, hoping for resolution of the basic conflict. Compared to such colossal mortification, the sacrifice of a few first-borns and virgins seems little enough indeed!

The conception of an already prepared ideal future, compensating present life, automatically dispenses with the services of Prometheus and renders his voice a sacrilege. The more he then struggles to return to consciousness, the more vigorously he is hated and disavowed. *The mind binds itself over to repress its own Promethean function, in return for the assurance of a heaven already Promethean, and man bargains away his earthly soul for the delusion of an unearthly one.* Prometheus is the sacrificial offering. The most valued thing, power to use forethought, is offered up.

The Freudians refer to the mental strain resulting from the feared sacrifice of the most valued thing as the *castration complex.* From a Promethean point of view we might in a similar manner refer to the supreme sacrifice as the *encephalectomy complex.*[11]

[11] Encephalectomy is, literally, excision of the brain.

Thus in our own religious tradition the personified Prometheus is offered up as a real sacrifice and crucified. He is crucified and buried deep in the remotely conscious levels of the mind, and there chained to the firmest rock, where a great bird, Conscience, continually guards and crucifies him anew.

Prometheus is generally crucified along with thieves and opportunists. But this is only half of the tragedy. There is a converse which is perhaps even more bitter. Not only is Prometheus thus denied by his brother, but wherever for a moment there breaks out some impulsive desire to *serve and protect* Prometheus, thieves and opportunists are always there first, eagerly awaiting a chance to impersonate him and to steal his well-earned reward. Opportunists rush in to seize Promethean laurels, as sparrows and starlings sometimes snatch the grain put out for rarer visitors. Prometheus then often starves in the very garden of those who love him and offer fervent prayer to his deified prototype.

Nowhere is the bitter irony of this tragedy more clearly seen than in that astonishing movement known as progressive education. In a wave of Promethean enthusiasm a number of colleges and schools were established in America during the late nineteen twenties. They were to be dedicated to the fearless pursuit of truth and to the magnificent application of it to the growing mind. Faculties were hastily built up, drawn chiefly from conspicuously "liberal," or "rational" Promethean imitators. In nearly all of these schools, the sifting of the years has brought to light essentially the same picture. Perhaps never in educational history was there gathered such a crop of unchastened, unmellow, and unmatured young expressivists as these progressive educators were.

There have been Promethean minds in the nets that were cast so enthusiastically into the sea of educational ferment, but the dominant trend has been far from Promethean.

These young progressivists turned out for the most part to constitute a hard-talking, hard-drinking, loud-living band of frolicking wasters, possessing little more insight into their own or other minds, than would be found in a random sampling of New York's Greenwich Village, or London's Bloomsbury. They were happy opportunists, revelling in the stolen rewards of Promethean suffering.[12]

But Prometheus is yet immortal, in the sense that mind is immortal, and although crucified he remains an element in every human life. Psychologically he becomes only dissociated from the conscious focus. Man sacrifices the life of his fore-brain in order in insure his -tion and his -ness, but the sacrifice can never be complete so long as there remain living forebrains in the world. Prometheus strives forever to return to his own, and it may be significant that in the Greek legend Hercules, himself the son of Jupiter, at last slays the vulture and releases the suffering god. We speak of the great wonder of the building of the pyramids, but it may be that future ages will speak with awe of the nearly absolute chaining of Prometheus through a thousand years of human life. It is one of the stupendous achievements of life on the earth, the supreme sacrifice of history, and everywhere the religious mind still carries the encephalectomy complex.

Yet today Prometheus is abroad. Experimental method

[12] During the past ten years I have had the good luck to be invited to visit a considerable number of these progressive schools, in America and England. The difficulty referred to here has, I think, been common to them all. Always the door has been opened to Prometheus, and always the waster has entered. But this is in no sense a condemnation of progressive education, or of the courageous idealists who have founded these schools. In many cases the school has stood the strain, and at the expense of enormous early faculty turnover has fought its way through to a genuinely Promethean atmosphere. In a few instances there has been wise and shrewd selection of faculty from the beginning, but more often the faculty turnover has been staggering. I cite these facts not to dampen an enthusiasm for what is probably the most significant and exciting sector on the educational battlefront, but to illustrate the relationship that exists between the Promethean and the waster mind.

has slain the vulture. Even a dozen years ago it was risky to teach Promethean psychology, for then the religionists themselves were distinctly less friendly to such an outlook. They were far more solidly Epimethean. Whoever in the early nineteen twenties tried to teach a psychology dealing directly with the Promethean controversy found himself shortly in the Promethean predicament, and it was exciting going. Yet now in the same university he could teach this point of view with almost total freedom. He would indeed often receive support and gratitude from the very sources that loved him least, half a generation ago.

So far as the outlook of the Protestant churches is concerned, there has been a nearly miraculous change of heart. Never was there a time when more challenging and more interesting careers lay open to vigorous minds than are now to be pursued in this overlapping field between religion and psychology. It is a strange paradox that such opportunities should lie open to young men and women in a time when the great majority of youths know not what to do with themselves.

> "Good was it in that dawn to be alive,
> But to be young were very heaven."

18. EPIMETHEAN AND PROMETHEAN TRENDS. BEHAVIORISM

Epimetheanism is the backward look, a straining back and a tight gripping of a morality. Among the characteristic Epimethean movements of our own times was the rise to power of the Methodist Board of Temperance and Morals. The great picturesque achievement of it was the struggle for prohibition, that tragicomic monster child of Epimethean religion and of a dissociated Promethean psychology, which sat for more than a decade upon America's shoulders like one of those woolly red flannel undershirts of New England boyhood days. Behind it there was the surging of a kind of aspiration for a better life that should go down in history as noble and heroic, though it may not do so; for Epimethean orthodoxy, the puritan reformer mind, does not sit well in the nostrils of the most widely heard critics of the day.

Recent Promethean trends have been mainly associated with the attempt to make a religion of scientific method and of rational thought. Examples of it are the literature in praise of the new scientific psychology which a decade ago was hailed with high enthusiasm; the movement toward freedom of the press and the popularity of the literature of "higher criticism"; the fact of survival at all of such periodicals as the *Nation* and the *New Republic, American Mercury, Forum* and the like; the astonishing popularity and success of a few brilliant religious minds who have departed radically from Christian orthodoxy; the enthusiastic reception of the later, urgently Promethean writing of H. G. Wells. The utopia, wherever it occurs, is virtually a Promethean literary orgy, and as nearly all of the later work of Wells may be regarded as a series of experimental attempts to write the utopia from different directions of approach, Wells may be taken as the literary prototype of Prometheus. A perfect example of purely Promethean literature is, I should say, his essay, *The Open Conspiracy.* The charming attacks of Mencken and his friends on the Bible belt are not only delightful and perhaps enduring American literature, but they constitute magnificent material for teaching social psychology.[13]

A very significant Promethean movement not always recognized as such was the behavioristic movement in psychology, identified somewhat inaccurately with John B. Watson. The behaviorists were for the most part young psychologists who had perceived the fearful damage that the magic word

[13] College sophomores readily perceive the play of Promethean idealism in this material, when it is pointed out to them, and it gives them an insight into the mechanism of the Promethean conflict in their own minds. It is of course not the thing he attacks that Mencken really hates, but the suppression of Prometheus.

can do—words like *mind, soul, instinct,* and *the unconscious.* They saw the human mind entangling and deluding itself in these magic concepts like a goose in a fishnet. Psychology, they said, had become an academic old ladies' tea party; indeed it was not so much a psychology now as a *psychologoguery.* It must get rid of all its magic words and must build a new scientific vocabulary of its own. There soon came into existence a great literature of the conditioned reflex, the stimulus-response mechanism, the patterned organic confusion (emotion), the subvocal verbalization process (thought), and the prepotent stimulus-response path (instinct).

The behaviorists had a keen recognition of the extent to which existing institutions had been smugly rationalized about the concept of instinct. All of the stupidities of mankind had long been accepted as irremediable, for were they not merely uncontrollable outgrowths of instinct and of the old Adam? The real objective of behaviorism became that of reëducating society concerning the *basic motivation* of the human mind. Man was not to be a creature of instinct, stamped with hereditary limitations predetermining him to make war against himself, to murder and lay waste, and to be forever obsessed with his little gods. But he was to be himself a potential god, capable of rising to unimagined heights, if only he could overcome his fatal subjective obsession and view himself with rational objectivity.

This was a Promethean declaration of independence. It carried the stamp of a noble enthusiasm, and was tremendously healthy medicine for academic minds accustomed to a monotonous recitation of the thirty or sixty imagined instincts of man. It awakened many slumbering psychologists and sent them bustling about for more defensible material, thus leading directly to closer coördination between psychology and the related biological disciplines. And it created a new sensitivity to the use of words.

Now among the avowedly religious, the Promethean conflict rides very close to the conscious threshold. Always the orthodox concentrate their hatred, not upon the heathen, the unbeliever, or the waster, but upon the unorthodox. Whoever is also deeply religious and seeks the light, but seeks it in a different quarter—let that one watch out for his skin. The terrific hatred of the orthodox for behavioristic psychology was not founded upon abstract principles, nor was it quite by accident that a large proportion of those psychologists who were in the behaviorist ranks were men who at some time in their lives had been intimately associated with the profession of religion.

Of a group of forty-one behavioristically inclined psychologists interviewed at the American Psychological Association meetings in 1925, twenty-nine, or seventy-one per cent, had either trained for the ministry or had at some period planned such a career. Watson himself is the son of a minister, and started in his father's footsteps. Yet priest and orthodox minister alike have risen to greater heights in their defensive castigation of behaviorism, than in their resistance to the genuinely anti-religious Freudian psychology which in the wider conflict represents their true antithesis.

The Promethean behaviorist in his intense wish to free the mind from its ancient obsession with instinct and from the dominance of self-focused biological nature, sought to divert consciousness away from the self,[14] to bring it to bear upon the outer relations, upon the *behavior* of people. In this manner the behaviorist hoped to bring psychology to an acceptable position among the objective sciences, but such a hope was foredoomed to disappointment, for no mind can ever comprehend either the outer or inner world except in terms of an equally adequate comprehension of the other.

[14] Behaviorism actually came into existence as a protest against the method of *introspection* in psychology. The isolated contemplation of the inner world precipitated a pendulum swing which became the isolated contemplation of the outer world.

As a psychology, behaviorism must take its place among the premature overenthusiasms engendered by the popularization of objective science; but as a philosophic and religious vitamin it was a magnificent Promethean gesture.

In its striving to free man from obsession with his instincts, behaviorism is the diametric antithesis of the Freudian plan of persistently rubbing the mental nose in those elemental sexual, digestive, and self-assertive preoccupations which naturally characterize the normal first awareness of the emerging child mind. The Freudian psychoanalyst restores his patient to wholeness by taking him back to instinctive, self-loving beginnings of life as the one safe and true foundation for an orientational outlook. This is simply *resolution* of the character conflict. From the Freudian bias, it is "character" that causes human conflict, and when this is amputated, the patient is successfully analyzed. He can then live a more expressive life, as a conscience-free waster. Freudian and behaviorist are the complete opposites in psychology, and the Christian Epimethean is the unreconciled brother of the Promethean behaviorist.

Behaviorism aroused terrific hatred, and nowhere was ever the Promethean conflict more bitterly fought out than behind academic walls. Here the two great camps of religious idealism were drawn up in a direct antagonism nourished and reënforced by all of the notoriously petty personal jealousies and little schemings of academic minds. Here the two eternally opposed trends of responsible thought were in direct competition for control, and the hostility was by no means limited to psychology departments. The civil war spread through all of the academic branches, and during the past twenty years the watchers of the intellectual trails have observed what must have been one of the bitterest open conflicts in the history of the human mind. Just as in the war over prohibition, it was really the Prometheans and Epimetheans who were quarrelling; and the waster element took advantage of the opportunity.

In prohibition the two camps of idealism were at war over the distribution of a commodity which neither of them wanted, while the common opportunists, bootleggers, lawyers, politicians, longshoremen, innkeepers, ammunition dealers and such like practical-minded men made merry over the spoils. By splitting the religious mind, prohibition shook a golden harvest into the lap of the waster.

It was essentially the same on the academic front. The Prometheans by permitting themselves to become identified —for the time being allied—with *all* haters of conservatism, gained the advantage of a certain numerical strength against the Epimetheans, but only at the cost of defeating the ultimate purpose of both camps, for it was through this successful imitation of Prometheus that many an opportunist established himself firmly in some position of academic power. Now it is hard to tell from university catalogues whether the purpose of education is to develop minds, or advertising managers, bond salesmen, public accountants, and athletic directors.

Chapter Six

A WORKING PICTURE OF THE MIND. THE GROUND PLAN OF A PSYCHOLOGY ADAPTED TO THE STUDY OF CONFLICT

The real function of psychology has always been to formulate a systematic *conception of mental life, and the central difficulty in such a task lies in building a system which will apply equally well to the inner and to the outer world of consciousness. A psychology which fails to describe individual human motivation and the outer patterning of the social order as coördinates and intimate reflections of each other, can be of little use to the student of conflict. The latter needs a systematic classification of mental life in which individual and social psychology are seen as inevitable reflections of each other, for he has found to his sorrow that otherwise both become isolated and cut off from real experience. Academic psychology has up to the present been of surprisingly little assistance in the study of conflict. The reason seems to lie in its tendency to try to separate individual from social psychology. This chapter constitutes a skeleton or ground plan of a psychological point of view concerned primarily with the study of conflict.*

Chapter Six

A WORKING PICTURE OF THE MIND. THE GROUND PLAN OF A PSYCHOLOGY ADAPTED TO THE STUDY OF CONFLICT

19. THE FIRST PREREQUISITE OF A PSYCHOLOGY. A SYSTEM

IF THE whole sweep of an individual's total awareness of his world is visualized as one continuous picture which has for convenience been drawn in a series of connected *panels*, like an early Chinese descriptive painting, then it may be possible to speak of a part, or facet, or panel of the mind without destroying the perspective or losing the relationship of that panel to the whole. This conception may also help to visualize the inter-relation between individual consciousness and its wider complement, which has sometimes been called the group mind. The panels may be thought of as constituting a plane of contact between the inner and the outer world. The social institutions and the inner individual mind are imperfect mirror images of each other, and they fit against each other, like the inner and outer parts of a mold. Whatever system of classification a psychologist applies to one, he must above all else be certain that it applies equally well to the other.

Thus the panels of an individual consciousness must fit, or correspond to the panels of the wider, outer picture which is the total social influence. If we were to picture the individual mind as made up of ten panels, we should expect to find ten corresponding basic social institutions. A constant check upon the adequacy and good sense of a system of either individual or social psychology can be made readily available simply by applying it to its complementary reflection and seeing if it works. If a panel picture of individual consciousness does not also provide a skeleton which seems to carry the observed social institutions fairly well, it is undoubtedly a false picture and should be discarded.

In my own approach to the human mind I build my thinking around a basic system which has five panels. There is nothing necessarily right or true about this system except that it enables me to cope with disorientation in all sorts of minds with a measure of effectiveness, to locate the foci of individual mental distortion, to trace the history of it, and to reveal its nature to minds in a position to profit by such assistance.

It is as if the mind were a tree, and the circumference of approach to its trunk were divided into four facets, which correspond to the four clearly demonstrable hereditary human motives, namely the need for sustenance, for physical and later for social security, for sexual happiness, and for orientation. The awareness processes which are rooted respectively in these four elemental life activities, give rise to what I like to call the four structural panels of consciousness.

Extending through the whole span of these four elemental panels, like a vascular matrix, and growing up from them, there is a universal craving for compatibility between inner feeling and outer experience—*a wish for the marriage of feeling and intellect, and a potential keen delight in the achievement of it.* When consciousness succeeds in becoming both an act of feeling and of thought at the same instant, that is, *when a meaning is emotionally felt,* this wish is fulfilled and the resulting awareness may be called, under various circumstances, a feeling of wholeness; the certainty of significance; a flash of insight or intuition; the aesthetic experience; and on rare occasions the mystic experience, or the intense experience of the soul. It is this experience of the soul[1] which

[1] To an Eastern this state of highest delight may be the state of *yoga.* Yoga is a transcendence and a complete abstraction from all of the four

seems to constitute the final goal of all human striving. It is the state of *feeling-awareness,* and when it is achieved, man is at home in his universe.

Feeling-awareness may be achieved in many of the relations of life or in only a few. Some find it mainly in material possessions, some mainly in social domination, some mainly in the "wild chaos of love," some mainly in religious meditation. This experience may extend evenly through the four structural panels, or it may occur largely in a one or two panel distortion. *The pattern or profile of the occurrence of feeling-awareness in a mind is what I mean by the fifth panel.* It may be visualized as the finer branching and the leafy interlacing of the tree. It is actually a *qualitative* element superimposed as a sort of over-panel upon the whole structural four panel picture. It is the panel of feeling, the panel of the soul.

These five general skeletal concepts provide sufficient canvas to paint in the outline picture of a mind so that it has a system to it and fits together, and at the same time is a meaningful reflection of the social institutions. The panels may be named as follows: (1) *Panel of Material Relations.* (2) *Panel of Social Dominance and Submission.* (3) *Panel of Sexual Relations.* (4) *Panel of Orientation.* (5) *Panel of Feeling-awareness.* Institutionally, they are the economic, political, sexual, religious, and aesthetic panels.

I cannot emphasize too strongly that this descriptive system is only a pragmatic device and not a didactic classification. If this essay were concerned mainly with individual

---

elemental panels of experience, even from time orientation. We of the West have what is probably a younger point of view. I think that our truest "soul state" emerges not from transcendence of the elemental panels of experience, but rather from the achievement of harmony and proportion in the various panels. The roots of true human unhappiness lie always in distortions, in placing false values on experience, and hence in destroying the health and balance, and the normal growth, of the fifth panel.

psychotherapy I should state the panels somewhat differently, and particularly would emphasize that underlying them all there is a constant undercurrent of awareness of the morphologic and physiologic self,[2] a kind of anchor or reference point of all consciousness in the biological reality. This underlying subsoil of a mind determines individual color and tone, and the buoyancy or heaviness of the personality. The condition of physical being is the first and deepest determinant of consciousness, and everyone knows the great temperamental variations which have their roots in the state of health, in the characteristic bodily tensions, and in the physiological and anatomical peculiarities of a person. The still unborn science of individual differences will rest upon an understanding of this underlying matrix of the mind, and the shrewdest psychologists of the future will be those who have developed great insight, not only into the constitutional types of structural make-up, but also into that still more obscure and interesting world of the continual interplay of physiological and mental individuality.

This is one of the great uncharted continents of human thought, and therefore an exciting hunting ground for observant minds. The present concern, however, is mainly with the social and educational problem of directing the conscious focus *away from* the instinctual self, and therefore I shall not in this book especially emphasize this biological subsoil of consciousness.

20. THE FIRST PANEL OF CONSCIOUSNESS

The Panel of Material Relations. Concerned with economics, with the acquisition and possession of things, with the wealth and property relations of a mind.

[2] Dr. George Draper in his book, *Disease and the Man,* has used the panel idea from the perspective of a medical clinician, describing the human personality as the clinician sees it. Thus he has three panels, which he calls *morphologic, physiologic,* and *psychologic.* He is looking at the total personality from very long range. Here we are making a closer and more minute examination of the psychologic panel.

This panel no doubt has its chief tap root in food-getting activity. The earliest wealth is always food, including air and water, though secondarily wealth soon becomes rather the power to control the potential supply of food, and also the supply of other things, some of which are more directly related to the other panels of consciousness. Thus wealth beyond a certain critical point actually means freedom or power in sexual and social and religious and aesthetic interests, as well as in food control. The institutional reflection of this panel is constituted chiefly in a group of habit patterns or "rules of the game" that have grown out of the early discovery of the efficacy of storing up for later use, first food and then other materials for the satisfaction of wants. Thus the idea of property came into the world; then the representation of property by various symbols, such as flocks and herds, or number of wives, and finally by money.

Psychologically, a unit of money is a release from the necessity of expending energy in the pursuit of basic wants. Money provides the individual who possesses it with the means of satisfying routine wants without specific effort on his part. He is released from food hunting and the like, and thereby is given freedom to seek to satisfy remoter motives; or if he has none, to do nothing at all. This is the important psychological meaning of money. It is society's guarantee that its possessor *ought* to be free to follow his own desires; that he is trustworthy, has earned the privilege of choosing his patterns of interest, and can be trusted with the responsibility of choosing wisely—that is, of choosing interests which will promote the wider social good.

If a society were to be functionally healthy in the first panel, money would be available only to individuals of relative maturity, who could be trusted to use their released energies toward the accomplishment of purposes pertaining to the ultimate social good. In a functionally planned society, money would then become, not the "root of evil," but a weapon through which responsible persons could control and penalize the waster. It would be a means through which the responsible mind could be freed for the application of its energies to purposes in line with its central desire to build character, while the waster would be automatically inhibited from wasteful activity, simply by being deprived of money. The latter thereby of necessity would become preoccupied with the basic first panel business of maintaining physical life, until he could rise perhaps in later generations, to a nobler and more responsible mental level. Money would be a means for putting the waster back to the foot of the class. Theoretically it is just that. Yet with the chastened, or responsible mind everywhere entangled in the Promethean conflict, the waster steals a march, finds a short cut to money, and so "gets away with" his unchastened way of life.

From the point of view of the first panel, it is possible to estimate the degree of maturity of a social culture and to put a finger upon the deepest sources of conflict and perplexity, simply by determining the extent to which the society has succeeded in keeping money away from waster personalities, and in guaranteeing its rationed distribution to more highly cultivated, responsible minds. If now we consider that almost the opposite of this ideal actually prevails; that we permit money to be distributed chiefly on the basis of persistence and cunning in getting it—when we contemplate the implications of this anomaly, we begin to comprehend the terrific handicap which man saddles upon his Promethean prospects here in the first panel. A deep wonder comes into consciousness that the idea of character should continue to hold its own at all. There must be strong character fortifications somewhere in the other panels. Somewhere there must exist a powerful enough reservoir of human Promethean resolve to overcome a terrific first-panel distortion.

As matters are arranged, the maturest and most developed minds frequently lack sufficient economic security to free their energies for intellectual pursuits, while persons in possession of wealth are often totally irresponsible in the character sense. The former group have grown souls at the price of weakness in the first panel, and the latter have achieved a distortion in this panel at the price of their souls. Both suffer from first panel social ineptitude. *The suspicion begins to dawn that after all there may be a cardinal first panel virtue, which is poverty in the sense of frugality; and a cardinal sin, which subjectively is the lust for wealth, and objectively is conspicuous personal expenditure.*

21. THE SECOND PANEL

The Panel of Social Dominance and Submission. Concerned with the dominance and submission relations between human beings; with social prestige; with law and order; with the political and social status arrangements of society; concerned particularly with protecting individuals from harm intentionally inflicted by other individuals.

The second panel has its main root in the need for protection from the danger of physical injury and pain, carelessly or intentionally inflicted by other individuals. The need for protection of life and limb lies at the source of all law and social arrangements. This panel develops into the ramifications and privileges of social prestige, and gives rise to the institutions that make for social security. It is on the one hand the effort of the individual to find stability and his safe, *right* place in the social hierarchy; and on the other, the institutionalizing of tabus which protect individuals from destruction and exploitation, so long as they keep to the rules of the game. Thus there is protection of the young; protection of women; of one's own family; protection of the weak, who are presumed nevertheless to possess some virtue of value to society; and protection of specialized individuals who, in devoting their energies to their chosen fields of effort, have neglected to arm themselves against the possible depredations of more practical-minded neighbors. These functions of protection become institutionalized and turned over to specialists who are the police, and in a still wider sense the army and the state.

From the point of view of the character conflict, the most important implication in this panel bears on the protection of relatively civilized individuals from exploitation by less civilized or less disciplined or less chastened individuals. It is well known that the more intellectual and the kinder a personality becomes and the less concerned with its own protection it grows, the more threatening is the danger of exploitation at the hands of watchful opportunists. This is the source of the Promethean tragedy. We worship the legendary Prometheus who suffered for us on the cross of human selfishness and practical-mindedness, but the Prometheus who lived next door had better get his mind down out of the clouds before we possess ourselves of his house and daughter.

If this social-protective panel of consciousness and the institutionalized projections of it were to disappear from the human mind overnight, the wasters of the earth would destroy every Promethean and the bulk of Epimetheans before the setting of the sun. This is a point upon which it might pay every young college undergraduate who thinks he is a communist or an anarchist to pause for a moment and meditate.

The less complex and mature, and the less tentative and tolerant a mind is, the more readily it agglutinates or combines with other minds at its own maturity level. It is very much easier to find a hundred low grade intellects that are like-minded, and so will fight readily for a common cause, than to create such a gregarious tendency at maturer mental levels. This is the eternal dilemma of both State and Church. There is always a strong tendency for the unchastened to combine against the chastened, for the barbarians to invade and destroy a civilization.

Similarly in the case of individuals, the sensitive and relatively fragile one is forever in danger of being caught out alone, and bullied or destroyed by a *gang* of less imaginative beings. There is eternal warfare in every public or private school, between the more solitary and the more agglutinative personality. Children carry these great fundamental conflicts closer to the surface than adults do, and whoever desires to understand the human mind as a psychologist must understand it, always does well to turn to the child for instruction.

In the eyes of normal, average children, the more civilized individual is often a sissy, a highbrow, a peculiar or queer one, one to be made fun of and persecuted if he is weak, and to be opposed and defeated *en masse* if he is strong. I do not mean to imply that all sissies or highbrows or queer ones are of a more civilized stamp, but only to point out that the child mind does not make any fine discrimination between the mentally and emotionally superior, and the inferior. To the "regular fellow" they are all in one group—the different—and the general tendency is to level the differences or eliminate the individual if possible. This same impulse is seen in cattle on the range and in herds of animals under natural conditions. It is deep in the human remoter consciousness, and the second panel is civilization's defense against its continual tendency to tolerate the destruction of that element of the social hierarchy which has gone on to more elaborate feeling and thought.

The great second panel problem of life is that of building institutions which will protect smaller and often maturer groups from conquest and exploitation by more numerous and, because less mature, more like-minded and closer knit groups. In general it is the protection of those who by choice or necessity have developed wider, more impersonal and extensive consciousness, from those who live at levels of narrower, more personal and intensive consciousness, and so have both intenser hatred in their hearts, and greater group strength to destroy. It is not only the problem of attempting to alleviate the hard life of Prometheus upon the earth, but also in the end a matter of protecting Epimetheus from the waster. *The cardinal second panel virtue is humility rather than obedience, as we now use these terms, and the cardinal sin is arrogance, or the lust to dominate.*[3]

22. THE THIRD PANEL

The Panel of Sexual Relations. Concerned with the attempt to harness and civilize the emotional and creative energy of the reproductive urge, which is known to be capable when under discipline of warming and supporting the whole tree of character.

This panel of consciousness has a double tap root, growing in part indirectly from the reproductive phenomenon and from the consequent familial organization of society; and in part directly from the emotional pleasantness and excitement that is organically associated with sexual experience and hence with sexual objectives. This emotional characteristic of sex interest, when under discipline, renders available the whole energy resources of a personality as a sort of vast reservoir for warming and enriching and supporting character. When out of discipline it can for the same reason devastate a personality almost as effectively and as quickly as can hunger or pain.

Sexual activity is perhaps the most dramatic instance in which the whole organism functions altogether harmoniously toward a single goal. There is a clear one-directional striving, which means that for the time being—it may be for only a moment—perfect orientation and perfect happiness

[3] Some psychoanalysts love to use the term *ego* and speak of ego domination. To me such a term seems pretentious, cultish and unclarifying. Ego refers, if to anything at all, to the whole consciousness of the relations of the self, in all of the panels. We need terms that can carry a sharper focus than "ego."

are achieved. Wholehearted integration of purpose becomes a reality, and biologically the great straining of animal energies toward the unknown finds expression in an adventurous, courageous, reckless upward surging of life. For this reason the third panel often becomes a highly distortional fifth panel focus; that is to say, the soul comes to find its main expression in sexual activity.

This sounds like religious language, and it is not surprising that psychologists have established a close identification between religious and sexual motivation. There is no doubt that religious experience at its best involves at least the redirection of some sexual energy. That is what religion actually is concerned with—the direction and aiming of emotional energies. Freudian psychoanalysts call religion a *mere* sublimation of sex, and therefore are not interested in it. Better, religion is a harnessing and utilizing of some of the normally wasted, lost, or *surplus* energy of sexual and other expressiveness that ordinarily does not actually contribute to the enjoyment of life at all.

Ideally, civilization focuses, applies, and makes the most of affective energy that *might* have been expressed in sexual channels. Yet an excellent civilizing influence does not really rob the sexual panel of any of its energy, nor does it take away any of the feeling value of sexual consciousness. Rather, it acts as a balancing and an invigorating stimulus upon both the sexual and the orientational panels of a mind. It lays open an avenue by which sexual energy can be made to yield a greater return in subjective happiness, and in the end, instead of lowering the feeling value of sex, it lifts it to a point where a higher feeling quality permeates *not only specific sexual relations but the whole range of consciousness.*

Here is without doubt where the character conflict rages in its clearest manifestation. Sexual desire is life at high intensity. It lifts the whole personality up out of itself, and opens the way for transcending the self. But in this very lifting power it also carries a certain volatility, a tendency to escape, to run off into the air, leaving the overly sexual mind in a depressed, unsupported state, like a collapsed balloon.

There is another and perhaps still more important aspect of the character conflict in the third panel. When in the early decades, at the time when the sexual tide is at its height, some emotional energy does get successfully diverted into intellectual channels, so that ideas once are *felt*, this energy seems to be permanently sustained, and even appears to increase in old age. It is not lost. But if it goes off through direct sexual, or other direct channels, the later decades of life may find the personality with no feeling support for its mind, and thus without intellectual interests in old age. This is possibly the worst of all human fates. Old age without an intellect is far more distressing than youth without sexual paraphernalia. To *such* a predicament there is no solution. This unfortunate person, instead of rising to the full human stature in the second half of life, must carry a deadened brain through what should have been his best years. He must read detective stories and play bridge and think about personal things, even at the very top of his life; and if he is a college professor, as is pitifully often the case, he will lecture from his notes of twenty years back. The interests which enrich and bring the second half of life to its fulfillment, seem to grow from seeds that must be planted back at the time when the elemental energies of life are at their full.

These are not really sexual energies at all, until they appear in sexual relations. They are drawn from the general stock of life energy, and they *may* be expressed through a very few, direct biological channels, or through a much wider branching of interest and desire. Which way they shall go is determined by the way the individual handles the character conflict. *The cardinal third panel virtue does not lie in sexual inhibition, nor in sexual expressiveness; but in the diffusion of sexual energies into enthusiasms, which will in later life lay the pattern of the growth of the soul. The cardinal sin in this panel, as in the others, lies in distortion of values; that is, in devoting too much direct energy, either expressively or repressively, to sexual phenomena. The moral prude is probably as scarlet a third panel sinner as the sexual waster.*

23. THE FOURTH PANEL

The Panel of Orientation. Concerned with maintaining orientation in time, through bringing feeling to the support of thinking, thus building a conscious hierarchy of values which will give zest and expectancy and point of life, and will lead a personality out to its fullest emotional and intellectual development.

The three panels now described may be considered the *biological* panels of life. They have clear and obvious foundations in essential biological process. There remain the *psychological* panels, which really come into existence through the emergence of the idea of time, though these also have roots extending back into biological function. At least two such roots seem intimately associated with the orientational panel. One of them, the universal need for awareness of direction, has been discussed. The other is the tendency of man to reach out and explore, to *wonder* about things, and to carry this *curiosity* over into overt manipulative action.[4]

The urge of curiosity and the need for time orientation make up the warp and the woof of a common fabric, for where the one leads the other must follow, or the drama comes to an end. Orientation may be simply the response of the living forebrain to the play of curiosity upon it. In any event the two ideas are intimately related, and both are

[4] Or to carry overt manipulation over into curiosity. It seems to make little difference which way it is put. Manipulation is probably much older than curiosity, but in human life the two have long since established a cyclic relationship.

involved in the mental activity which I have been calling orientation in time, that activity which leads to the development of personality beyond the satisfaction of the elementary biological motives, and on to the growth of character. This is the activity which psychologists and religionists together must learn to harness, until it can be used everywhere to prevent the dying back of the brain.

Religion is concerned with the development of character, and one of the most important purely religious problems arises from the fact that no single orientational or theological formula can ever be made to apply comprehensively to character. Yet the religious mind must needs produce theologies, as a crustacean must secrete the carbonates which harden into his shell. Then the first fourth-panel perplexity becomes that of maintaining a balance between the Epimethean defense and protection of these theologies, and the Promethean defiance of them, without in the process crucifying Prometheus between a communist and a fascist, and without selling civilization over to the despoilage of the waster.

Theology is the natural *end product* of a life of religious thought. If an agreement could be reached among all religious teachers that no person under sixty be permitted to teach or lend the authority of his approval to a dogmatic theology, and then only in the presence of and for the benefit of persons past fifty, the perplexities of religion might be greatly alleviated and the Promethean conflict might lose its bitterness.

Theology is a natural product of intellectual maturity, but to teach a *child* a theology is to run the danger of warping and distorting the child's life. Premature theology may be as fatal to mental growth as cast iron clothing would be to bodily growth. Yet to fail to stimulate and develop the child's religious thought and wonderment is to starve the superpersonal levels of his mind and very possibly to stamp out the essential significance and happiness of his life.

There are no absolutes in these matters. It is necessary to use judgment. It is possible to teach religion without prematurely teaching a theology. This book is for better or for worse an attempt to do so, for though it is concerned essentially with religion, you will look in vain for a theology in it. The Christian Bible is a magnificent assembly of literature and philosophy and poetry; yet it is ruined for generation after generation of young minds, just as are the best fruits of later literature, by the unimaginative and untimely presentation of such material. Here is Epimetheus without a trace of the spirit and imaginative aspiration of his brother. The best time to enjoy the Bible is late in life, and education should lead in general to a reading of the maturest of human literature in the second, rather than in the first half of life.

A man need never be afraid to talk to his son about religion, and about his God, if he will remember and make clear to the child that in so doing he is really talking about a panel of his own character, about his time-dimensional aspirations, and his noblest dreams. Hour for hour, it is likely to be of far more good to a person to talk to a religious child about such matters, than to talk to a psychoanalyst. *The cardinal fourth panel virtue is reverence for character, and the cardinal sin is premature orientational certainty, which produces inevitably either a Promethean, an Epimethean, or a waster distortion.*

24. THE FIFTH PANEL

The Panel of Feeling-awareness. Concerned with the development of sensitiveness to the subtler, less obvious meanings of things; with the imagination of pain and joy; with warming and vitalizing the aesthetic experience; concerned in short with the growth of the human soul. The panel of the soul. The aesthetic panel.

There is in human life an experience that is both a feeling and a thought at the same instant. It is the experience of simultaneously seeing and *feeling* a meaning; this is the aesthetic experience. The highly aesthetic mind is, I think, simply a mind unusually sensitive to a system of meanings, and capable of quick emotional participation in them. It is the mind that *feels* itself over into things in its environment. There is in English only the rather inexpressive term *empathy* for such a quality of mind, though the Germans have the much richer term *Einfühlung* (a feeling into something). This priceless gift may be developed with respect to a very wide variety of things in the environment.

There may be a fine, quick, rich feeling for form, for color, sound, taste, or for movement in the world about; for living things of every kind or any kind, from the smallest insects to the largest animals; for the human face with its infinitely changing nuances of expression, and its play of emotion and feeling; for the signs of intellect, of character, of humor, and all the countless other revealing signs in the human personality; for the enormous differences of personality in children and dogs and birds and in all animals; for the characteristics of different trees, the personality of them, and of different leaves on a tree; for the grasses, flowers, weeds, the smells of the earth, the changing moods of the weather and the seasons and the rain; for the personality of pieces of furniture and of old clothes and old houses. To some persons these things are *people*, and they can be talked to, and in this there is fine play of feeling and affection, at times perhaps the finest and rarest blends of the affective life of rich minds. There may be feeling for pictures and for other artificial attempts to catch or reproduce beauty; for the dance and for the flight of birds; for the happiness and the pain of creatures who cannot speak an overt human language, such as insects caught in houses and trying to get out; and finally and perhaps in the end most important of all, for ideas.

In short there is in the manner of movement and in the behavior and in the mere existence of all things, a rich world of aesthetic experience for the mind that is sensitive enough or observant enough, or richly enough supplied with feeling, to respond. These experiences make up the fifth panel consciousness of a personality. Sometimes they are called aesthetic, and sometimes they are called religious. They are, I think, always characteristic of the truly religious mind; yet the term religious at its best connotes more. It also carries the idea of orientation, the sense of time perspective, and vision of the future. *The most highly religious personality is he who has combined fourth panel maturity with fifth panel maturity, and thus not only has thought his way through to an orientation, but has a strong sense of feeling identification with his world. Unless the idea of fourth and fifth panel integration is implied, there is, I think, no need of using the concept religion at all.* One may instead refer respectively to the orientational and to the aesthetic aspects of a personality.

The really great differences in human personality lie in these last two panels. Fifth panel consciousness is to be compared to the upper branches and to the finer interlacing leafy detail of a tree. The first four panels are the heavier branches. The main trunk branches play a part in the tree's personality, but it is an underlying or background role. The impression of the tree that lingers in memory is usually the upper and outer shape; the quality of the finer branching; the character of the leaf and flower and fruit; or perhaps its fragrance or the sound of the air in its leaves; or its silhouette against an evening sky. These, we may fancy, are fifth panel tree characteristics. To some minds a tree is a personality with all of these qualities and more. To others it is merely wood or shade. It is the same with life at large. To the waster, life is principally an opportunity for *expression,* and the world *a thing to be used.* To the chastened mind life is an opportunity for contemplation, and the world *a thing to be understood and felt with.*

There are people who are aware of and responsive to an aesthetic range many times greater than the normal, common average, and it is not inconceivable that there may be far more difference in this respect between a really sensitive mind and the normal, than between the latter and that of an inarticulate animal who has, such people say, no soul.

In an earlier chapter religion was defined as a process of bringing feeling support to the character pattern of a personality, and character has been pictured as consisting of a somewhat more deep-lying fabric than fifth panel fabric. The fifth panel is concerned with *delicate* appreciation of the meaning of things. I have once or twice referred to it as the *highest* panel of consciousness. It might better be called the most delicate, or most sensitive panel.

The fifth panel has to do with the integration of feeling with the awareness of common, simple things, in contrast to the orientational panel, which carries the function of integrating feeling with the profounder sense of purpose,[5] or direction. The fifth panel is concerned with vitalizing and supporting the most peripheral and delicate twigs of consciousness. It is quite a separable concept from the idea of orientation, for highly aesthetic minds are often not in the least religious. A person may have developed unusual feeling sensitivities with reference to some sector of human experience, without having built any general organization of character at all. The "arty" personality is sometimes a case in point.

To the arty personality the idea of character in the sense

[5] In earlier lectures, and in an earlier draft of this chapter, I have called the fourth panel the teleological, rather than the orientational panel. As I see it, these two words carry about the same meaning, but the more classic term is in much more violent disrepute in scientific circles, and I have omitted it, hoping to lure two or three thereby to read the book. For any who prefer this term, the fourth panel is the *teleological* panel.

of social responsibility is frequently quite out of the focus, a strange other language, though there is not necessarily an antagonism between the two types of mind. The waster is the open antagonist and the enemy of character, but the arty individual is merely in a different world. He has a different focus of consciousness altogether. Arty people are sometimes aware of this difference, and often speak of themselves as merely "unmoral," in contrast to the waster who is anti-moral.

The Two Worlds of Aesthetic Awareness

There are two rather different worlds of aesthetic consciousness, and in considering the aesthetic panel of mind it is convenient to speak of *natural* aesthetics and *artifactual* aesthetics. The boundary between them is not always sharp, but try to visualize in your mind's eye what the term arty personality means to you, and then compare that with the picture of an observant, eager, though quiet and humble child watching a muskrat build his house. You will then have the essential difference.

Whoever is widely aware of the world of *natural* aesthetic stimulation dwells in a kind of Forest of Arden. He comes to live "With thoughtful, searching eyes, to look with love on things and men, and to find in all he meets a constant sweet surprise." A human face or a new insect becomes not merely a thing to recognize, but a new personality, and there is a warm delight in it; the insect as well as the face. A child who has never spent happy hours watching hens, and chuckled with delight over their astonishing social hierarchies and their vagaries in the first and second and third panels, may have missed the matrix which would have grown in later years to the kind of imagination which is a true sense of humor. A mind alive to the natural aesthetic world is independent, and it has a natural buffer of resiliency and recoil, in which it perpetually recovers and is recreated, even in the face of the inevitable shock and tragedy of a world of life and death.

To have established in childhood a permanent emotional and intellectual rapport with the outer living things, is to have found an anchor in *something alive which yet does not change.* The living things of the woods and meadows and fields and marshes are immortal. They never die and leave you. They are always there. They are always the same. They have eternal youth, yet are older than you are. They have the greatest simplicity and humbleness, yet they carry the wisdom of the ages. They are artless. To commune with them is to commune with all who have lived before you in the Forest of Arden. Whoever has felt the wish for that quality of consciousness which is *to be as a little child,* has it in the hollow of his hand, if he but live where he can escape beyond the concrete and the noise and the swamp draining and the eternal covering of the earth with "improvements" that mark an urban, overstimulated civilization. It is well if a man had wise parents who took him as a child feelingly among these immortal living things that have eternal youth, for then his whole life can be a unity, and he will have no second birth to go through in order to find a character and a religion.

Only the mind well sensitized to this tremendously broad field of contact with warmth and life should ever be trusted with the responsibility of teaching children, and with implanting in young consciousness the early impressions of the world. Such people are very possibly our closest approach to the Christ ideal, for they are in a position to maintain the heart of a child through life. By the heart of a child I mean simply the prolongation into adult life of the quick curiosities and the warm emotional imaginings of childhood. When this quality somehow becomes combined with unusual intellectual maturity, a great mind appears on the earth. It is almost certainly the cardinal prerequisite of a great mind, and as it is a distinctly more common quality in women than in men, there may lie an unsuspected source of hope in a human society which seems likely to be more influenced by women in the future than in the past.

That now rapidly increasing group who find their main fifth panel life in some art love present quite a different mental profile from the natural aesthetics group. These people do not often have the heart of a child personality; they are only rarely simple; their personalities are frequently greatly complicated by profoundly conflicting orientational trends; they are often wasters in many of their affairs, though they are seldom vulgar wasters—seldom the typical big automobile, fur coat, loud radio sort of waster. The fourth and fifth panel growth of these people seems distorted, yet not destroyed, and they have turned for their higher panel ecstasies to things that the human mind has artificially produced for itself, even in urban, crowded, hysterical environments. In making and possessing and handling, sometimes even in seeing artistic things and in witnessing performances, the artifactual aesthete salvages some of the ecstasy and reassurance of the significance of life that he seems so nearly to have missed altogether in an overstimulating world.

I do not mean to imply a condemnation of the training in art appreciation and in art expression that is now in many places so heroically taught to children, but only to point out that compared to what these children *could* be taught, with only a fraction of the effort and waste, this is a poor, dead, weak thing, which substitutes but thinly for the warm and simple rapport with life which an overstimulating atmosphere obscures.[6]

[6] This point of view may seem rather an intolerant one, stated so bluntly in three short paragraphs. I am of course referring here mainly to the religious implication of the matter. I am sure that many thousands of naturally character-phyllic minds turn away, and escape, from the most interesting and important problems of life, by embracing one or

Music borders upon both natural and artifactual aesthetics. It offers a most fascinating field for the study of the fifth panel, and also one of the most important diagnostic opportunities for the psychologist. I believe that with a little further experimental work music can be shown to be of greater use than dream material in the analysis of the motivation of a personality.[7] It may be that by means of it the main drift of the major conflicts in a mind can be made out in a fraction of the time required for useful dream analysis.

Music reveals the picture of the Promethean conflict in a predominantly religious mind with nearly uncanny clearness. The natural aesthete almost invariably is most responsive to

---

more of these artifactual interests *as religious orientational substitutes*. Art interests which fit into a wider orientational picture enrich and expand a mind, but art taken as central purpose, or as central interest, is fatal to a mind. Again and again in psychotherapeutic practice, I find people who through fearfully distorted early education have *founded their religion* upon the dance, the drama, the plastic arts, some branch of music, even upon the art of dress and personal appearance, or upon "interior decoration." When through later accidents of circumstance these people develop minds, they have to go through the tragic second birth which William James described in *The Varieties of Religious Experience*. The second birth is really the breaking and resetting of the orientational backbone.

[7] The technique of this work with music will be discussed in the second book of this series (see p. 230). I have been using music in analytic work for some time. The method seems very promising and it appears to carry the advantage of being somewhat less open to wild subjective error on the part of the analyst than is dream interpretation. Music "does things" to every mind and there are fairly clear-cut response patterns to different kinds of music. These vary enormously in differently motivated minds, but they seem to vary in patterns. Through careful analysis of a number of personalities and through recording respective effects upon them of a wide variety of musical stimulation during analysis, it has been possible to pick up astonishingly useful clues, at least, as to the significance of musical preferences and antipathies. In my work these clues have proved distinctly useful material from which to construct a systematic map or profile of the fifth panel structure that exists in a patient's or student's mind. This mapping of the fifth panel constitutes, I think, the main purpose and the main value in any psychological analytic process. To reveal clearly where the distortions in the soul lie, is more than half the battle.

simple vocal music. But the determination of the dominant theme of musical love in such a mind seems to depend squarely upon the status of the Promethean conflict. The Epimethean religious theme song is that of resignation and dependence upon a higher power—the song of faith, as in the typical Protestant hymn. But the Promethean mind, far from being stirred, is profoundly irritated by this theme, and seeks instead the imaginative romantic ballad or serenade, with its long-sustained powerful chords, its expression of superhuman strength of aspiration and of heroic transcendence of self. Many of the old English ballads contain fine Promethean music. Those who know the song, *The Holy City,* can see in it a fascinating mixture of Epimethean and Promethean music.

Waster music is rapid rhythm music, often with a tone of arrogance or a repetitive expressivistic, self-assertive theme. It is simply the vulgar, assertive voice of the forgetter of time expressing itself in a harmony. For three decades now in the West this note has carried a rising intonation, like the swelling crescendo of a savage dance as it moves on toward orgiastic culmination. What the culmination is to be will depend upon the power of the character-phyllic mind to find its strength and intellectualize its Promethean conflict, ahead of a general collapse of first and second panel institutional structure. Waster music reaches a certain pathos at times, but it is never quite a sincere pathos, and always carries an understrain of mockery. The waster is never willingly caught serious in a sentiment, for sincere sentiment inevitably involves the *remembering* of time. When the radio entertainer sings in his sentiment-mocking rhythm the pleading refrain of "My baby has let me down," the Promethean does not feel a choking throb of compassion, but rather a throbbing passion to choke the entertainer.

Waster rhythm is not for a moment to be confused with the music that the artifactual aesthete loves. The latter has made *a religion* of aesthetics, and if it is music that he loves, it must be music into which he can project the whole complex panorama of the conflicts and stresses of his life. Music comes to be a main channel through which his threatened soul achieves a place in his consciousness, and therefore it is made the matrix, or habitual setting, of a vast imaginary amphitheater in which the mind recurrently carries out the drama of life. Such a person loves complex instrumental music, especially symphonies, and in response to such music he rises at times to utterly transcending heights of emotional imagination. It is as if his soul had itself become a complex reverberative instrument, and through the impingement upon it of vibration patterns into which a character can be read, the soul achieves that character for the moment, and it expands and takes life and soars to the skies of human feeling.

The artifactual aesthete is a tremendously discriminative and sensitive person. He is often generous and rich in eclectic insight, and is sometimes capable of heroic self-sacrifice. He is likely to possess all the qualities of the Promethean mind *except one. He is rarely simple.* It is not often that he can stand the strain of being considered a fool, and he flinches at the prospect of being caught serious. To be despised and villified by fools is too much for him. He cannot make the supreme sacrifice of humility. This, I think, is the true differential in the matter. This is the fork in the road where the artifactual aesthete diverges from the heart of a child personality.

The mind grounded in natural aesthetics has a certain security in the time dimension, and a sureness of its emotional foundations, for which probably nothing can substitute. The foundations will stand, even in the face of physical pain. Only a person with this sort of mind[8] is capable of withstanding the terrific strain of carrying a Promethean purpose in a world full of wasters and people who are themselves so unsure of a foundation that they dare not be caught

[8] That is, only such a person and a fool.

with any fourth panel objective at all. During the first half of such a person's life he is likely to remain incredible to his contemporaries. He is different, and it seems as if he must be concealing something. But in his later decades he tends to become either a great man or a beloved recluse. It seems to be a general principle that if the Promethean personality can hold out and remain true to itself past the thirty-fifth year, the second half of life is likely to be immensely happy.[9] Hercules (great strength) slays the vulture in the end.

I suspect then—though indeed it is only a suspicion—that individuals who love symphonies, the drama, the dance, or other works of human art overly well, are generally people who could have carried the child heart through life, had circumstances given them in early childhood the intimate influence of adult minds who were themselves safely past thirty-five and well grounded in natural aesthetics.[10]

In any discussion of the fifth panel the concept of the *mystic experience* must at least be mentioned. This is a loosely used term, but in it the two elements of thought and feeling are very clearly implied. I have elsewhere defined the mystic experience as *an aesthetic response to the intuitional*[11] *apprehension of meaning*. The mystic experience seems to consist in an emotional ecstasy following the sudden realization of a general meaning. The psychology of it may lie in the relation between the fourth and fifth panels of consciousness. We have seen in discussing the fourth panel that the

[9] In discussing this observation with Dr. Jung, I find that he too regards the middle thirties as a sort of critical threshold for emotional life. It is excessively rare for a person who has good emotional orientation at thirty-five, to lose it, and there is good reason to regard this period as the ideal one for analysis, or for psychological reëducation.

[10] This raises the very interesting question of optimum age for parentage. Psychologists have for some time noted a statistical tendency for later children to surpass earlier children slightly in mental tests and in similar performances. This may be physiological, and it may be due purely to the greater wisdom and mellowness of older parents. Possibly as we grow wiser we will tend to have our children later in life.

[11] See Appendix, Section 2, for discussion of the meaning of this term.

mind does normally strive to make head and tail of things, to maintain orientation, to get the data of experience into a system, or into a meaningful relationship. This striving constitutes the basic fabric of religion. And when suddenly a whole block of experience hitherto resistant to meaning, does as it were *jump* into a perceived meaning system, there may follow an ecstatic emotional wave not altogether unlike that of well-earned sexual fulfillment.

The resultant sense of emotional warmth spreads out into all the finer consciousness of things, and the person is aesthetically whole as well as orientationally whole. This often happens in association with a *conversion*, of one kind or another. The mystic experience is a common phenomenon in enthusiastic personalities, especially in those who have a child-like emotional life combined with an active intellect. It is often associated with a religious enthusiasm, and it is this in part that gives rise to the common explanation of religion as sexual sublimation. Wherever sudden and enthusiastic release of emotional energy occurs in human life, men who think shrewdly, but not too deeply, will doubtless always "explain" it as a substitutive sexual reaction. The mystic experience occurs in the natural aesthetic mind, at calmer levels, in connection with the appreciation of the meaning of such a thing as a pine tree, or a beetle's antennae, or a child's innocence. Similarly it occurs in the appreciation of artifactual aesthetics. Once in the Louvre in Paris I watched a woman put on a performance of writhing ecstasy in front of a Rubens painting, which I am sure a Freudian analyst would have called a sexual manifestation. She was, it is almost needless to say, quite a stout lady.

Summary

In summary, it is of help in considering the nature of consciousness to visualize it as if it were spread out in a convenient number of panels, or surfaces of experience contact. We can then think of a mind in terms of consistencies and conflicts; can look for main trends in the basic, biological panels; and can trace them through in the more complex psychological panels. In this manner we are able to keep a sort of psychological orientation, and to contemplate individual minds and social problems in terms of each other.

These five panels are somewhat arbitrarily set off and defined, but they are far from a random classification of human mental experience. They follow fairly clear natural demarcations. Most students of social science would agree to the definitions of the first three, the biological panels. The fourth and fifth could be presented with some plausibility as a single panel called, possibly, the panel of religion. In teaching this psychological conception to students, I always encounter the desire to reduce these last two panels to a single concept, and there are always a few who would subdivide the sexual panel into two rather discrete sectors of experience; namely that built around the family and reproductive and educational affairs; and that having to do with the pleasure of the personal sexual adventure. This cleavage certainly exists, and such a presentation is fully as "right" as the way I have presented it. There have been suggestions that the educational institutions occupy a sufficiently basic place in human consciousness to justify the inclusion of a sixth basic panel, that of institutionalized education. However, this relationship is purely a derived one. Education is built up through all the panels. There is economic, social, sexual, religious, and aesthetic education. It is not biologically inevitable that a person become educated. Indeed the opposite often seems closer to the true picture!

Finally, there have grown up in Western society a vast number of more or less related and more or less institutionalized activities which are really escape channels for frustrated minds; institutions of amusement and titillation. Most of them have come into existence in the name of *recreation*. But the developed mind continually finds its own recreation everywhere—in its sense of humor; in its feeling contact with the earth and with natural life; in its love of children and of the child mind; in its study and exploration of new fields of knowledge; in its reading and conversation; in its music and art and games and lectures and hobbies. A developed mind has little need for institutional recreation. Yet not many minds are developed, and these diversions and drugs and escapes play what may have become a necessary role in the maintenance of mass toleration of life, as the prohibition experiment would seem to indicate. The suggestion has been made that recreational and intoxicational interests should be included as a basic panel of consciousness, but I believe that psychologically these represent a quality rather than a sector of consciousness. Everybody tends to find his recreation at his own level, in each of his panels.

Perhaps one further note of definition is needed. I have already on one or two occasions used that feared and beloved term, *the soul.* It is one of the most valuable words in the language, and possibly of all words the most feared. We fear to contemplate the soul as the miser fears to look in his hiding place—*the thing may be gone.* This word should therefore always be handled with the utmost respect, and whoever uses it should be required to make clear just what he means. In this book I use it in a purely descriptive, and in a purely psychological (not theological) sense. By it I refer merely to the pattern of the fifth panel, that is, to the total occurrence of consciousness in which feeling and realization become one, or intermingle. Wherever a thing is both perceived and felt, there is the experience of the soul; and whenever a thought and a feeling become indistinguishable, there is the soul. Soul means oneness, unity, union between the inner wish and outer reality. As man moves toward acceptance of the universe, toward compatibility between what he feels as the wish from within, and what he perceives as the arrangement without, and as both elements expand, the soul moves toward greatness.

Chapter Seven

THE GREAT CONFLICT AT WORK

In this remaining section the vocabulary now built up, and the psychological point of view, are to be applied to the problem of tracing the elemental orientational conflicts systematically through the panels of consciousness. In this idea of using the panel method for systematic study of the sources of trouble in human life, there is nothing new. Every doctor of medicine has been drilled for years in the development of a panel picture of the physical personality. For medical students the body consists of five or six basic systems. Doctors carry this picture in their heads, and they know just what questions to ask in order to bring out a connected account of the physical history of the patient. With a system in their heads, all the information they elicit fits together into a related whole. If the psychologist is to think effectively in the field of the social relations of a mind, he too must have a system in his head, as William James so often used to say. Such a system has now been outlined, and it remains to apply it, in a sort of long-range survey, to the conspicuous perplexities of consciousness.

Chapter Seven

THE GREAT CONFLICT AT WORK

25. THE PSYCHOLOGIST, THE DOCTOR AND THE MINISTER

IN THE course of time it has come to be recognized that in mental as well as in physical life there are cardinal symptoms that reveal pathology and indicate the course that events have been taking. It is relatively easy in medicine to pick up the trail of these cardinal indicators, in one or more of the five or six great bodily systems; and having once picked up such a trail, say in the respiratory panel, one becomes at once eager to know how things are in the digestive, the muscular, the circulatory, the genito-urinary, and the nervous panels. Clear medical thinking derives from (1) knowing intimately and automatically the various systems of the body in their relationship to each other; and (2) a wide experience and knowledge of the typical patterning of common recurrent bodily ailments as they crop out in these related systems. As I have used the term panel in psychology, it has almost exactly the same connotation as the term system in medicine, for I became convinced long ago that clear thinking in psychology must in the end be grounded in the same kind of system approach as that used in medicine.

The main difference between a good medical mind and a good psychological mind is one of emphasis. The doctor relies relatively upon objective data and upon things that can be measured and weighed and matched in colorimeters and the like, though in the last analysis a first-class medical mind uses these things only as aids in the final diagnosis, which is in the first place largely intuitive, and judgmental. The psychologist has a relatively small array of objective aids or crutches, and so is much more dependent upon the quality and richness of his intuitive perception.[1] A doctor can earn a living and may make out to be a fairly good physician, even when conspicuously lacking the delicate mental sensitivities that constitute a good intuitive mind. He can make it up in part by extra attention to detail and by care in his laboratory work. I have known fairly good doctors, and of course absolutely top-notch students of medicine, who had no more insight into the minds they dealt with, than one would expect in a biologist. But a psychologist without these finer intuitive qualities is like an artist without appreciation of form or proportion. He is simply an impostor and a charlatan, however numerous his academic degrees, and however astounding his capacity for secreting statistics.

Yet the keenest and most delicate and active mind must also have a system to follow in its approach to the problems of psychology, or it flounders about uselessly and goes off at any sort of bizarre tangent. The psychologist simply must have both sides developed.

In this chapter the task is to tie in and give solid meaning to a system of social thinking by which naturally active minds, of whatever professional bent, can grapple with the problem of orientation. Society at large has suffered the loss of its healthy enthusiasms and there is a great sickness upon the educated mind; we now have a system of procedure to follow in conducting an examination, and a sort of clinical clue or preliminary bias as to the fundamental nature of the pathology. The problem is to see if this hypothesis can be

[1] At the moment the main attention of psychologists is turned disproportionately toward objectification, but there are also moments in the life of a duck when he seems to devote his attention to land navigation. So much the better for the duck, unless he in the process forgets how to swim. To try to make of psychology a "science," in the ordinary meaning of that term, is not unlike trying to make a land bird of a duck. Psychology is systematized insight into human personality.

made to save the data; that is, to see if further available facts bearing upon the social relations of a mind will fit into the system, and lead to a diagnosis.

The hypothesis is that the character-phyllic mind has lost ground on all fronts to the waster, essentially because of the internal ravages of the Promethean conflict. If that hypothetical diagnosis can be established more firmly, it will then perhaps be worth while to consider some therapeutic indications. We have also in mind a hunch or clue as to possible therapy.[2]

With a clue and a system in mind it really makes little difference where the physician begins his systematic inquiry, for wherever he begins he will in the end have covered all the ground, and in much the same manner. He may start with respiratory symptoms and end with a urinary inquiry, or vice versa. We are thinking now from the standpoint of the clinical diagnostician, examining a patient with complex and extraordinarily interesting symptoms. We are after implications, hints, subtle relations, common recurrent patterns showing up in the different panels. In short we shall be striving to combine the point of view of the medical clinic with that of the consulting psychologist and to focus it in a single perspective upon a problem, perhaps then to turn the patient over, if possible, to professional educators and religionists for treatment.

Few doctors or psychologists are at the moment willing to risk much hope on the professional religionist, for on the face of things he is in fairly desperate straits. Yet of what I suppose are the three cardinal elements of a great mind, namely *enthusiasm, intuitive insight,* and *systematized factual equipment,* the minister surprisingly often carries both of the first two. And these are the more vital two, for they

[2] This consists in part in the educational application of the techniques of psychological analysis; in part in the better teaching of history, and in all educational methods by which the meaning of time can be more feelingly and more intelligently imparted to human minds.

cannot be acquired if a person has reached adult life without them. The third can be taught to any normal individual if he can be made desirous of mastering it, that is, if he already has the first. Education is far more a problem of motivation than of factual instruction, and the quality of enthusiasm is inestimably more vital in education than the I.Q.

I have lived for many years among psychologists and among doctors, and I have found both, as groups, a little lacking in these first two cardinal elements of a great mind. This may be because the academic training that they have received not only ignores these elements, but at times actually eschews them. The young psychologist is often selected and encouraged on the basis of his alacrity in taking to objective, measuremental problems, and in manifesting characteristics that reveal a freedom from or hostility to these other traits. As a general proposition I believe therefore that I should as lief attempt to teach my particular approach to the human mind to a group of young men trained in Christian theology at its worst, as to a parallel group trained in the common variety of academic psychology.

The training of the medical clinic almost necessarily develops and encourages some degree of insight, but all of the associations of the practising doctor, and the grave personal responsibilities that he constantly carries, tend to render him a very cautious, conservative person. The Promethean outlook is therefore not very dominant in either the British or American Medical Association, and the medical mind looks upon all sudden or child-like enthusiasms with a certain denunciatory skepticism.

I rather suspect that there is more of the quality of child-like enthusiasm in the professional religious mind than in any other professional group in human society, and unless I am mistaken this is the element that is conspicuously missing from the equation which is modern social life. For this reason the general conception of a profession of religion may be worth saving, however shockingly the present practice of it has fallen into disrepute among the other professions. Somewhere there must appear a new kind of psychologist, and he must be a person of enthusiasm and insight, as well as capable of carrying a systematized, trained mind. It may be a better bet to attempt the development of such a personality from the ranks of those who tend toward the ministry, than to try to build him out of the material that is now to be found in the ranks of labelled psychology. I do not suggest by this that psychologists are emotionally inferior to religionists, but simply that for the particular job of averting the social catastrophe that seems to hang like a thunder cloud over our heads, psychologists typically lack one vital trait that the religious mind possesses.

We shall then seek in the various panels for further light on the problem of conflict, with an eye to its bearing on the central orientational conflict, and see if a diagnosis of the social sickness of society can be made.

26. CONFLICT IN THE FIRST PANEL

The Lust for Massed Wealth

There are forces in human nature which impel man to strive toward the development of character; yet we commonly set before children the first panel ideal of *getting rich*, and this ideal runs directly counter to the character ideal.[3] Matters are so arranged that young people are encouraged to *want* the first panel distortion of surplus economic power; and the most likely way to get surplus economic power is of course to want it, and to sacrifice other things for it; that is to say, to sacrifice higher panel development for it. In this vicious circle man plays a sardonic joke upon himself.

From such a strange anomaly of civilization there arises a conflict from which few emerge without lifelong mental scarring. Young men and women may be encouraged to "think of higher things," but if they direct their attention upon development in the higher panels, they run the Promethean danger of exploitation from below by less civilized creatures whose minds are more intensely focused in the first panel. The young person is everywhere pressed upon persuasively by the temptation to stop, and to throw his energy into the elementary struggle, to "let all that other

[3] The lust for massed wealth is psychologically simply a first panel distortion, as a dominating lust for social influence is a second panel distortion. These are the things that first block the development of character. It is not wealth or fame that destroys character, and hence curtails the mind, but it is the *desire* for these things; or once having them, the desire to keep them. No society can hope to move over into an era of psychological development until it first succeeds in rendering such lusts unpopular and therefore pathological. But it is not only the lust for wealth that constitutes a first panel distortion and cripples mental development. There is also a pathological negative aspect of the picture. Vocational ineptitude, improvidence, and the failure to face economic responsibility, are negative first panel distortions, as the "inferiority complex" is a negative second panel distortion.

go until later." And then of course there is no "later," for even if the individual turns out to be one of the very few who do in later years return to the wish for mental development, by the time he has done so it is generally too late. The long-neglected brain has died back to the three basic panels, like an unused muscle, and it can be brought to full function again only by Herculean effort. At best the mind may settle into a conventional religion, and then it becomes perhaps a three and a quarter panel mind.

With the general breakdown of the old religious formulae, there was an unprecedented compensatory piling up of youthful energy in first panel interests. Men turned to a sort of religion of business, and the business man stereotype came to be the dominant goal of youth's aspirations. Yet it is almost always regarded, even by business men themselves, as merely a *temporary* goal. Business is looked upon as something necessary, but not final—a hard and dirty game, to be played and won. Many youths feel that business is hard, and vulgar. They themselves are going to be business men, but only for long enough to make their fortune, which they hope and often expect, will not be for the greater part of their lives. So they go into business as a compromise, feeling that though the life before them conflicts with their best ideals, yet the end justifies the means, and they will tackle the thing in the spirit of the prospector who faces hardship for gold. For a time they carry the vision of the something beyond, which they will reach later on, after they have got the gold. Business, it is true, is narrowing and hardening work, but later on one can retire from it and can develop the better self. Then instead of yielding, like the genii of legend, to the magic touch of the hero, business reaches out its tentacles, and it gets the hero. Men and women find themselves caught, like monkeys in a trap, in a lifelong treadmill of preoccupation with matters down in the first panels of consciousness. At the beginning there is a struggle—all this is going to be over after a little while and my mind will be freer—then deeper and deeper the victim is sucked into the habit patterns of a business mind. Finally a hardening, a spreading numbness, and the struggle is over, forever.

We watch wave upon wave of young men and women as they enter this conflict and struggle in the grip of it. It is like watching an endless chain of marching soldiers. They are marching toward the promised land of maturity and understanding. It gleams and seems to beckon in the far distance. But a deep ravine intercepts the line of march. There is a fault, or cleavage in the earth. It seems an easy jump at first, and as each marching line arrives at the near bank, it hesitates for a moment, then the soldiers graduate, break ranks, take a little running start, and they jump; hundreds of thousands of them seem to jump, as into a bank of mist. And now and then, at long intervals, one or two reappear on the other side. The rest have been offered up as living sacrifices to human conflict in the first panel. You will find a few of the luckier ones sitting away the last decade or two of their lives on the front porches of little hotels somewhere in the Southwest, now and then talking a little and reading the newspaper, or playing bridge; but for the most part, just sitting. Their poor distorted brains have died back to the very stalk, like plants kept in a sunless room.

We muse in revery upon this endless parade of healthy young human brains to the sacrifice, and a vast question-mark takes shape in the mists of imagination, as animals sometimes appear in the clouds that drift near the horizon. Can it be that with all the ingenuity and resourcefulness that the human mind has shown in so many matters, it still must fail forever to bridge this elemental cleavage? Must a potentially five-panel mind struggle out its life with its energies so piled up and telescoped, even in a world richly filled with all of the reasonable material wants of a reasonably regulated population?

It is certain that the answer does not lie simply in the first panel itself. The problem will never be solved by changing the rules of the game, nor by manipulating the gold value of currency, nor by declaring for communism, nor by wars and political revolutions. These things can only drain off surplus human energy and alleviate the pressure for a generation or two. It is a problem of opening human eyes to perspectives, relations, time values; of building in a form of character which extends in some consistent, coördinate manner through the economic and political and sexual and religious and aesthetic panels, until minds in general can come to *feel*, not merely think, in terms of movement through time.

It is a great mistake to attempt to deal with these matters as purely economic problems, and similarly in the second panel, to attempt to deal with war and political corruption as second panel problems. In trying to check the overuse of the escape channel of drinking by putting it on a second panel basis and making it a matter of law, this country only succeeded in revealing itself as naive and absurd. But if the amount of money and energy and thought that went into prohibition had been put into the establishment of clinics for a five panel psychological analysis and reëducation of perplexed adult minds, the problem of resorting to alcohol might in time have worn a different aspect in America.

The Strain of Keeping the Pace

A very few irresponsible minds in a community, if in possession of money, can exert a tremendous disintegrative influence upon character. The young men are impelled to keep the pace, and to do it they are powerfully constrained to find a short cut to wealth. It is this quest for the short cut that plays such fearful havoc in the first panel of character. There is no short cut to the general maturation of a personality, and therefore a successful short cut to power in one panel is inevitably a distortion. A fully mature personality must be built through the creative effort of a succession of lives. But our traditions ring with legends of the rapid climb to wealth, and youth is stimulated to seek short cuts to a power which when so reached is actually a great evil. The young man soon learns in his quest for first panel power, that business is a sort of game, at which people bluff, and turn tricks, and join together in little agglutinations for mutual advantage against the common good. There is an easy tolerance of trickery, and it is understood that in every business there must be a little "racket," where some smart person gets more profit than would appear on the surface. Soon the young man realizes that the racket has spread beyond the first panel, that the political system itself has become in one sense a spoils system, and that people unite in mutual benefit agreements to promote their own advantage. He finds that the men who get rich are men who have a trick up their sleeves, and get in on something.[4]

All this constitutes a terrific strain on character and perhaps its worst feature is the inevitable levelling down of the mental horizon that follows the necessitous banding or ganging together in groups which characterizes the successful business game. In a society in which it is important to get a material advantage over other persons, the young man must surrender or hide his individual ideals and adopt instead as a mask the ideals and purposes and language and philosophy that make up a kind of common denominator for some group

[4] This statement may not be quite fair as a generalization. All large fortunes have not been built by trickery. Yet certainly all large private fortunes have been built by distorted and unmellow minds; for no balanced intelligence could desire a great overdevelopment in the first panel, or the continuation of such overdevelopment after a little of it had been achieved. I believe that even within another generation, it will be generally regarded as a little vulgar to crave private wealth. The vogue of the successful business man is passing, just as the vogue of the military leader has passed. The profession of arms no longer absorbs the best brains, except in uncivilized countries, but most of our best brains are still preoccupied either with making money or with keeping it.

that is bound together in the common quest. Typically he finds himself a member of several such groups. It pays to "kick with the right foot." And in becoming a joiner, he surrenders up the last hope of ever growing a mind. With each new group identification, the limits of the mental horizon are brought inward, and the soul is enmeshed like a school of fish in the tightening seine.

Finally the borderland between business trickery and dishonesty becomes merely a legal quibble. Is it dishonest or merely good business to sell a tube of toothpaste for fifty cents, when the commercial value of the material itself is really less than three cents, though you are paying thirteen cents a tube for advertising, and giving the druggist a rake-off of twenty-five cents a tube for the effort of handing it over the counter? The buyer is actually paying about sixteen times as much as the stuff is worth, and here is a sixteen to one handicap that the forces working for the building of character and simplicity must somehow carry. It is a sixteen to one victory for the waster trend over the character trend. The buyer gets cheated so outrageously that the thing would be incredible in any civilization, except for the fact that most of the buyers are themselves trying to do the same thing somewhere else in the game. Fully eighty per cent of us are somewhere identified with a racket too, and in order to keep up the general public tolerance for rackets, we are willing to submit to this one, and to other obvious first panel immoralities.

This is the kind of arrangement of things that creates an abyss between youthful Promethean resolve and the development of adult character. Here is one tap root of human disillusionment, and a primary cause of the dying back of the brain. It is not strange that so few succeed in jumping the abyss. Nor is it strange that now and again the thing should grow top heavy and out of hand. Now and then financial crises and panics occur. Then there is always a hesitation for a time between two tendencies; one toward retrenchment and reconsideration, toward facing the loss and returning to simplicity; and one toward inflation and further stimulation of an ever wilder and more dangerous distortion of values. For the waster mind, the thing to do is increase sales and speed up turnover, at any cost. Anything to get people to spending again. To aid in this all sorts of devices are brought into action, but none so devastating to character as advertising.

At least two very serious major character problems arise from the practice of advertising. First, the general spirit of wastefulness is tremendously augmented; there is conspicuous waste both in the enormous sums of money and materials that are used up in the advertising process itself, and in the pressure that is brought to bear upon the consumer to purchase unneeded goods, to waste his money. Second, advertising develops a toleration, first for exaggeration, and finally for frank untruth. An appetite for overstatement comes into being and soon creeps over into the general language. People grow accustomed to exaggeration, develop a taste for it, come to feed on it, and it subtly destroys their sense of truth. The stern thrift and economic virtue that may have been built into a personality through many generations of human life is yielded up and despoiled, and there is left a jaded, insatiable appetite for more and more of the enervating stuff of overstatement. The process is not unlike the development of a drug habit. There are hundreds of thousands of people who buy magazines primarily for the advertising material. They enter into the game, following the competing extravagances of rival claimants for the cigarette and mouth-washing championships, as they follow the baseball scores. In so doing they contribute to the general weakening of character. The problem of orientation in such a society grows difficult enough to be interesting, for the essence of character lies in modest statement.

Since getting along successfully in business is largely a matter of personal alliances and of general popularity and reputation, one of the most vital concerns of the ambitious business person is to keep up an appearance. He must keep up the sort of appearance that favorably impresses waster minds, for these are the men who are most prominent in the game and carry the greatest influence. This calls for two things: an appearance of prosperity; and a conformity to the dominant style, in dress, in behavior, and in conversation and mental outlook. Here is the source of the business of keeping up with the Joneses. However thrifty and simple a man's deeper economic morality may originally have been, if he enters into this competition of appearances, he must become a conspicuous waster. It is an unwritten rule of the game that a man's prosperity is to be judged somewhat by the expensiveness and wastefulness of his wife's appearance. And when his daughter goes to college she must not be out of style. These are levelling influences. They can keep men from thinking with more inexorable certainty than can a pint of alcohol or a quarter grain of morphine a day. Yet from a character point of view, material thrift and simplicity in the first panel are more vital to the ultimate happiness of society than possibly any of the other moralities.

The conspicuous waster is the most immoral person in the world, in the sense that he does the most damage. Almost every human life that is exposed to his presence is thereby laid open to some degree of low-level conflict. A restlessness is stirred up down in the first panel, where all should be serene and well ordered. People who have money to spend, but lack economic morality, are many times more effective in the war on character than people lacking in sexual responsibility. They carry the keeping up with the Joneses business one step further, and set a pace that poor Jones cannot keep. It is hard to bring up children with a family of this sort for neighbors.

The Tragedy of Specialization

A major psychological problem growing out of confusion in the first panel is that of specialization. In order to get into an earning position sufficient to satisfy the common ambition, and marry young, the young man or woman generally finds it necessary very early to delimit the field of intellectual interests. Thought must be focused upon economic or vocational matters at a period when all of the interests and abilities of the young personality should still be in a formative and plastic condition. The youth is forced to narrow down his curiosities and must vigorously deny the Promethean voice within him. It is like cutting all the main roots of a young tree except the tap root. The brain dies back to an intense central core.

This is a nice problem, this matter of finding a balance in the specialization of interests. To specialize too early is fatal to the mind. Yet to fail to arrive at a vocational focus in the middle and later years of life is usually to fail to make an achievement.

Early specialization, before maturity has been reached, constitutes one of the cruelest ineptitudes of life, and it is due mainly to first panel pressures. It is not only cruel to the individual who gets into the wrong pigeonhole and often is never able to get out of it again, particularly if he combines this misfortune with early marriage, but overemphasis upon early specializing settles a certain poignant penalty upon versatility. Versatility, or quick adaptability to a wide variety of activities and interests, is very probably one of the most important criteria of intelligence. Yet versatility is often a serious disadvantage in the struggle for success in the basic panels, and every practical psychologist knows well the problem of the patient whose real unhappiness arises from the fact that he has been able to do too many things well, and so has never concentrated his powers.

Many neuroses arise from unhappy adaptation to a social situation which demands of a person a specialized achievement in a field so far below his potential achievement level, that he becomes finally unable to direct his energies at all. These unfortunate individuals are like men equipped with wings who instead of being permitted to fly are forced to walk all of their lives, and finally are judged upon their skill at walking. This is a dilemma that in recent decades has come to occupy a place in human unhappiness, out of all proportion to its recognition. It works selectively, affects chiefly the best individuals, cripples them, and puts them out of the running early. Countless thousands of the most intensely unhappy persons in society could have been among the happiest, if only it had not been necessary for them to select a permanent vocation until they had passed, say thirty. If they could have been allowed to intellectualize and carry in their minds for ten years of adult unmarried life the basic doubts and vocational uncertainties that must necessarily reside in any unusually capable mind, many of these people whose brains are dying by the fourth decade, could have been saved for Promethean achievement.

The overemphasis on this first panel, which so notably characterizes the present trend of life, and may in a measure be regarded as an over-reaction to the long Christian attempt to deëmphasize it, tends to reward and to perpetuate those personalities that are closest to the instincts, and to cut off from the tree of life the complex, versatile, sensitive, intellectual personalities.

The Youth Movement in the First Panel

If the impressions a psychologist gathers in his routine work are accurate indicators at all, one of the most alarming changes that have been taking place in the general outlook of the past two decades is a rapidly increasing fear of old age and of death. Following the war, we have experienced something like a youth movement all over the Western world. Young spokesmen, young leaders in every field, young college presidents and state officers and business executives have come rapidly into vogue. In general a higher value has come to be placed on the years of youth, and a correspondingly lower one on the later years. The extreme manifestation of it is found in the Freudian expressivistic psychology.

Nowhere is this trend more clear than in the first panel. The normal values of the second half of life, essentially the intellectual and spiritual values of life, have been educationally deëmphasized so universally now that nothing seems so fearful as an old age without lots of compensatory material accumulation. The young mind growing up in the midst of this drama cannot fail to be strongly impressed by it, particularly as the struggle for economic security still generally ends in defeat—for only about a sixth of men and perhaps less than a twentieth of women at sixty are in a position to supply their own physical sustenance.

In a functionally directed society, i.e., one in which the basic business of the first three panels had been reduced to the fairly automatic operation of a reasonable plan, old age should be the halcyon period of life. It should be the flowering time of the mind. This we know, because it is so in a number of little circles and eddies of society where fourth and fifth panel culture has become dominant; in a few old families; in friendships that have grown through a period of decades out of common effort and interests; in minds that grew into perspective when young—in such little corners of society old age is the high peak of life. But in an essentially acquisitive society old age is a period of pain, of regret and uselessness; for where provision was not made in youth for the growth of a mind, the whole later consciousness must needs be a personal one, and attention must then be centered on the morbid process of physical involution. If in addition old age carries the specter of economic dependence and the mortification of a sense of dead weight, then the gradual sinking of life finds the dying soul a withered, frustrated, and pitiful thing indeed, and no dramatization can make the end anything but a mere cessation of suffering, in sharp contrast to the triumphant setting forth that a noble death can be. A society which tolerates the common occurrence of unhappy death must turn repeatedly with religious intensity to youth movements, which is actually only a turning back to the elemental panels for reassurance.

This contemplation of the spectacle of ignoble death is a powerful fear influence for the young mind, and it deals the inherent Promethean impulse a staggering blow. With the picture in his mind of an unhappy death in poverty as the closing scene in a parent's or grandparent's life, a youth can hardly be blamed for resolving to devote his life to the slaying and overslaying of that merciless dragon of human ineptitude, insecurity in the first panel. There is one eminently important purely economic step with which every government ought to concern itself. This has to do with guaranteeing a physically comfortable old age and a dignified death.

In summary the conflict between the craving for an expanding power over materials, and for an expanding participation in spiritual insight, can become a most profound and devastating struggle in sensitive minds. It can never be *preached* away. The only voluntary human interference that can affect it much, will be the teaching of a psychology carrying sufficient orientational insight, and sufficient practical virility, to penetrate to the motivational springs of consciousness and to lead personalities out to a balanced multi-panel development. Yet to teach such a psychology to individuals can perhaps be only a waste of effort, until it is at the same time educationally available as a religious orientation. Until ministers and psychologists can again talk a common language, no "economic planning" will ever reach the human soul.

27. CONFLICT IN THE SECOND PANEL

If the fourth panel is concerned with maintaining the *direction of movement* in the time dimension, the second supplies the structure by which society maintains the *certainty of existence* in this dimension. The second panel is the conscious projection of the social dominance-social submission attitudes of a mind. Brought into order or pattern, these attitudes[5] constitute the matrix of the social order and give rise to the formulation and observance of law; to the definition of the body politic and to patriotisms; to the formal and informal social status arrangements and pretenses; and finally, to public opinion. It is in the second and fourth panels that the Promethean conflict becomes most clearly manifest. One might say that in the second panel Prometheus is the aggressor in Epimethean domains, while in the fourth, the situation is reversed.[6] Both conservatism and radicalism represent an early, unhealthy, premature resolution of conflict, and both conservative and radical minds fall in readily with the popular psychology which assumes conflict to be an unqualified evil and a thing to be eliminated in the quickest way. Yet mind is built up not by eliminating conflict, but by intellectualizing it and by lifting it out of the basic

[5] When out of perspective and out of control, these attitudes of social relationship lead on the one hand to *megalomania* and the lust for power, and on the other to self-depreciation and the conviction of inferiority. When idealized and intellectualized and projected into the time dimension, it is possible that this *will to dominate* becomes the Promethean aspiration, the will to extend human understanding and the desire to be as the gods. Under the same influences, the will to submit and follow becomes perhaps the Epimethean resignation to the will of God, and the craving for a formula of -tions and -nesses. At intellectual levels, then, the principal second panel conflict centers around the divergence between the conservative, and the liberal or radical outlook. This is one of our clearest manifestations of the Promethean conflict.

[6] Law is essentially conservative (Epimethean); religion essentially aspirational (Promethean).

panels, up to the fifth panel level of play where it can be handled and manipulated and laughed about.

A mind is built a little as a bridge is built across a stream. The problem is always to make the two end supports balance each other. In the mind this balancing is carried out by ideationally trying alternatives, thereby arriving first at an abstract rather than a concrete appreciation of their consequences. This is mental problem solving, and it is as important to the growth of the mind to keep problems alive as to keep human beings alive. There is no happiness in beating a man you know you can beat; in hunting game that is tame; in overcoming feeble objections; or in owning things, in social deferences, in sexual favors, or in a religious faith, unless these things have been arrived at in the course of difficulty and self-discipline. It is important to keep problems alive.

Now a law is always an arbitrary resolution of conflict, an attempt to kill a problem, and the more laws a society finds it necessary to create, the more of these low-level impediments does it throw in the path of sustained happiness. To have no law in a society is to have no skeletal foundation upon which to build the second panel relations of the mind, but to have too many laws produces the same state of chaos in the end, for where all is skeletal foundation there is no opportunity for the development of that element of consciousness which is moral responsibility. Too many laws destroy character quite as effectively as too few, for they destroy the virtue of simplicity.

We pass laws concerning everything, as children in their play readily "rule" on this or that question as it comes up. In Tennessee a motor vehicle may not legally be driven along the public highway without a herald preceding it on foot at a distance of a hundred yards. It is against the law to smoke a pipe in a public park in New York City. There is a law in South Carolina prohibiting hip pockets—they furnish too handy a place for bottles. These three laws are well over on the funny side and they bring a smile. But there are thousands of laws that are only half funny, and some of them are at times enforced.

The multiplication of laws is a sure indication of general loss of orientation. It is a barometer of religious confusion, and every law that is passed weakens every law that was previously in existence, thus contributing further to the breakdown of character. Law is at its best but a palliation of irresponsibility and a sort of surgical substitute for character. The piling up of laws is like the piling up of a drug habit. The mind builds up a tolerance for them and takes them ever more lightly. Yet *respect* for law remains one of the cornerstones of character. Here lies a serious second panel perplexity, in a land teeming with ambitious young legislators.

The Perplexity over Democracy

The magic word democracy has created profound bafflement. The term is used in two quite different senses. In one sense it is a name for an ideal goal of human life; and in another, the name of our present pattern of government. The first is a religious and the second a political meaning.

Children are taught in American schools that in democracy all men *are* equal, which is nonsense. Later this gives rise to cynicism, and to failure to grasp the real vision which lay behind the founding of the nation. The same problem arises in the fourth panel with respect to the use of the term *heaven*. Conceived as a place or a state that already exists, it can lead later only to impatient disgust with the religious mind, or to mental stultification. We confuse the static with the time-dimensional conception of life. Children are taught a static conception both of religion and of government, through the inadequate definition of key concepts.

Democracy is full maturity in the second panel, as heaven

would be full orientational and aesthetic maturity and final understanding of the meaning of time. It would be a tragic misfortune to be *born into* either democracy or heaven, for there could then be no happiness. Happiness is the process, not of having these things, but of moving toward them.

Possibly the most perplexing of the dominance-submission anomalies in a democracy arises from a second panel manifestation of the same conflict that was basic in the first panel. We have not yet succeeded in arranging for any very *discriminative* distribution of political power and social influence. Power in this panel is as it were left lying around loose for those who most want power. Political influence can be achieved by scheming for it and asking for it, and consequently it goes most often to personalities that are focused back at an unchastened level of personal desire. These personalities then become conspicuous patterns or guides for young minds, and a vicious circle is established. Social influence comes to abide not where mind has reached its best maturities, but where it is least matured. There is in consequence an intimate tie-up between economic control and governmental control, and both come to be manipulated largely by the more aggressive, acquisitive minds of society. The final result is, as some wag has put it, "Instead of a rule of experts we have a rule of extraverts."

The real problems of life in a democracy center round the creation of techniques for developing the superpersonal levels of the mind. Until religion and psychology become a common enterprise it is probable that little progress can be made against the central human stumbling block of the continual gravitation of power and influence back to the more instinctive levels of life.

In a society arranged about some sort of aristocratic ideal, or oligarchic plan, the second panel patterns will withstand for a long time the breakdown of fourth panel influences. But in a society aiming at democracy and thereby giving over to fourth panel care many of the earlier second panel securities and safeguards of human life, the pulse of things is tremendously sensitive to what is happening in the fourth panel. When in such a society confusion appears in religious matters, it is felt almost at once in political and social matters. This is the situation that we in America are now facing. We have placed our hope in a democratic plan, which is really to say that we are banking on the ability of the fourth panel elements of society to maintain so clear and strong an orientation that character-forming influences will necessarily exert in the long run a stronger pull upon the average mind than will relatively disintegrative and egocentric influences. In America, however, the democratic dream has already been blurred and nearly buried beneath a rapidly rising and angrily muddied tide of population on the one hand, and the destruction of the old theology on the other. We are not at the moment actually moving toward democracy, as Franklin Roosevelt would possibly bear witness. He has felt it expedient to advance heroic first and second panel policies running rather clearly counter to the democratic point of view.

A modern democratic government may be defined psychologically as *an arrangement in which a society has attempted to substitute fourth panel maturity and responsibility for the artificial restrictions and hierarchies that less Promethean cultures have found it necessary or wise to set up in the second panel.* When we attempt the life of democracy we make the presumption of great orientational stability, and if it turns out that the presumption was premature, the consequences are likely to be severe. The collapse of religion in a democracy is a far more immediately painful thing than in any other form of government. Yet in the pain of it may lie our salvation. If cancer were in its early stages a painful disease, its mortality would be greatly reduced.

Patriotism and Pacifism

War is the most dramatic of the second panel symptoms of ineptitude, and many thoughtful persons question the wisdom of any patriotism. Rational thought leads directly to the postulation of a world without patriotisms, and at some time in its life every healthy brain ought to feel a mounting indignation that anywhere a group of human beings should set themselves apart and arm themselves against the common cause of mankind. Therefore let us disarm, and I will sign a pledge never to take up arms in the service of my country under any pretext. There can then be no more war.

But it is not so simple. Here is almost exactly the same problem that we find on examining the nature of democracy. As an ideal, we look to the ultimate political brotherhood of man. Yet it is well to make a distinction between ends and means, and the best means to an end is not necessarily to assume it at the beginning. There is wisdom in Vaihinger's philosophy of *As If*. Live *as if* wisdom and virtue were in the ascendancy over the earth. Do unto others as you *would have* others do unto you. Every day I am growing better and better in every way. God is love, and the *true way* is the Christian Science way. Disarm, and the world will disarm. In all of this there is a common theme, and it is a wise theme, but there is also a flaw in it. It is too soft; too easy a way out. It produces the illusion of having faced problems that actually still remain unfaced, as when in the morning I dream that I am up and shaving. I do not wish to hold a brief for the militaristic point of view, for all of my personal sympathies are for good reasons on the other side of this perplexing question, but I do wish to point out that the problem of the military relations of a nation is by no means disposed of by signing a pledge that one will not bear arms. It is not wise to kill problems so offhandedly. Their ghosts are so troublesome.

You cannot escape the problem of dealing with the arrogant and destructive tendencies of relatively uncivilized human groups, in so simple a manner as by the verbal abolition of war. The American experiment with the abolition of drinking ought to be a case in point. Yet the religious mind is forever entangling itself in some economic or political or sexual reform, like a great ape in a grapevine. Such entanglement is always a tragedy, for it always means the loss of perspective and of influence in the end. We must look deeper than the abolition of things. The essential problem of religion is not to abolish war, but to develop the human mind.

Whenever a man in the name of religion signs a pledge, "I will not fight," he weakens the power of religion, even though he may for the moment strengthen the cause of peace. We must do better. The leaders in pacifism are the true Promethean spirits of their day. It is vitally important that their energies and their influences should not be wasted. We can at least *expand* the pacifism pledge a little, and try to direct this splendid impulse toward some positive program of planned attack upon the underlying causes of war. These underlying causes are first, second, and third panel distortions —greed, arrogance, and overbreeding. Let anyone then, if he must sign a pledge, pledge himself to conquer these things, first in his own personality and then in the outer social influence. Pacifism can never become a significant movement until pacifists clearly recognize and accept the militaristic impulse that rides just below the surface in their own consciousness. Happiness lies in moving *toward* a goal, in the *positive conquest* of something, not in an abolition. Whoever can weave this principle systematically into a religion at a high intellectual and cultural level, may achieve great psychological effectiveness in the war against war. Mussolini has done it, at his level.

Psychologically, the cause of war is a condition in which the character conflict has been impatiently *resolved* in one or both warring groups, and relatively uncivilized desires have taken the upper hand. The resulting dominance of instinctive expressiveness over the inhibitory power of the civilized elements of the mind may have its roots in any or all of the three basic panels. It may arise chiefly from greed for possessions, from arrogant craving for social dominance, or from the consequences of indiscriminate and unchastened reproduction.[7] It is to the control of *these* things that religious minds must apply their energies and their pledges. To sign a pledge abolishing war is like signing a pledge that the Mississippi river shall not overflow. Behind floods lie forestation problems which may yield to control.

Large Group and Small Group Psychology

With the rise of the large town there has come into being a second panel problem which may in time loom large enough to overshadow all other considerations in this panel. It is the problem of what I like to call the *urban sacrifice*. Life in a city is in certain very fundamental respects a different order of existence from the country life of most of our ancestry. Here we need not consider the degenerative effects of it upon the physical organism, but some of its psychological implications are so important from the point of view of religious conflict that they cannot be omitted from the picture. The outstanding psychological effect of urban life is continual overstimulation.

Conscious happiness lies in reminiscent contemplation of the meaning and the relatedness, and of the essential simplicity of the things of this world, not in the rapid presentation to the senses of the things themselves. The capacity of human consciousness to rise to its fullest and richest possibili-

[7] All of these three cardinal sins, greed, arrogance, and overbreeding, are natural enough instinctive expressions of life. There is actually only one *sin*, namely failure to develop the higher panels of consciousness and thereby to hold lower panel impulses in good balance.

ties is conditioned upon such influences as induce the moods and the opportunities of reflective contemplation. An overstimulated mind comes to respond in the only way that it can respond to the tumbling welter of its social contacts, namely in a superficial and habitually dissociated manner. All things are cheapened, hurried, and attentive consciousness is so swamped with stimulation that there is little chance for the development of the richer levels of awareness. Overstimulation is, I think, the essential cause of dissociation, and therefore possibly of the bulk of human unhappiness. It certainly produces the phenomenon of extraversion, which means the loss of integration of a mind with its own deeper levels. Such a mind comes to depend upon the outer relations of things for its support, and the setting is then laid for the emergence of the unchastened, waster personality.

It is possible for a rich person to live in a city and to shut out in a measure some of this overstimulation. He can live most of the day out of hearing of noise and out of sight of artificial contrivances and of rapid movement and shifting faces, but no one can create the environment of natural aesthetics in an urban setting. The solitude of the deep forest, the sweep of open country, the unspoiled natural life of the great marshes and swamps, the ever-alluring and ever-mysterious night life of the woods, the intimate rapport with weather and with the meaning of the seasons, the continual panorama of simplicity and sincerity of life, the expectant meaningfulness of all things that happen—that is the magic secret of happiness. In urban life human beings are shunted off, dissociated from meaning, little by little, more and more, until at last the whole meaning system of a mind is destroyed and replaced by something fast, artificial, and unstable and untrue, and in the end tragically dissatisfying. Overstimulation carries a mind more and more to its own surface, and farther and farther from its deeper reality, until consciousness is a twoness instead of a oneness. This is the urban sacrifice.

Everywhere there is a certain amount of conflict between the faster and more dissociated and more hysterical mind, and the simpler, more intuitive and reflective, chastened mind. It is the conflict between large group psychology and small group psychology, and the two points of view are not very far separated respectively from what we have termed the waster outlook and the chastened outlook. One of the most serious implications of the conflict is to be found in certain educational trends. There is a "progressive" educational influence which seems to be founded on the supposition that human life is to be progressively more of a quantitative and less of a qualitative consideration. Children are to be developed mainly for the purpose of leading well-adapted, urban lives. They are to be as expressive as possible, as extraverted as possible, and free from "complexes." They are to be discouraged from phantasy and meditation, are not to be disciplined in any manner, but must adapt expressively and continually to groups of other children. This is the trend of influence of the Freudian psychology, which springs from a racial and social outlook that has been almost exclusively urban and essentially unhappy for many centuries. That formerly happier and mellower cultures should now turn eagerly to such a religion in a time of orientational chaos, may some day appear to historians as a just balancing of accounts.

Different in principle from such a philosophy is the "small group" point of view that the mind of a child should be cultivated with care and discipline; that children should especially not be hurried in their social development; and that as much care should be exercised in chastening[8] the too aggressive, or too extraverted child, as in "bringing out" the shy and inexpressive one. There is a good deal of evidence

[8] It is not to be supposed that by this term I am advocating the use of violence with children. Whoever resorts frequently to physical punishment in dealing with children is a highly unimaginative educator.

that the best minds of later life develop in children who mature late, and are often notably shy and behind their fellows of like age, both in early physical development and in the emergence of social assurance. The small group psychology is especially concerned with the protection and buffering of these sensitive, late maturing personalities. In the course of my own work with children, I have become convinced that far more damage can be done to these late maturers by hurrying them into "expressiveness" than is ever done to the more vigorous and physically precocious individual by too stringently chastening or repressing him. *I am not sure that for the best ultimate development of a mind the greatest educational need may not lie in slowing down and postponing social maturity.*

It is certain that many of the tragically jammed and confused conflicts of later life are related to this matter of the relative inhibition and free expression of early second panel impulses. Whether the main cause of such conflict is to be attributed to too much inhibition; or to unwise and inadequate inhibition; or to too *little* inhibition, is a matter of point of view. The answer depends somewhat upon whether you belong to the character camp or to the waster camp in your psychological outlook. We have been living recently in a high wave of waster psychology, but there will probably follow in its wake a trough of character psychology which may be as deep and destructive as the wave was high and destructive. The function of psychologists ought to be to keep a level head in the face of these actions and reactions. Just now[9]

[9] There are quite a number of writers who still urge us on toward the "new freedom." They do not seem to realize that we have swung well past the freedom point and are already out near the waster end of the cycle. Bertrand Russell still harangues and rallies his cohorts into a battle that was fought and won, a whole generation ago. The psychologist must play the part of the rider on the beam in these pendulum swings, and he should always try to so apply his weight as to shorten the excursion. The danger which the next generation of psychologists must face, probably lies more in a fundamentalism than in the waster threat; yet it will be well for the psychologist of today to keep a watchful eye on the waster.

a psychologist ought surely to counteract the waster and expressivistic influence as strongly as he can, though a generation later it may be just as imperative to keep the pendulum away from the other extreme, as was in fact the case a generation ago. The psychologist is theoretically one who can be trusted to keep a balance in these matters. The religionist should be another.

As a practical suggestion for those who deal educationally with children, and have become aware of the universality of this conflict between the aggressive and the retiring personality, I think that one key to successful handling of youngsters lies in keeping them in very small groups, and in putting extremely aggressive personalities together. Aggressive personalities seem sometimes to supply the influence needed to inhibit and chasten each other, as nothing else will. Of a group of four overly loud, extraverted children, one or two, or even three, will often come out at the end of a short period together, far more civilized and thoughtful. Similarly the plan of putting very shy personalities together tends unmistakably to bring out stronger social character. It is a question of tact and skill in grouping, and of keeping the groups down in size. When children are mixed indiscriminately, the aggressive ones tend to become more so, and the shy ones retreat farther and farther into their shells. The same phenomenon can readily be noted in adult life. Put any sensitive adult into a company where there are one or two aggressive or loud personalities, and you cannot get a word out of him with a crowbar.[10] But put half a dozen sensitive people together, all about equally shy, and soon they will all warm up to quite a sociability. It is good fun to observe the atmosphere of various dinner parties and social gatherings, and to note the operation of this principle.

The indiscriminate mixing of young minds in large groups seems to produce either the intensification of differences, or tragic, emotionally charged conflict and frustration. For this

[10] Unless indeed you resort to the physical violence of alcoholizing him.

reason I have come to regard the practice of sending young children away from home to school[11] as on the whole a harmful one, even granting that the adult influences in most schools are individually better and wiser than those in the average home. We cannot of course prevent the necessity of a child sooner or later facing an urban world as it is, but it is well in the early formative years to build in as solid and as *individually indicated* a personality foundation as possible, before these inevitable strains are applied. The problem is always to develop in the child a character which will stand the test of time.

Parent-child Relations

There is in the second panel a particularly conspicuous reverberation of the character conflict. One of the dominant trends of the waster influence has been a progressive repression of the *feeling* element of consciousness. There has been a great war on the sentiments, and the impression has filtered out into educational philosophy that in order to achieve a rational mind you must be free from sentiment of every sort, especially from sentiment built around the natural attachment between parents and children. The Oedipus complex lurks like a ghost in the attic, and stamps natural parent-

[11] Even more harmful, I suspect, is the practice of sending children indiscriminately to collective camps, where they attend long enough only to become overstimulated and hysterically delighted, or to feel inferior and left out of things, not long enough to become really acclimated. I have had to deal with a number of cases of childhood unhappiness which was apparently directly traceable to the confusion and overstimulation of summer camps. Such experiences doubtless speed up the development of "personality" in youngsters, and certainly make them more socially adaptable, but is this necessarily wise, and is there not a very great danger in bringing children prematurely through their shyness and reserve? To develop social personality and expressiveness too early may be one of the very worst things we can do to a child. It may lead to early loss of zest for life, and to early dying back of the brain. I think that there is little doubt that sexual precocity is associated with just these phenomena. It may be the same with second panel precocity.

child affection with the sickly pink tint of "sexual perversion." This sort of jolly nonsense ought to be good fun to read; yet there are college graduates who take it, not merely seriously, but verily as holy writ.

There are young parents in the land, who under this astonishing influence have proceeded to attempt to rear children in an objective, impersonal, or disinterested manner, as if both they and the children had through some extraordinary purification lost the affective quality of mind. The children are to be made independent, presumably of a sexual fixation on one or both of the parents. Yet actually the only kind of parent who ever produced sexual fixations in children is of course a sexually obsessed or vulgar and unimaginative parent, in which case the child is fortunate if he escapes with nothing worse than an "Oedipus complex." Children are enormously sensitive to the attitudes and ideals of a parent, often indeed far more aware of such attitudes than are the adults themselves, and no mother need ever worry about the "Oedipus complex" if her own sexual life is moderately well in order, and if she is glad in her heart to let the child grow beyond her when the latter begins really to grow up. If she fails on these counts, she has no business having a child in the first place.

Parental sexual fixations of remembered childhood can be suggested readily enough to neurotic minds, and can be teased up delightfully into the dimensions of a general alibi, but so can anything else. If I can win the confidence of an uncritical person (establish a transference), I can make him believe that he has the soul of a blue heron and can plausibly interpret every dream in such a way as to prove it. I can even "cure" him by convincing him that he has made a great mistake in trying to be something different from a blue heron, and now he will be happy imitating the habits of that noble bird. He will be whole, having found the light and the true way.

So far as I am aware, a truly sexual fixation of a practically important nature between parent and child rarely if ever occurs except in low-caste families, living under conditions of bad domestic hygiene. It is common enough for unhealthful, unwise, or selfish affectional and dominational relations to become established, especially between mothers and sons and between fathers and daughters. *But these are not sexual problems, even by greatly stretching the meaning of that term.* They are dominational, second panel problems directly,[12] and more indirectly they are problems of perspective and general self-control, that is, orientational problems.

One of the most important experiences, if not *the* most important, in a child's life, is constituted in the feeling of rapport and in the mutual enthusiasms and affectional interests that tie his mind to that of both his mother and father. Here above everything else in the world, is needed the influence of an adult mind the dominant quality of which should be *child-like* enthusiasm and candor. These qualities are readily taken over by the child, and they lay the foundations of his future soul. I am not sure that these early bonds of enthusiasm between parent and child are not more important in the lives of both, than are any of the contemporary relations that are built up during life. Yet it is these irreplaceable associations that young tasters of psychology would throw overboard, in order to insure that their child shall be "independent" of unhealthy fixations. Such mistaken modernism is comparable to a tragic affair which came to my attention two years ago, in which an insane mother had cut off both of her child's hands in her zeal to stop him from masturbating.

The poor mother in her distorted and fissured consciousness thought that she was doing something for the child's

[12] For this reason it seems logical to discuss these vital relations between parents and children as predominantly second rather than third panel considerations.

good. And there are many other poor mothers who have in almost as tragic a fashion cut off both themselves and their children from the strongest anchorage that a human system of values can ever find. In most personalities the affections and the mutual enthusiasms that are shared by parent and child supply the grounding for virtually the whole values system. Yet in the past half dozen years I have again and again and again had to reassure parents *who have been through college,* that it is "all right" to show spontaneity and playfulness and delight, even a little affection, in their relations with their young children. These people in their silly and credulous horror of the Oedipus complex, had proceeded to shut and bolt all of the doors and windows that lead to maturation in the fourth and fifth panels of consciousness. They are like children I have known who, their heads filled with tales of the bogey man, missed all of the mystery and the beauty of the night.

The psychoanalytic slang of Oedipus and castration complexes and of overshadowing parental sexual fixations, has filtered into the common consciousness not through the psychological fraternity—I have never known a trained psychologist to use such language except in fun—but through a certain borderline element in the medical profession who, except for their technical instruction in their profession are sometimes incredibly immature and unimaginative persons. Also much of this slang has come in by way of cheap journalism, and through books on psychological subjects written by grossly incompetent people whose claim to psychological maturity may rest only upon the fact that they themselves have been made "whole" by being psychoanalyzed. If the process of being treated for neurosis gives a person mature psychological insight, then to have one's leg broken and set should constitute adequate training for a certificate in surgery. These people have been *converted* to something, and that in itself is almost proof positive of profound psychological distortion and mental bad health. The mind that is suddenly converted to something is a mind without balance, stability, or dependability. It is an unmellow mind. There is ground for extreme skepticism of any adult who suddenly "gets a new religion."

The human personality needs a strong anchor in the second panel, some personal relation or relations in early childhood, that are immensely beautiful and immensely secure. Children need a sense of comradeship and a feeling of common purpose with an older and stronger mind, perhaps the mellower and maturer the better. Only with such a background, I think, does a personality very often find the later drive and inspiration to grow up. Probably the most important decision a human being has to make is what is to be the attitude toward the second half of life. Is this to be the time of full fruition, or shall it be a period of decline and mental dissolution? About this question rages the central conflict of civilized life, and the attitude that a person finally develops toward it is determined in large part by (a) the trend of his parents' ideals at the time when he first came into consciousness, and (b) the extent to which there was established in early childhood a deep sympathy and coöperative rapport between himself and at least one parent.

If a father wishes his child's mind to be fairly certain to develop to its best possibilities, he must see that he himself is well along toward the fulfillment of his own highest mental development when the child is young, and he must possess a genuine craving for rapport with the child mind. Fortunately these two qualities are generally associated. It is usually the wisest and maturest men who are naturally closest to their children. This may contribute to the reason why it is so often the younger children of families who go on to mental maturation. It may be that because the parents are older they have in many instances learned the wisdom and the delight of rapport with the child mind. It should be remembered however that children of parents one or both of whom are very close to the end of the reproductive period, where such children do not show evidence of glandular or nutritional insufficiency, are very frequently more sensitive, fragile, and apparently more imaginative than the older children. These younger ones are likely to be more shy, more introverted, and more tender-minded than the older ones, and they may be naturally more susceptible to fourth and fifth panel influences. It is possible that these later comers maintain such characteristics through life, and that they tend toward intellectual and aesthetic careers, though I have not yet known a sufficient number of them to generalize.[13]

In summary the second panel of consciousness grows up essentially from the effort of society to civilize the dominance and submission relationships between human beings. In every mind there is perpetual conflict between these two opposed tendencies, leading especially to perplexities concerning conservatism and radicalism; attitude toward law; patriotism and loyalty to democracy; pacifism and militarism; small group and large group psychology; and most important of all, concerning the relation between parents and children. All of these perplexities of the second panel recede a little and become more elastic and buoyant when we cease attempting to resolve them, but instead pass them one by one through the focus of the light that is shed by a sympathetic understanding of the nature of the elemental human conflicts.

[13] This is the sort of research in psychology that seems eminently worth carrying out, but it cannot be done in laboratories. So far as I am aware there is no short cut to results in such a field. It is a matter of carefully and systematically collecting observations through a long period of years. This was the Darwinian method of research. It is a very different conception from the sort of research in which you set up an apparatus in October, make observations in November, crank a Monroe calculating machine from December until April, write it up as a thesis in May, and either graduate or publish in June. This is not psychology. It is a sort of transitional mongrel offspring of science, born of a questionable three-cornered marriage between physiology, physics, and statistics.

28. CONFLICT IN THE THIRD PANEL

Population Pressures

The deepest third panel perplexity centers finally about the problem of population control. There has been a steady biological increase in population, which is in itself a serious enough problem, but this fades to negligibility when compared with the increased psychological proximity of people that has been brought about by the development of automobiles, by the telephone, radio, electric illumination at night, and the like. It is as if some giant force had suddenly laid hold of the world and squeezed it like a puff ball until it contracted down to a hundredth or even to a thousandth of its former size. This psychological telescoping of the world has moved up the problem of population control and selective reproduction, from a vague, future speculative philosophy to the status of a vital and immediate urgency.

Men have begun to face the disillusioning possibility that the hard-won freedoms and surpluses and opportunities for the development of the human soul, for which countless generations of their forbears have consciously sacrificed and striven, may all come to naught. The institutions of education are swamped and clogged beyond hope of perspective for years to come; national arrogance and the animal craving for revenge and power and expansion sizzle and threaten to break out at many points, like a teakettle under increasing head of steam[14]; and there is such competition even for food in this world of magnificent human possibilities, that the vast majority of men and women still are devoting most of their energies to getting it.

When relatively scarce, human life is a passingly noble and significant thing. There is beauty in it, and it is good to con-

[14] In the face of this, men talk of pacifism. They must learn to strike deeper.

template. But life has become so common and cheap a thing that the fifth panel significance of it has been steadily falling. Automobiles present the same anomaly. A few hundreds of thousands of them in the United States would have added beauty and zest to the human world—they did indeed do so when at that number—but sixty millions of them have created a situation in which all but waster minds tend to regret their invention. This is likewise true of radios. There may come a time when the same may be said of human beings.

The essentially orientational nature of these manifestations of conflict is borne home forcibly when one contemplates how futile and weak have been our attempts to deal with the reproduction problem directly from the sexual panel approach. We have our little attempts at birth control, and afternoon clinics in contraception, but doctors know that these are but dams of sand built against the tide.

Christianity originated as mainly a fourth panel attack on third panel problems. We may be about ripe for another such movement. If so it may be just as well for it to take shape fairly soon, for when too long held at one extreme the pendulum has a way of swinging violently, and there lies ahead the danger of reaction toward some third panel "fundamentalism."[15] The rampant waster has for some time been tweaking the whiskers of the tiger of fundamentalism. Once fully aroused, we know well enough where the tiger will first strike. He will *leap for* the waster, but he will *get* the Promethean. In the bonfire will be the Christ, not the Caesar.

There is a growing sensitivity to religious influence. In many quarters a restlessness can be sensed, and a tendency to sniff the air, such as is seen in a flock of wild geese before they take wing. It is a good time for religious minds to look

[15] That is, toward another emotionally sustained effort to suppress the sexual motive in civilized life.

earnestly into their deeper consciousness, and to face as squarely as they can, the question of what kind of sexual controls they really would like to see on the earth.

The truly pertinent third panel question is, can the human mind achieve mastery over biological reproduction, through the exercise of will and fourth panel control, or must such control continue to be exercised in the future as in the past, through the infinitely more painful, blind, overt trial and error process of perpetual economic and political struggle? The central conflict is very clear and sharp here, but the Promethean conflict has at this point gone over into a fearful snarl. The Epimethean has been obsessed with the sacredness of the whole sexual business. It was a Christian obsession, and the religious mind is still pressed upon by vestigial Christian influences to recoil in righteous horror from the problem of population control.

This pressure is still the most dominant influence to which women in the average intellectual ranges of life are exposed. The Promethean in the meantime has been driven far out to the opposite extreme. To him the whole third panel problem seems more and more to hinge upon restricted and wiser reproduction. And so here the Promethean and the Epimethean come into their most violent opposition. In the third panel they are at complete juxtaposition, and hence are wedged so tightly against each other that the waster holds the field virtually in his own possession. If institutional religion has become an ineffectual voice and is now seldom heard to utter effective speech in the reconstructive relations of the first two panels, it has in the third panel receded to something less than a voice at all, but resembles rather the barking of dogs in the distance.

The Charges Against the Family

The great conflicts may be seen in fine perspective in the study of the psychological implications of the family, which though an outgrowth of reproduction, is mainly a second panel unit. The family inevitably implants in young minds the ideal of perpetuation of its own pattern. Therefore universal parentage becomes inseparably associated with happiness, and the child mind is exposed to a powerful influence blocking the development of the ideal of selective reproduction. Thus while the family is the focus of most of the civilizing influences of society, it is also a source of leverage through which powerful waster influences play.

In the family the child is very early stamped with the same limitations that sit upon the parents, especially if the parents are young and unmellow. He is heir to all of the prejudices, weaknesses, even vices, of a unit of society which is generally not sufficiently strong or sufficiently enlightened to have made contact with those sources of human thought which could stimulate the young mind to the development of its best possibilities.

The problematic stresses resulting from unwise attachments and antagonisms between various members of the family have been made the pivot and the main focus of psychoanalytic theory. There are families in which the dominance of parents over children extends far into physical maturity, and often full grown men and women are found intellectually dependent on their parents. The parents have clung to the children with all the tenacity of their grip on life itself. In this manner the family gives rise to a form of parasitism by which parent minds, themselves without purpose or direction, hold fast to the younger organism that it may not escape from them and leave them alone and old in their purposeless world. This problem is orientational, not sexual.

Possibly the most serious of all the complications produced by the family scheme of life will in the end prove to be the first panel complications. The idea of family inheritance of wealth tremendously complicates and brings emotional reënforcement to the struggle for wealth. The family certainly accentuates the acquisitive motive, both through the idea of passing on wealth to children as heirs, and through the peculiar personal dependence of women that the family has created. Women become things to be privately supported and to be kept for private purposes, like yachts.

These are serious problems, all of them, and the conflict that rages in the third panel must in time produce profound modification of the family relationship. Yet these problems go so much deeper than the external structure of families that it is perhaps a great mistake to place present psychological emphasis upon the outer form of this third panel institution. To change all the external third panel rules of the game would effect little change in the human mind. We need a technique for going deeper.

Man's One-sided Third Panel Psychology

The social structure is man made. It is still man's world, and women for the most part try as individuals to be what they think men want them to be. But men have lost their own orientation and no longer know what they want in women. The male mind oscillates conspicuously between two alternating desires concerning women. Man wants a slave-wife, and he wants a mother-goddess; rarely can he make up his mind either to one of the polar extremes, or to an adaptable compromise.[16] And so man continually strives to approach woman "both as conqueror and as refugee." Men and women alike are caught in the back and forth play of these sharply opposed tendencies, and it is rare to find a young individual of either sex who has fought out the battle with himself or herself and reached a serene perspective. This

[16] The causes of this alternation must lie far back in the character conflict. When the unchastened waster mood is on, man is the exploiting conquerer, the user-up of things. When the chastening time-conscious mood is dominant, he is the little boy, and he wants to look wide-eyed out upon the world, from the protecting arms of the time-wise earth mother.

is one reason why young educators are so often abominably bad educators.

Man long ago hit upon one happy solution to the conflict, simply by deciding to create for himself two different kinds of women. He would have pure, noble, monogamous, goddess women to worship and to win and marry; women at whose feet men could sit as little boys and be purified; women like angels, set apart, and protected from the dross and corruption of an evil world. In these women only the purest and simplest thoughts might exist, and their minds were to remain as protected as their bodies from life's experience. So man created goddess-mothers for himself, sexless, appetiteless, mindless, but true and noble creatures to reassure him of his own somewhat more distant, though more convenient relation to heaven.

And he also created *fallen* women, to be given over to the play of his third panel delight, and thus to be overcome by evil and altogether condemned and spoiled—women with sexual appetite and available, warm bodies. With plenty of these scattered about in the environment, men were able to live a fairly good life of it, to have their cake and eat it too. For being of somewhat coarser and more durable stuff, by convenient hypothesis, men could be exposed to contact with these fallen women without themselves becoming corrupted.

Man made out to have a good time without sacrificing the hope of heaven. He had already, in his fallen women, given over living sacrifice to take care of that. He succeeded in projecting the great third panel conflict upon woman, whom he had subjugated and conquered; and by thus incorporating the problem of the opposites in visible flesh and blood, it was possible to arrive at a satisfactory individual compromise with life. But in the process women had been exploited, and where exploitation occurs there is always sooner or later a reckoning to be paid. Within the male mind is a powerful female component, and presumably there can never be a safe development of minds, which is not at once both a male and a female development. To isolate or subjugate either component is to lose touch with the feeling side of life, and the inevitable consequence is confusion in the orientational, and starvation in the fifth panel. Never will a morality sit well for long upon the human conscience, if founded upon the suppression of part of the mind. Sooner or later, "emancipations" are bound to come.

From a purely male point of view not the least disturbing of the baffling emancipations of modern life has been the general disorganization and diffusion of the prostitution patterns. Prostitution has become more expensive, far more secret and dangerous, and at times as much an exploitation of weak and foolish men by shrewd opportunistic women, as the reverse. It has been taken over and is now run by the criminal elements of society, except for a scattering fringe of worn-out, undesirable women. Prostitution has gone over into the hands of bootleggers and gangsters and politicians, and has become an unclean, corrupt, and unsavory thing. The double standard of morality is passing among the better educated levels of human life, and with this change it becomes increasingly necessary to think, to reconsider basic values in life, and to reformulate the entire program of the relations between men and women. We can only predict remotely what will turn out to be the wisest patterns of sexual morality, but one thing we know: that the old projection of the conflict upon women will no longer work.

We struggle, weakly perhaps, but we struggle toward the ideal of the fully adult mind. This is not essentially a male or essentially a female mind, but coming as it does to full fruition only in the later decades of life, after the turmoil of sex is over, it is both male and female. It is a mind conscious of itself, capable of seeing itself in perspective as a focus and as a reflection growing out of experience which extends far back of the individual life into an ancestry which is equally masculine and feminine.[17] Such a consciousness must embrace the point of view and the feeling of both polar components. There is not very much difference between mature male and mature female minds, though there may have been sharp differences at earlier points in the lives of individuals who have grown to maturity from these opposite sides of the biological tree. Male and female converge as both approach understanding.

In the light of the concept of maturity as goal, the meaning of the traditional antithesis between virtue and sin begins to clear a little. Virtue resolves into that which promotes, and sin into that which interferes with the development, not merely of character in the Christian sense, but of wider and better balanced thought and feeling in all of the panels of a mind.

The Strain of Premature Marriage

The conflict associated with the question of the optimum time for marriage plays a part in almost every consciousness. It is still the social tradition for both sexes to marry about as soon as economically feasible.[18] Yet if the child mind is to receive its early impressions from the parental mind at the latter's best, this must be quite late in the parents' lives, or at least late in the life of one of them. Ideally the child should have the advantage of early intimate association with the maturest, wisest adult influence available, and in those, alas, still rare cases where parental minds are moving in their later decades toward mellowness and a rich philosophy, it seems a tragedy that children should come too soon. Indeed

[17] Jung loves to put it in this manner. "Now remember that you have inside your mind a two-million years old man-woman. Let us see what *they* have to say about [this problem]." The metaphor may be a strained one, but it is an excellent approach to the remoter levels of a mind.

[18] There has been a slight trend recently toward later marriage. Yet the average age of first marriages, in six states in 1932 was: men twenty-six; women twenty-three.

the early burden of a family is often an insuperable handicap not only to the children but also to the parental development that would have gone forward if the family had been postponed. Further, from the point of view of a woman who is selecting a husband, it is very difficult to predict what the course of a young man's development is to be, while he is still in the twenties, though a little later he cannot conceal his true calibre and the real nature of his gifts. At thirty-five a man has almost inevitably given good indication of his career, and a reasonably safe guess can be made as to the future curve of growth. Therefore if a woman desires to assure herself, and her children-to-be, of association with a mind that is going to mature, it is a fearfully risky business to marry a very young man. The chances are overwhelmingly against her. The percentage of minds that do mature is still so fearfully small.

It is rare for people under thirty-five to possess insight into their own temperamental constitution. I think that two-thirds of the cases of marital unhappiness that have come to my attention have been traceable in part at least to an attempt to build a marriage upon a relationship in which one partner had dominantly sensitive, tender-minded, intuitional, feeling qualities, while the other tended toward extraverted, objective, outwardly focused, waster identifications. Whatever descriptive language is applied to this central temperamental divergence, whether we call it introversion and extraversion; tender-minded and tough-minded; subjective and objective dominance; intuition type and sensation type; one-minded and two-minded; mystic and rationalist; the poet-dreamer and the dynamic-waster; or simply soft-hearted and hard-headed, there remains here a fairly clear mental polarity and a lively problem of the opposites. It is a pretty serious tragedy when a marriage takes place between two individuals who are well out on the opposite ends of this distribution. Such a marriage cannot work at all unless the tender-minded one, usually the woman, submits completely and obliterates her own personality. Ordinarily, to the more subjective member of the partnership, the marriage means bitter pain and affectional starvation; while to the more objective, or tough-minded member it is a source of perpetual irritation and cramping of life. In the past two decades this tragedy of the opposites in marriage has been markedly on the increase, for the waster has not only greatly increased in numbers, but his popularity has risen like the tide, with a corresponding slump in the social value of the more chastened types of both male and female minds.

There is conflict here in the mating business, which is too involved and far-reaching for any formulary solution. It is really only a special instance of the central antagonism in human life, between the two elemental trends. Later marriage seems the only way of meeting it. The secondary perplexity, concerning what to do about individual sexual happiness and maturation in the meantime, is still altogether in flux. The Promethean temperament courageously goes on with its light bearing and with its dangerous experiment, and it occasionally wins through to a happy individual adjustment of the matter. There are quite a good number of men, and certainly some women, who seem to have handled the matter of pre-marital sexual relations without harm to themselves or to others, though where one has found the way to such an outcome, there are many who in the attempt have lost their perspective and irreparably damaged the feeling qualities of their minds. Happy is the stern self-disciplinarian, and happy the waster in these elemental matters. The rest must think, and must carry the conflict, and muddle through.

The Changing Meaning of Chastity

The conception of chastity as a cardinal virtue is changing. It is coming to carry less of a physical and more of a psychological connotation. There has come into existence the idea of a psychological chastity which is not necessarily quite a physical chastity. With the realization that the danger in sexual relations lies far less in the relations themselves than in their emotional associations, that is, in what people make of them, it grows clearer where the true character problem lies in the third panel. A strong character is a person who can be trusted with responsibility in sexual as well as in other matters, who will ring true to his best purposes, and will never exploit or waste either material things or the affections and loyalties of human life.

Chastity may perhaps be taken as a Promethean cardinal virtue in the sense that *a chaste person is one who has so ordered his sexual outlook, that he and those with whom he associates are adequately protected from the psychological as well as from the physical consequences of unwise or ill-advised sexual behavior.* This Promethean conception leaves the way open to those who believe they are wise and strong and kind enough to maintain a high level of character in the face of, or even because of, some degree of dispersion of sexual interests. Then the problem of character in the third panel changes over from a morality to a responsibility.

The great paradox in this outlook lies in the fact that to substitute responsibility for morality in sexual matters requires all the judgment, and the freedom from emotional imbalance, of the fully mature mind, and ordinarily by the time a mind is mature, the period of intense sexual interest is long since over. It is indeed open to question whether there can be such a thing as a mature mind, while there remains sufficient susceptibility to sexual excitement to develop subsidiary or temporary relationships. Therefore when Bertrand Russell and similar Promethean speculators concerning the sexual philosophy of the good life, suggest the wisdom of wider and richer sexual impingements, they always appear to be thinking in terms of some ideal person endowed with physical youth but with the maturity and responsibility of the true philosopher, a combination which does not occur in natural life. Russell aims his books at youth, yet as he writes he does not seem to visualize a youth sitting across the desk from him, but only a half youth, a physical youth, and the practical problem remains at about the point where it was.

If we go over now to the Epimethean camp in this matter, and throw in our lot with the champions of a morality, we shut Prometheus out of the third panel, and thereby defeat the true educational objective. For the objective of education is the development of character, not the resolution of conflict. In this morality controversy the Promethean conflict looms so prominently as to overshadow and obscure the deeper and more vital conflict that lies beneath it. Most of the war over sexual morality is waged between Prometheans and Epimetheans, and just as in the prohibition case, the wasters meanwhile make merry over the spoils.

Confusion in the Concept of Romantic Love

In a time of religious confusion, most lives seem rather humdrum, yet there are few who do not at some time or other, or at several times during the course of life, succeed in getting their feelings into some integrative focus with a romantic love idea, and then they are stirred, transformed, ennobled. The idea becomes central to the whole mental organization, and there is brought about a condition of psychological wholeness.

This happy eventuality is by no means limited to the sexual panel. The same *kind* of thing happens in all of the other activities of life. When a person gets his ambitions and his aspirations centralized around any articulate goal, he has a pivot about which to build a system of values. That the central idea is so often marriage is an accident of the order of society in which we live. If there were no such thing as marriage, this phenomenon of focused enthusiasms would still occur, though it might not be built essentially around the sex relation at all. It might indeed more often rest upon common enterprises carrying greater intellectual content than is usually the case in the sexual enterprise.

Love is an emotional, really an enthusiasm phenomenon. The essential nature of it is sexual only as the mind is sexual.[19] But through tradition and through the very close tie-up that has existed between Christianity and sex, the love emotions have become so intimately identified with the sexual relations that to many it has seemed plausible to construct a psychological system around the basic hypothesis that in sexuality lies the central principle of human motivation.

In this confusion of the sex motive with the general vital stirring of enthusiasms, lies one of the most immediately troublesome ineptitudes of modern thought. Through the strained social emphasis that is placed on the conception of love as a sexual relation between two persons, this kind of love is artificially rendered the greatest thing in the world, and the loss of it or failure of an individual to achieve it becomes by the same token a most fearful tragedy. Thousands of personalities smash themselves to wreckage and despair on imaginary rocks of disappointed love, and ten times as many more rationalize and justify wasteful or insignificant lives on the basis of such imagined smash-up. The distortion of values that this emphasis has produced in women's minds is utterly staggering. Most women are still taught to measure the success and the happiness of their lives almost exclusively in terms of a third panel conception of success.

One very important function of the idea of a panel picture of consciousness should be to help clear the confusion that exists between love in the third and in the fourth panel. The

[19] Love is sexual only when applied to the sexual panel of consciousness. It is also a religious phenomenon, when applied to ideas carrying time-conscious orientational significance, such as, for example, God. Religion is not sexual sublimation, nor is sexual behavior religious sublimation.

affection bonds between two people who are persuaded that they love each other may set up a highly nourishing and enriching focus of feeling-awareness, leading to the realization of purposes that transcend personal consciousness; or on the other hand such a love may amount to little more than an intense, mutually reënforced selfishness. The evaluation of personal love is always relative to the consequences that it induces in the higher panel consciousness of the minds involved. The waster too, may be an intense lover. He is almost always an enthusiastic one. And so is the cheerful sparrow.

The Third Panel Monkey Traps

Many secondary strains are thrown upon character by the peculiar nature of the third panel relations. Goaded by the general tendency of women to gravitate to men who are strong and able to protect them from the things that they fear, young males frequently fall into the pretense of strength as part of their armament for the game. Strutting, boasting, and arrogant pugnacity may then become habitual, and may greatly modify the whole pattern of the personality. A certain intellectual arrogance often characterizes the male who is ill-endowed with native sexual attractiveness.[20] In more sensitive, tender-minded males, *lying* to women sometimes progresses to such proportions that the general distinction between truth and falsehood is lost, and the personality surrenders its integrity altogether. Many careers of crime owe their origin to this motive of keeping up a show of strength and success, in the effort to hold the attention and preference of women. At more complex levels of mind, strutting and boasting often take the form of a sort of chivalrous or man-of-the-world swagger, producing a bluffing personality, which frequently brings defeat in the end to naturally gifted

[20] Dr. Alfred Adler has developed this theme in detail in his penetrative work, *The Neurotic Constitution*.

men; if not direct first and second panel defeat, then the defeat of warped purposes and of ultimate loss of simplicity. In all of these cases, the male is caught in a *monkey trap* of his own creating. The artificial, inflated picture of himself with which he now has to live, is constantly in danger of bursting, and there is forever the shadow of a vague fear of some great humiliation and revealment. The *fear of being found out* will haunt his dreams, and will create painful conflict in his mind.

Another monkey trap into which the somewhat less intelligent male mind is inclined to fall, is laid in the traditional dominance-submission relationship that men have established between men and women. Man dominates over woman, thereby taking upon himself a great responsibility. He presumes to possess superior insight and wisdom in the conduction of affairs. Woman yields up her intuitional wisdom in deference to the stronger and wiser male, and we then have the picture of a great ape beating upon his chest for attention, but forever with nothing to say. There are few traditions in the human stock of habits that can make quite so conspicuous a fool of a man as the lord and master stereotype. This too sets up a false *persona*[21] in the mind, and foredooms that every attempt to face reality shall end in basic conflict.

Sometimes the business of sex obsesses an individual to such a degree that he becomes a sex glutton, falling back to a level of living essentially for the sex pursuit, as people sometimes live essentially to eat. Then most of the life energy escapes through third panel foci. At a more introverted level, a routine of masturbation may become actually the main business of life, or one of the so-called sex perversions may dominate the personality. These last two patterns of sexual focus, the introversions and perversions of sex, are activities

[21] Jung uses this term to designate the picture of himself which an individual carries, or tries to carry. It is the picture of character *without* the element of remoter consciousness. The *persona* was the mask used by Roman actors. It derives from the verb *personare,* to sound through.

in which *imagination* plays a powerful part, and they are therefore primarily problems of sensitive, subjective, aesthetically developed and tender-minded persons; while the pattern of sexual gluttony is dominantly associated with the tougher minded, extraverted individual. There is also a fairly close relation between alcoholism and sexual life. The sex glutton or sensualist requires the inhibition of his imaginative functions, and therefore finds the use of depressant drugs greatly to his liking. He is frequently, if not usually, alcoholic. But the excessive masturbator and the homosexual have in a sense partially sublimated sex and have transferred it to delicate, imaginative levels, where they have got it wedged, as it were, at a point somewhere between normal physical integration and complete sublimation or spiritualization. These people are *almost never* alcoholic. The practice of psychotherapeutics is always heavily weighted with patients who are disturbed by inability to make peace with masturbational or homosexual tendencies, but in my practice I have yet to meet a male[22] homosexual who is clearly alcoholic; or to meet a clear case of alcoholism in an excessive masturbator. These two partial or abortive sublimations of sex are problems of the over-delicate, aesthetic temperament, and consequently they seem to constitute one of the peculiar dangers of the naturally religious mind.

Opportunities lie about in every direction for the mind to lose its perspective and to frustrate itself in the third panel. Many become fanatic on the question of the *control* of sex, and fill their minds so full of morality that they boil over with it, like a kettle of oatmeal. There are people who gauge the major personal judgments of their associates, of institutions, of races, of literature, of everything, in terms of apparent moral implications in the third panel. Unfortunately,

[22] Female homosexuality is, I think, quite a different problem from the male form. We cannot follow that interesting side trail here. We are not yet sure enough of the ground.

this is generally done in the name of religion, and then religion becomes identified with a distorted sense of the enormity of sexual sin. For minds caught in this particular tangle, Freud is sometimes a delivering angel. He rubs their noses in sex, throws them into it as one would throw a water-shy boy into the pool to teach him to swim; and now and then the treatment works. Sometime ago I sent a woman to a Freudian analyst. She had been chiding me for years about my own too easy tolerance and looseness of thought in the third panel. Recently I had a talk with her, and before we had finished she had called me a prude, a moralist, and—worst Freudian epithet of all—a *Christ-er*.

One of the lighter and more amusing third panel monkey traps is the almost universal Western custom of commercially exploiting the fashion idea in women's, and to a lesser extent, in men's clothes. The phenomenon of fashion in women's clothes and the riotous advantage that the exploiting mind takes of the opportunity that it offers, present to the student of psychology one of his most enlightening rays of insight into the weaknesses of the human personality. Women feel the pressure of this waster game so strongly that devotion to it becomes for large numbers of them the central life purpose. It affords a lever by which men with money can control women individually, and at the same time it gives to unintelligent women a sense of achievement. To be a little more conspicuously adorned than some other woman, to give the impression of being more expensively dressed—this is something worth while, and life is after all good, and has meaning. One then has a purpose. The third panel has been made to yield a fourth panel satisfaction. The business of conspicuous waste in the third panel may be observed at its best on formal evening occasions, and on Easter Sunday, when all good Christians throughout the land gather with humble and simple hearts to indulge in reverent, reminiscent contemplation of the triumph of the chastened, self-effacing

Jesus, over the rampant waster influences of his day. Easter provides an unusually inviting monkey trap. How the waster loves Easter and Christmas, and how the crucified Promethean at the Court of God must bite his lips on those days!

Christianity Has Been a Dominantly Female Religion

Much of human literature and philosophy is built around the overt or tacit assumption that the male physical and mental character are standard. In the Christian theology, and in Greek mythology, woman is an afterthought, created from a non-essential part of the true human body, and the female mind is by implication an imperfect replica of the male mind. Typically men have tried not so much to understand the strength and unique powers of the female mind, as to measure it by male standards, and to see how far it falls short of the dominant male ideal of the period. The momentarily dominant Western male ideal is a highly distorted, objective, rational, three panel outlook. A few decades ago, there was very little questioning of the male standard, for the common male outlook was then closer to an adequate compromise with the more subjective feeling and intuitional qualities of the female mind. Even now it would doubtless be possible to produce wholeminded acceptance of the supposed masculine objective view of life, if the male mind were to get at the children young enough. But things are so arranged that women typically have first chance at the child mind, and sometimes they utterly corrupt it by encouraging the heart of a child outlook. Once this has taken place, there is no peace for the child afterwards in less than a five panel world, except at the price of the encephalectomy complex.

In later years when the growing mind is trying to adapt itself to the objective standard of a three panel consciousness, it becomes inevitable that earlier attitudes should be forced down into the deeper levels of consciousness[23] and there they

[23] That is, they are "repressed."

become vague yearnings and give rise to a poignant restlessness. Life seems forever incomplete and unreal. This may be the source of the persistent adult impression that something very vital and important has been left out of the modern consciousness.[24]

Children see the world in the earliest years chiefly through their mother's eyes, and their earliest ideals of life are female ideals, carrying warmth, feeling, mystery, phantasy, imagination, unashamed enthusiasms. This idea lies deepest in their minds all their lives; it remains the most real, ultimate, and true life picture. In a world dominated by Christian theology it was possible to carry this kind of world-idea close to the surface all through life, whether you were man or woman, for the whole Christian picture was overwhelmingly a female picture. Except for its outward form, Christianity must go down in history as the one great *female* theology. Christ is psychologically far over toward the female side of consciousness.

The weaknesses of Christianity as well as its strength are female weaknesses.[25] It carries all the danger of a highly sub-

[24] The Freudian explains conflict and the deep, unsatisfied yearnings of life, in terms of repressed lower panel (sexual) desires. The view advanced here merely reverses the Freudian picture, and regards the difficulty as due, instead, mainly to the overexpression of lower panel, and the consequent repression of higher panel desire. The Freudians use dream material to support their view. I think that this same material, the same dreams of the same patients, can be even more plausibly interpreted to support the opposite view. In the long run, either view is bound to be a distortion, for the objective of education is to bring balance and perspective and wisdom into all of the panels. Yet the psychologist must place his emphases in accordance with his judgment of the needs of his time.

[25] It is often said that women are more critical of each other than of men. In this connection it is interesting to note that women in college seem both more hostile and more friendly toward the Church, than men are. In a project designed to measure conservatism and radicalism by the graphic rating scale method, at the University of Wisconsin in 1929, I secured attitude measurements from about 1500 men and the same number of women. The questionnaire called for the expression of an attitude with respect to seven or eight key problems in each of the five panels.

jective view of life, and for fifteen hundred years remained so incapable of response to rational influence that finally it brought upon itself the full fury of a storm of objectivity which had been gathering during many centuries of repression of that element of mind. This looks to many psychologists like a destructive and fatal storm, though there is a nucleus of Christian theologians who are heroically resolved to pull the old ship through, in its wrecked and battered condition. I hope they can, but that problem lies outside our field.

Christianity has been a religion of one-sided emphasis, and it may be that many generations of human life will pass over the earth before the human mind will again know the child-like happiness, the serenity of purpose, and the supportive moral character that seemed for so long to obtain in the fool's paradise which men created by chaining Prometheus to the Christian cross. The reaction that has set in against the old theology is bound to run its course, and it is a hard, disillusioned, and unhappy outlook that is taking the place of the dominant thought patterns of our recent predecessors. We have swung sharply away from the subjective component of consciousness, and already the conflict has grown uncomfortable, between the now repressed subjective higher panel desires, and the objectively permissible hypotheses. This may be the oldest of all conscious conflict, this struggle between the half-articulate wish and the inescapable data of overt sensory experience. It may be much older than the present differentials that seem to exist between male and female. It may be a relatively recent and accidental tendency for the female mind to cherish the child-like feeling

---

The questions in the fourth panel dealt mainly with attitude toward the Church. In this panel, seventy-seven per cent of the number five reactions, that is, of the most extreme hostile reactions, came from women. Also, seventy-one per cent of the number one (most extreme conservative) reactions came from women. No such proportions were found in any of the other panels.

aspects of life, while the male assumes the more intellectualized point of view. There may be something older than sexuality behind the conflict. In a prolonged period of matriarchal culture such a relationship might be profoundly modified, or even reversed. We should therefore perhaps be unwise to build a psychological explanatory system as solidly upon the bi-sexuality hypothesis as one school of analytic psychology has been doing. This does not go quite deep enough. It is unfortunate that we have no psychological knowledge of what a matriarchal society comparable to our own culture would be like.

Be these matters as they may, here lies a vital conflict. Hundreds of thousands of unhappy adults in America and Europe who are psychology-shy, might successfully find their best personality patterns if wise and shrewd minds *in the name of religion*, rather than in the name of psychology, could make clear to them, by any of half a dozen techniques, the real nature of the central conflict in their minds. These people are not yet ready to seek psychiatrists and psychologists, and it may be that the more is their good sense for that, but many of them are dependent upon the minister of religion, and if within the next two or three decades, before it is entirely too late, the profession of the ministry can equip itself with applicable psychological techniques, it may win through. The ministry cannot much longer go on, clinging blindly to a theology and ignoring the real needs of the religious minds of society. I think that the salvation of religion in our culture lies in sending ministers to school to study conflict. It may be well in the meantime to let theology rest for a time, until we can return to it with fresh minds and a better perspective.

It was a strange arrangement from the beginning, that of the Christian world outlook. It was man's world, and he had outwardly succeeded in splitting woman into two very different creatures, to solve his own third panel problem of the opposites. Yet through a compensatory compromise with the repressed side, *in religion* the Christian world became actually woman's world, and so the dominant orientational outlook of both men and women was really a woman's outlook. Man *ruled* his world with a masculine arm, but always he *saw* it with female eyes, much as New York City, though outwardly under Irish rule, is in all except the second panel more of a Jewish than an Irish city. This was not altogether an unhappy arrangement, and if only some provision had been made for leavening the intense Christian suppression of the Promethean element of mind, Christian theology might have carried the balance for thousands of years, and might have provided an integrative matrix between feeling and thought upon which man could have built a structure of both, transcending all of his dreams.

Religion was woman's compensatory strength and her assurance of significance in the order of things. She had virtually nothing else, and had been forcibly placed in the position of carrying all her eggs in one basket. But now science has dropped the basket. In all of the three basic panels, woman was a secondary consideration, practically a chattel, but she ruled in the fourth, and through that, also in the fifth. With the undermining of Christian theology, this balance was completely destroyed, and woman was as it were thrown overboard to sink or swim in a world now entirely foreign to her natural gifts. The waster in the meantime, now unleashed and rampant, broke out in a wild first and second panel scramble for money and position; and of course contributed gaily to third panel chaos.

The Hope in the Female Mind

The young woman faces quite an interesting world today, in her "new freedom." She has already been going to college in some numbers, and has been exposed to methods and ideals of education that have grown up under exclusively male dominance. She studies the things that men study, and thinks the thoughts that men think, and of course she is heavily influenced by the dominant philosophic trend in education, which is that of endeavoring to apply the statistical method to everything conceivable. Psychology she finds to be almost exclusively the construction of devices for trying to measure things. Psychology has become a "science"—no place here for female qualities of mind. The social studies likewise she finds a great confusing welter of statistics, objective data, and remote, intellectualized, superficial measurements of things. Nothing for her there. She might as well be a mathematician! Even literature and poetry have changed. No longer are there poets that anybody can understand. Poets, like painters, now reveal a horror of sentiment, and to be caught serious is worse than being caught naked. Likewise artists and dramatists seem everywhere to have transferred the Christian body shame to a sort of modern soul shame, and they have covered up their souls as a Victorian lady would cover up her body. Everywhere soul prudery has grown up where sex prudery has been stamped out. Everybody hides his soul behind some heavy drapery; behind statistics, objectivity, intellectuality, or behind some vague distortion of lines and color which for designative purposes he calls modern art. We live in a Victorian age transposed.

In such a strange world the female mind, guardian and cherisher of the soul, finds itself vastly puzzled. Women know that something is wrong, but they are still new in the world of intellectual development and up to the present have been mainly occupied with the mistaken business of trying to play the game as men play it, and of trying to do what is expected of young persons who are emancipated and educated. They have adopted masculine habits, as a guest adopts the ways of his host, and have been very statistical and objective, thus sacrificing their most valuable gift and undergoing amputation of the soul. There is one compensatory feature in it. A few women of high intelligence who yet so lack beauty or grace or physique that they would have been unable to compete successfully in the marriage market, and would therefore in the old order of things have been condemned to a life of idleness and frustration, have been able to live happy lives in the masculine competitions of business and the professions. They become business women and lawyers and doctors with a certain intensity and professional earnestness, behind which one senses centuries of tragic repression, and it is good to see them. It is good fun to watch women surgeons, and women psychiatrists.

A few thus find orientation, but the vast majority of women already grown up will never find peace or fundamental happiness in life. Their little fragmentary hoard of conflicting loyalties and impetuous incohesive starts and thrusts at life must rattle about in a great fourth panel void for the few brief decades of their lives, and most of them will go to sleep without the dismay of full awakening. If they wake too much, there is some gentle anesthetic nearby: alcohol, gasoline, rhythm, drugs, bridge, the movies, piety, love, the arts, literary clubs, the drama. For a few there is humor.

But somehow the women not yet come into being must find a way of restoring to a baffled and bungled world the balance and invigoration of a developed female consciousness. This may happen rapidly, if once women can emerge from the first blundering attempt to adapt to the male order of mind, and can realize that there are great sectors of human consciousness in which the female mind is not only more at home than the male mind, but which demand *primarily* female thinking, and cannot possibly keep pace without it. These sectors are the fourth and fifth panels of consciousness. This, I suspect, is the real reason for the intimate historical tie-up between religion and the third panel. Men have written religions, but the female mind is vital to religion.

The Tragic Strains Involved in Sexual Precocity

There is a relation between the third and second panels, which may be of the greatest educational significance. The problem of sexual interests among youngsters of secondary school and early college age, important as it undoubtedly is in its own third panel right, carries a still more significant second panel reverberation. In a post-adolescent atmosphere where there is encouragement to develop early sexual interests, most of the spotlight of desire and attention comes soon to be centered upon a very few individuals of each sex, and around these all things revolve. A bad strain is thus thrown not only upon this minority, but also upon the majority, who though also stimulated and also made prematurely restless and adult-minded, are relatively neglected, and often develop a feeling of being out of it. In this manner, through an entirely artificial third panel influence, many growing minds are subjected either to a false exhilaration arising from a distorted sense of social importance, or to discouragement and a sense of personal inferiority. It is difficult to say which is the more unfortunate group.

This problem of social-sexual status on American college campuses, particularly where fraternities and sororities are permitted, expands to such proportions that it comes to dominate and overshadow every other consideration in the minds of an astonishingly large proportion of the students. Students become obsessed with the business of the social and sexual "rating" of themselves and of each other. It is by no means altogether a sex question, for it arises from a mutual reënforcement of distortions in the third and second panels. These young minds are not thinking as growing minds need to think in the basic relations, but they have been overstimulated to come to a quick unnatural maturity, and to make vital and dramatic decisions in matters that ought to await at least a dozen years of maturer reflection. I mean such matters as the choice of mates, the selection of vocations, and the determining of the kind of associates that are to be considered permanent friends.

An early settling of these things is an early death to a developing mind. It is like picking fruit green or like cutting flowers before they come to full bud. It makes for a premature hardening of the mold of character, far ahead of the fulfillment of the best possibilities of the personality. It produces in the twenties and even in the 'teens a world-weariness, a sense of having experienced and done all that there is to do and feel, and now in place of the eager enthusiasms of a developing mind there is sophisticated boredom. There can be little doubt that the tacit encouragement of early sexual exploration during school years throws a very great premature strain upon the further growth of character, not only in those who are thus encouraged, but throughout the whole youthful environment. A sophisticated worldly outlook, at any age, is a potent destroyer of the bridges to further mental development. Sophistication is very possibly the worst enemy of the human mind. It drives many youngsters either to premature vocational decisions or to an early marriage which will end their growth with even greater certainty.

Encouragement of early overt sexual activity throws an especial strain upon that group of young people to whom I have referred as the late maturing stock. These are the ones who seem to develop most frequently into the good minds of later life. They are never among the precociously attractive, but tend rather to be known among their fellows during school years as queer, shy, taciturn, immature. They are sensitive, quiet, and inconspicuous. They are invariably late in sexual maturing. These young people are made to feel trenchantly their position of isolation and loneliness in an atmosphere of precocious sexual pursuit and of consequent early preoccupation with social status. They become restless and worried, and their minds are not infrequently thrown off the track entirely by the intriguing and cliquing and sexualizing that seems to be going on around them. For when the spirit of sexual expressiveness gets into a very youthful community, it is like the effect of the smell of blood on wild cattle. Sex becomes the great end in life and the disturbance is by no means limited to those directly concerned. We have no way yet of assessing the final values that are at stake in this conflict, but we can see enough to realize that the conflict is there. If some of us can remember an educational outlook in which sex was so completely hushed and repressed from consciousness that even well-educated adult minds were characteristically green and undeveloped in the third panel, it may be well to remember also that human happiness lies not in the reversal of repressions, but in the intellectualizing of conflict.

There are two antithetic poles in the human rational system, and life dances back and forth between them like a monkey on a string. There is the metaphysic that no reality exists but God, that human biological nature and the natural wishes of man are all illusion and nothing but conceit. Suppress them, ignore them, reach with your soul out toward the true reality, the absolute. And then there is the much older metaphysic, now modern, that only the feeling self, the ego, is real. All else is an illusion and the projection of a wish, even the projection of a sexual wish. Therefore express the ego, know it richly, and extend it outward through all the universe. To the first metaphysic, every natural desire is unhealthy, for it is a symptom of imperfect soul concourse with God. To the second, every thought which shifts the focus of attention away from the ego is an illusion and a symptom of repression, and the mystic experience is a cardinal sin, for it is an offense against rationality. Good minds have expanded and to some extent humanized both these extreme points of view, but they still stand as the two essential metaphysics of the world. Sex, being so clearly a thing of expression or repression, is forever tossed back and forth like a basketball between these opposite poles. For almost every mind of the Western hemisphere, it is a little sinful either to express, or to repress a sexual impulse. That is why the third panel plays so important a role in the determination of character and in the understanding of conflict.

29. CONFLICT IN THE FOURTH PANEL. ORIENTATIONAL PERPLEXITY

Religion is mainly concerned with the application of techniques for the development of character, which is functionally the ability to maintain an orientation in the face of conflict. Character is really a sort of buffer system of protection against the pain of conflict, built up by the mind in its continual effort, (a) to protect the orientation already achieved—Epimethean function; and (b) to penetrate farther into the unknown—Promethean function. The deepest human conflict lies in the fact that man is engaged in a continual struggle against the disproportionate gravitation of interests back to instinctive needs; and against the narrowing of consciousness from the contemplation of the future and the past, down to the purblind focus of the present.

This main conflict between the waster and the characterphyllic mind is always present in a human culture, but it is a rare opportunity to live in a time like the present, when the waster trend has the upper hand. Such periods are necessarily rare, for no civilization can for long stand the strain of one of them. In a short time the balance must always swing back the other way, or the civilization goes to pieces. We are as psychologists excessively fortunate to be able to study the human mind under rare circumstances. It is like being an astronomer in the time of a great comet. We have to be careful in such times as the present, to avoid the common mistake of writers who have lived in similar periods and have described human nature as essentially bad. A pessimistic note always dominates the literature of a period of waster dominance. It is really an exciting time to *study* religion, though the situation is a little hard on the individual who is himself directly involved in the religious institutional struggles. It is more fun today to be a psychologist than to be a minister.

The central conflict is too deep and too general for specific educational attack. It is the Promethean conflict that concerns us most, both as psychologists and as religionists, for this is the conflict that splits the religious mind against itself, as a civil war splits a nation. In this section we shall therefore contemplate in further perspective[26] some of the conspicuous problems which act as diversion dams in the splitting process.

Perplexity Concerning Objectivity and Subjectivity

Modern man has succeeded in establishing the virtue of disinterested, or objective thinking, though the Epimethean mind has fought this development with violence, every inch of the way. Any student in the sciences will now tell you that the first principle of scientific method is to learn to keep wishes, feelings, and desires out of the picture. Scientific thinking depends for its efficacy upon a certain degree of dissociation between feeling and thought. This is what the term *objectivity* means. An objective mind is in relatively closer touch with outer objects than with inner feeling. A subjective mind is in closer touch with the inner feeling-awareness than with outer objects.

Together these two outlooks represent a perfect abstraction of the problem of the opposites, and the relation between them presents as clearly as it can be found, the real problem of the human mind with reference to conflict. The free development of *both* of these points of view is vital to the happiness and to the further growth of the human mind. The one is responsible for poetry, song, romance, for all of our awareness of beauty, for the bond of attachment between individuals, for friendship and affection, in short, for the entire sweep of consciousness in the fourth and fifth panels.

[26] This section constitutes a general summary and a review of the theme of the book as a whole.

The other has produced everything for which science stands, namely such consciousness as we have of the *true*, or *tested* relationships that exist in the universe. Dispassionate objectivity builds the ladder upon which the human mind climbs toward understanding.

These two elements are opposed at every level of mind. The will to accept the universe, to love it, to feel the tune of it, to feel the good of the world as it *seems* to be, "I do not ask to see the distant scene, one step enough for me"; and the will to *know*, to extend the little circle of cold light into the unknown—the struggle between these two wills is the ancient Promethean conflict between the prophet and the priest, and the key to the further development or destruction of a civilization very probably lies in the balance that is kept between these two elements of mind. They have to support each other as the two spans of an arch, or the whole structure inevitably collapses. When they do so meet, the mind is whole, there is spirit in it, and its energies are available for the graver problems of the deeper, central conflict. A first-rate human intelligence tolerates both objective and subjective wisdom, though perceiving the profound conflict between these two kinds of wisdom, and the primary function of both psychology and religion is to elevate this conflict to the toleration, or play level of consciousness. Between science and religion there must always be conflict, but there need not be intolerance. If the psychologist can turn the method of therapeutic analysis to educational purposes, he has at his command what may prove to be a tremendously powerful weapon in lifting the conflict. When a person has lifted his Promethean conflict well up into full consciousness, and has insight into his own temperamental quality of mind, he is well insured against the chaotic inner doubt which is often so characteristic of middle life. When the present wave of waster rule recedes, and it is no longer popular to desire to "make money," I think that the primary vocational decision will rest between a career of science and a career of human amelioration. In order to make this decision wisely it will be necessary only to have clear insight into one's own temperamental predominance. Am I most deeply a person of objective or of subjective wish? To help answer this question for people is the most practical immediate function of the ameliorative facet of psychology, whether applied in the name of education, religion, or medicine. It is at this point that the three ameliorative disciplines meet.

Practically, the first great obstacle to religious wholeness, the perplexity that is often called the conflict between science and religion, is simply the continual temptation to dissociate the problem of error from that of conflict. The historical Christianity devoted its energies almost exclusively to the Epimethean business of eliminating conflict from the mind. Its conscious objective was a life of faith, which is a life free from conflict. It let error go. In such a world intellect became an evil thing and a hindrance to happiness, and it was sacrificed. All Christians through the Middle Ages who achieved any education at all, must have suffered fearfully from the *encephalectomy complex*. The world of human consciousness was simply given over to rampant error, in return for release from conflict. This was of course not religious wholeness, unless one is willing to define religion in such manner as to omit the intellectual variable.

The present reaction to the prolonged intellectual restraint which Christianity exercised, is a swing over to the Promethean business of eliminating error from the mind. We have been tearing error out by the roots, wildly disregarding conflict. If this trend could be carried to its natural conclusion, it would in the end render all feeling an evil, and the human mind would become completely insensitive to conflict. In the process, we should all go through an *animec-*

tomy complex.[27] The method of science is the perfect antithesis of that of faith. Untempered by any religious influence, science would aim to produce an entirely rational mind, which is simply a mind incapable of feeling. But such a program can never be carried out, for the mind cut off from feeling automatically dies. The animectomy complex, unlike the castration complex and the encephalectomy complex, is merciful and fatal.

An overbalanced Epimethean civilization might live on in a functionally decerebrate state for thousands of generations; even indefinitely. The ants and many crustaceans seem to be getting along about as they did a million years ago. But an overbalanced Promethean civilization will destroy itself almost overnight. *It makes mistakes.* Prometheus is a fearfully dangerous god, and that is why human tradition is so heavily loaded with his crucifixion and repression. When he gets loose, fire starts, and things happen fast. There is a great healthy fear of him deep in the remotely conscious levels of the human mind.

If there is one point which above all others I should like to bring out in a study of the religious mind, it is this: *Religion must carry the balancing, or compromising function, between the rational and the feeling elements of consciousness. No other articulate social influence is likely to do it. The religious mind must always hold itself ready to swing either way, as the situation demands; either toward Epimetheus or toward Prometheus.* It is for this reason that the truly religious person must be so entirely a chastened and humble person. He must be mellow, careful, sensitive, and *unsure.* He lives continually in a cross-fire between powerfully

[27] Literally, amputation of the soul. This mixing of Latin and Greek (*Anima* + *ectomy*), though it has become very common in medicine, is doubtless still a bit vulgar. I apologize for it, and only hope that the bad usage will be forgiven in the warm delight of poking good-natured fun at the Freudian psychoanalysts. Their *castration complex* is *such* a good one. If only they could chuckle a little more over it.

opposed influences, and is caught in the resentment of extremes. Yet his function is to integrate extremes and to force them to support each other in a progressively higher arc. He must act as a counterbalance to every arrogance, to every distortion, from whatever source. The religious mind is the antithesis of the arrogant mind. That is why there can never exist for any length of time a muscular, or expansive, or arrogant, or Rotarian, or other waster conception of a Christ.

The religious consciousness is torn between the pull of the intellectual vanguard and the deep feeling qualities of the less elaborated mind. The price of the compromise that it needs must always make, is a profound and a genuine humility.

The Great Fourth Panel Temptation; Cheap Religions

A cheap, or escape religion is an orientational system which a mind embraces at some level below that of its own best development. As in other matters, what is an escape for one mind may be the finest achievement for another. There are no objective standards, and every mind is faced with the necessity of finding its level for itself. Yet in the hurry and push and rush of trying to make a place in an urbanized world, most individuals grow bewildered, forget their morning wish, and after a varying experience of doubt and conflict, seize hastily upon some wrapped-up orientational formula; some little loyalty; a romance or two; a modified or restrained piety; and from these things a twinge now and then of warmth and insight and participation is derived. This is my "religion." I have bought it at a bargain, perhaps for only a few cents a week, and into the bargain I have thrown my soul or my intellect or both. I will now stop growing, and my brain will become mainly an organic waste. Such a religion is not an influence in the direction of further development, but is an escape from the conflict between the will to grow and the craving for certainty. The conflict is resolved by the repression of the will to grow.

All of these escape religions are not to be found in the churches. They occur in every panel of consciousness. There is always something to join, some party, some movement, some mutual benefit organization of a semi-religious flavor, some -ism or some -ness. And these play upon the emerging mind like so many blind alleys in a maze. They are fourth panel monkey traps. The bait is always the offer of a short cut to happiness. Conflict is to be resolved by taking sides somewhere. Then all things come at once to be either right or wrong, and with respect to all things, I am now either *for* or *against*. The problem of steering between this temptation to sell out too cheaply, and the equally serious danger of never coming into any hierarchy of values at all, presents one of the nicest and most delicate of life's alternatives.

The churches are filled with thousands of individuals who have bought a cheap religion, and have promptly become a dead weight. They call themselves religious, and in the eyes of the observant young they pass as the religious population. The influence they wield is labelled religion, and it produces fearful confusion. That is what makes it necessary to devote such a study as this almost altogether to the definition of elementary concepts, and causes half or more of the men and women I know whose opinions are worth while, to feel that the wisest course is to abandon the concept of religion altogether, to leave it to these people who have cheapened it, and to let them wallow in it until it disintegrates entirely, in the meantime replacing it if possible with better-built psychological concepts. The contempt for religion created in the best minds by the loading of religious institutions with people whose fourth panel development seems to have come to an abrupt end when they joined the Church, constitutes one of the poignant perplexities of our culture. Many of these people are kind; some of them are of the salt of the earth. In *something*, they must ground a faith, for it is by faith that one must live, after selling over the chance to grow a mind. Whatever substitute may in time appear for the present formulary religion, this will likewise become the source of the faith of kind but unintellectual souls, and then it too will be, in the same sense, a cheap religion.

The religious mind is torn between its desire to fall back to a simple and heartfelt faith, and its will to grow to the kind of integration between intellect and feeling that it dreams of in its strong moments. This is a painful conflict for those whose thinking carries back to the old order of things; who can remember not only the heavy stupidity and the dreary piety of a Protestant horse and buggy Sunday in New England, but can remember also the bond of personal affection and the warm sense of significance of individual life in a community, that the simple religious fellowship carried. Somewhere the religious mind must find a compromise which will embody the simplicity and humility of the old religion of faith, and yet support the wider intellectual sweep of a point of view capable of tolerating, though perhaps mellowing a little, the sort of urban mind that would *without a smile* explain life in terms of castration and Oedipus complexes.

Religion and the Urban Sacrifice

The general tendency of urban life is toward overstimulation, and toward the consequent sacrifice of maturation in the fourth and fifth panels. With the stupendous psychological increase in population of the past two generations, it is almost as if the great urban centers had reached out with relentlessly seeking tentacles and had embraced and urbanized the whole countryside, until nowhere is there escape from overstimulation. This has created an acute religious dilemma, for when a religious mind makes the urban sacrifice, surrendering simplicity and humility and attempting to step into the rhythm of a faster stride, it generally succeeds only in stepping into a confusion from which it may never recover.

Probably a relatively greater number of ministers than of any other profession have in the past several years sought the aid and counsel of psychologists. For a goodly proportion of these men mental conflict has been sufficiently severe to produce neuroses. In my own practice I have known only a relatively small number of these baffled ministers, but in nearly all of the cases with which I have been familiar, much of the trouble has proved to lie in the inevitable incongruity[28] between the religious outlook and the overstimulated life that ministers have often been seduced into living. Some of them try to make the urban sacrifice and at the same time to teach the fourth panel, contemplative life. They dress up, step briskly, drive a waster automobile,[29] live in a situation unprotected from radios, and walk mostly on concrete. Then they attempt to throw their minds into human perspective, and to make some head and tail of the problem of orientation. It is not strange that so many ministers should consult psychiatrists.

The problem is not so simple that it can be solved by avoiding cities. For in cities, unfortunately, are often to be found the centers of learning and the rich contact with that wide diversity of knowledge and experience that alone can lay the foundation of a good intellect. As we now live, it is almost as difficult to develop a good intellect apart from urban life as it is to develop a great soul in a city. Yet the religious mind must achieve the integration of the two. The

[28] I say "proved to lie" in this incongruity. We all know that what a psychologist finds as the cause of conflict depends as much upon the psychologist as upon the patient. That I find the urban sacrifice so often in the religious mind may mean only that I have never made peace with having to live in a city. What I here call the urban sacrifice, Freud would call the castration complex, and Adler the masculine protest. All these terms are good fun, if they are used in fun.

[29] That is, one larger, louder, or more conspicuous than necessary.

conflict therefore calls for some kind of compromise. The young man must *know* that these things call for compromise, and must be prepared to live in cities for a large portion of his life; yet must so pitch the outlook of his mind that to live in cities will not lure him into the urban sacrifice. The adult religious mind must also make its compromise with this conflict, and must carry its vision of simplicity and of life-renewing communion with the vapors of the earth, through many years of the clatter and crowding and concrete of cities. If a person can resolve to do this with a stiff upper lip, he is likely to come out all right in the end.

It can be done, if the vision is solidly grounded in the early years of life; *but under no circumstances should a human child ever be born in a city, or allowed to spend any of the growing years within reach of the urban influence.* This handicap is too much for any mind to overcome, and I do not understand how those individuals who had to spend their earliest conscious years near the environs of massed population, ever succeed in living at all, beyond the period of sexual interest. The human mind is a delicate structure, and the upper panels of it do not grow under crowded conditions unless they are given an unusually good start. Let those people who *must* raise something in a city, raise a dog; but let it not be a dog of consequence and delicate sensibilities, such as a setter dog. Let it be rather one of those ill-tempered, degenerate, wizened little animated sausages that one buys in bird stores. These surely cannot dream painfully of a better world.

The Most Dangerous Study

Theology is speculation concerning the nature of the unknown. This is the most fascinating and exciting of all human thinking, and it should be approached with awe and respect, as a man would approach the greatest pleasure of his life. It may be a very great tragedy to become entangled too young in a theology, for theology is to the latter half of life, for maturing minds, very much what sexual fulfillment is to the first half of life, for maturing bodies.

If, as my observation would seem to indicate, it is better as a rule not to study psychology until after college graduation, it is altogether possible that theology ought not to be touched for another ten years. To teach a theology prematurely is to run the danger of resolving the conflict by chaining Prometheus; yet to turn away from theology entirely is to turn away from the highest human level of integration of intellect with feeling. Theology is an effort to carry the sense of feeling-awareness into the contemplation of the unknown, but it is identified in the popular mind with the idea of *answering questions* relating to the unknown. It cannot exert a healthful general influence until the popular conception of it changes over to the idea of *thinking into* the unknown, not quite as one dives into a river, but rather as one tentatively tries out the coldness and the feel of the water on the first day of swimming in the spring. When the theological mind *plunges* into the problem of the unknown it loses all of its virtue: its humility, its simplicity, and its reverence. It is then transformed with surprising rapidity into an arrogant, dogmatic, unchastened, and essentially absurd figure. On the whole, the flavor of the term theology in minds that count is not as good as it should be. Many of the most deeply feeling persons of the living generation think they are anti-religious, because they despise some theological ineptitude. They then never penetrate to the seat of their own conflict, but add their voice to the general religious confusion. Much of this unhealthy and premature resolution of a profound human conflict may have its roots in an insufficiently cautious or reverent approach on the part of religious teachers to the most dangerous study.

The Perplexity of Protestantism

It is always a nice problem, that of what to do about some rapidly changing concept. What shall I do about the concept God, religion, democracy, patriotism, love, morality, success? What shall be done about the concept *Christianity*? Shall I be a Christian, or shall I abandon the whole notion, and be rid of all its ramifications and distresses as I would rid myself of an obnoxious acquaintance? The more deeply religious a person is, the more difficult does this decision become, for the more poignantly does he feel the ineptitudes of established Christianity, and the more sensitively does he recoil from identification with a cheap religion, yet the more urgently does he need fourth panel fraternity and feeling rapport with his social environment. For a long time now this conflict has been somewhat mitigated by a progressive budding away from the main trunk of Christianity, which has called itself Protestantism.

The history of the rise of the Christian Church is beyond the horizon of our discussion. We believe that Jesus lived, that he was a Promethean idealist, and that he was crucified by the Epimetheans of his day. The overt reasons for, or rationalization of his crucifixion are of little significance; we know why Epimetheans crucify Prometheans. His theology, or a theological system attributed to him, became the central principle about which an extraordinarily humble religious organization grew up. In time ruling minds of the Mediterranean world perceived the practical usefulness of such a religion of humility, and by accepting it or becoming "converted" to it, gained practical control over it. It thus became institutionalized primarily as an instrument of social control in a world whose future seemed far from democratic; a world in which the main purpose of the ordinary man's life was to do his duty, rather than to develop a mind. During the course of centuries, much of the older religious and theological lore of the race was gradually incorporated into Christianity, until there came into existence one of the richest collections of religious scripture that the world has known.

Ultimately, Jesus' name became permanently identified with a world-wide religious and theological institution which probably by this time more closely represented the thing against which he as a Promethean had fought, than that for which he had laid down his life. The Church became rapidly entangled with political and sexual and economic affairs, but in spite of this it retained its homogeneity and essential wholeness through many centuries, by practising the most rigorous and merciless repression of the Promethean side of consciousness, never hesitating to kill and to torture with the utmost savagery, wherever the stir of Promethean life could be scented. The power to kill was bought by a compromising alliance with the ruling second panel powers.

Throughout all this period of Church power there were continual schisms, two or three major truncations, and innumerable buddings, but most of the buds were successfully destroyed. Then at about the time when scientific method was at last gaining a secure foothold in that realm of human thought which is farthest removed from man's immediate and personal interests, namely in the world of the remote outer environment,[30] one of these buddings finally broke away into successful life. This was modern Protestantism, and it carried the germinal seed of Promethean aspiration.

Protestantism attempted to follow the star of intellectual

[30] Modern science first found its secure foothold in the realm of human consciousness which has become astronomy, physics, and mechanics. This was only five or six human lifetimes ago, counting a lifetime as seventy years. It spread slowly into the thinking that has become biology and physiology, against terrific resistance. Only in our own time has objective thought achieved any serious foothold in psychology. Man became objective first concerning those matters farthest removed from his interests; then applied the method closer and closer to his own vital concerns. The healthy half-light of objectivity has now pretty generally reached the human body. It is reaching the mind. It has not yet reached the soul.

exploration, and at the same time to maintain its rapport with Christian theology, which was still the main source of reassurance in a world full of death and social ineptitude, and the main cohesive bond of the Western mind. The inevitable consequence of such an attempt has been a continual further budding and splitting off of Protestant sects, each sect carrying a progressively attenuated twig of Christian dogma, until one comes to find little in common between the most liberal Protestantism and the original Catholic Church. There are now Protestant churches that have no creed at all; to which membership is to be had by simple declaration of desire to live "a wise and Christian life"; there are churches that have come to regard Jesus as a perfectly natural human being, born from natural parents; churches that place the Christian miracles on a level with other folklore; that regard prayer as a healthy manner of thinking out problems—an excellent communion with the deeper self; that look upon the Bible as a sourcebook of human philosophy and folklore and poetry.

These changes constitute very fundamental divergences from the Roman Catholic dogma. In the face of such differences there is strong feeling in the more conservative and reactionary quarters that "liberal" Protestants are not Christians at all, and often in the minds of Protestants themselves there dwell uneasy doubts on this matter. Still farther out, beyond the liberal Protestant fringe, are strung many if not most of the best trained minds of the day, fairly certain that they are not Christians, yet uncertain as to whether or not they are religious. Some of them are Unitarians; some are members of an ethical culture society; a few good minds devote their fourth panel energies to a hobby of psychic research. A good many think alone.

There is a continuum of Christian identification, extending from the Roman Catholic dogma and its Greek and Anglican modifications, through a range of more than two hundred varieties of Protestant sect and of related organizations of a semi-Christian or perfunctory Christian flavor, and finally twigging out to independent religious minds who though feeling no institutional loyalties, yet in some vague, shadowy depth of their consciousness still think with many of the Christian concepts, and loosely consider themselves "Protestant."

The perplexity of Protestantism is like that of a man who, straddling his boat and the bank, finds that the boat is drifting out into the current. At first it is rather a pleasant stretch, but it soon develops into a first-class predicament, and the straddler shortly finds himself struggling in the depths of purposive disorientation, unless he can swim the waters of doubt and arrive at a purposive formulation of his own. Protestantism has been an attempt of the Christian mind to span the waters of doubt, and the question is simply, how far can the concept of Christianity be stretched without breaking? Or has it already broken?

By acting as a buffer between the Catholic dogma and the Promethean thrust which we call modern rational thought, Protestantism has brought about the postponement of a final or fatal open clash between these two elements of mind, and so has protected both. The movement has to a degree intellectualized the Promethean conflict and brought back to life the Promethean element of mind. Protestantism is in one sense responsible for the safe-rooting of scientific method in the modern world.[31] It has accomplished a heroic straddling of diverging trends, but in many minds the strain has become too great. People weaken and grow nervous if not neurotic. Some return to Catholicism; some find temporary exhilaration in the religion of atheism; some merely die in the fourth panel; and many break over into the waster freedom. Only

[31] In an indirect manner. Had it not been for Protestantism, the Church would certainly have continued successfully to destroy all Promethean beginnings, and the merry torturing and burning of Prometheans would be as common a spectacle today as it was a few lifetimes ago.

the first of these four alternatives is likely to solve the problem beyond a single lifetime, and even this possibility will not long be available unless the Protestant buffer is in some way made to hold out, for without Protestantism as a protection, the Catholic Church would now almost certainly crash to the earth like a stricken monarch of the woods.

With the great continuum of Protestant thought stretching between Catholic theology and the growing point of scientific thought, the conflict between the two extremes is graded, softened, absorbed, and it is possible for mature and sensitive individuals to move in a measure between the two poles, to partake of the beauty and the aesthetic nourishment of Catholic rituals, even to *belong* to that Church in all senses except the intellectual, and yet at the same time to maintain a vigorous intellectual or scientific life. Thousands of well-trained people are living in this manner in Europe and America. There is dissociation in their religious thought, but they know it, and have made peace with it. In the music and the dignity and the great age and tradition, and especially in the subtly suggestive odors of a fine old Catholic Church, an urban mind may experience for a moment some fleeting twinge of that sense of significance and at-one-ment with life that a more fortunately born person learns to feel daily in his awareness of living things, in the atmosphere of the seasons, and in the voice of the forest.

The Protestant movement has created a great strain in the Christian mind, for it has forced the expansion of the concept of religion until religion *begins* to embrace the idea of intellectual growth. Protestantism has brought Prometheus up into religious consciousness, and now it becomes necessary for every individual to make peace for himself with the Promethean conflict. In this way many minds are forced to grow, though it may well be that under such a strain not a few *souls* are lost that otherwise might have been saved. That is to say, some persons doubtless fail to achieve a wholeness and a character, a sense of sure identification with life, who in an intellectual dead calm might have been happy. But there is no longer a respectable intellectual dead calm to be found. No church founded upon a dogmatic theology any longer commands any significant *intellectual* respect in the world.

Protestantism has brought religious conflict up into consciousness, and has so precipitated the serious question of its own survival. This is actually the question of the survival of Christianity, for if Protestantism suddenly goes out, the Catholic Church will be caught in the full fury of a very advanced Promethean conflict to which it has itself made no adequate adaptation, and it may collapse with a crash. If this should happen before the religious mind has adapted itself to a new set of orientational concepts, it might be the end of our little drama of civilization. Christianity, certainly, seems likely to survive or perish with Protestantism.

It is gradually growing clear to the religious mind that religion must be a development, a culturing of personalities, a differentiation and an individuation of consciousness in the higher panels. In differential development lies the element of full maturity. Yet religion is a social enterprise, and the element of cohesion and sympathetic identification with other growing minds is the necessary life-giving principle in the fourth panel. This means that a high degree of fourth panel development can take place in a mind only if in immediate association there are other minds who are going through a *somewhat* similar development. No one consciousness can ever extend *very far* beyond the position of others with which it is in contact, and the feeling support of a mind must reach all the way back to the solid warm earth, through a series or pyramid of supporting minds.

Whoever therefore would find the way through to both emotional security and intellectual maturity, must prepare to pay the price of a toleration for the converging pyramid of religious thought which must needs lie strung out between his position and that of the least Promethean of contemporary theologies. These intervening minds protect him, support him, nourish him, and make possible the great intellectual span between him and the most Epimethean of his fellow beings. So long as there exists this *continuum* of orientational outlook, a position even at the extreme growing point of it is protected and fairly safe, but if the string is broken, then the two ends must consolidate and the Promethean conflict will break out in blood and fury until the weaker side is destroyed. If the Protestant mind has succeeded in intellectualizing the conflict between Christian theology and the Promethean element of modern consciousness, and has thereby protected and buffered the Catholic Church, it has been at the same time the very life support of those Prometheans whose position lies *out beyond* Protestantism. Without the intervening presence of Protestantism, these people who represent the vanguard of human thought would not be permitted to live a week, but would be cut off from physical life like the outer blossoms of a tree in a sudden frost. The Inquisition would be revived almost before the sun could set.

But if Protestantism is to be salvaged, I believe that three important steps must shortly be taken. 1) The confessional needs to be revived and brought up to date. It could be made an instrument for the systematic and intelligent application of empirically effective psychological techniques. 2) The sacraments must be recovered. They should be recognized as vitally necessary psychological way stations whose function it is to provide the skeleton of emotional continuity and cohesiveness in individual lives. Yet we need quite a different set of sacraments from the old set. Perhaps the attainment of first, second, and third panel self-mastery and responsibility ought to be celebrated by sacraments to be administered between twenty-one and thirty-five. The emotional crisis of thirty-five should certainly be the occasion of a sacrament. And we badly need a sacrament to usher in the period of full mental maturity, possibly to be administered normally at about fifty-five. 3) The practice of preaching must give way to more up to date and more individually qualified educational methods. It is certain that preaching and public exhortation are doomed, for these have already become far more of an irritant to good minds than a solace to weak ones. If the Protestant Church could face this reality squarely and could substitute individual and seminar teaching for the pulpit, this one change might save the day and might pave the way to other, still more courageous steps.

The immediate conflict in the religious mind reduces essentially to the question of whether to support Protestantism, and to suffer and tolerate the heavy drag of those millions of sluggish minds who really "protest" only against the occasional necessity for thought—whether to suffer a partial identification with these intellectually weak ones in order to gain the human support that is vital to existence out at the growing point of thought—*or to cut away from everything that institutionalized religion has come to stand for, and with a magnificent Promethean resolve to try to go it alone in the fourth panel.*

In this essay we are concerned more with the problem of conflict than of error. It may not be an error to despise the Protestant Church altogether, but one may be sure that this manner of resolving the conflict must hasten a violent and destructive clash between the Promethean and Epimethean elements of society; more specifically perhaps, between the Catholic Church and fundamentalism on the one side, and Promethean scientific and intellectual influences on the other. To precipitate such a clash may be a wise thing to do, or it may be a very tragic thing. If there should result a definite swing either way it would be fatal to civilization, for the consequence would be either a great wave of revived fundamentalism and heresy hunting, and a theological dictatorship once more in the world; or general dissociation between feeling and thought, and chaos. Either an Epimethean or a Promethean overbalance will destroy a civilization. With a Promethean dominance, we crash in a magnificent Icarian fall; under Epimetheus the brain dies back and consciousness slowly recedes.

The Protestant mind has been playing the part of a buffer between two opposed and excessively powerful distintegrative forces. During the relatively few generations of this drama, human consciousness seems to have penetrated more deeply into the unknown than ever before in any similar period. It may therefore be well to weigh the consequences and the dangers in any movement which too sharply would upset this delicate balance. The question of attempting to preserve a Protestant theology should occupy scant attention, for this by definition and in all of its implications is transitional. The deeper question centers upon the practical usefulness of Protestantism in keeping the Promethean conflict up in the light of full consciousness, where it can be handled. The impatient impulse to throw aside the *impedimenta* of Protestantism, and to try to emerge thereby into the clear air of rational thought, is of the same origin as the second panel impulse to create democracy by declaring for communism. A completely rational fourth panel consciousness is to be carried in mind as a distant heaven toward which to aspire and to yearn, but it is folly to attempt to declare it into existence, and thereby to sweep away the machinery by which the mind is enabled to move a little toward such a goal.

The conflict between the impulse to leap in a single bound from Main Street to Prometheus, and the impulse to crawl back under the warm bedclothes to Epimetheus, is the great conflict in the religious mind. Protestantism is like a temporary scaffolding which supports the conflict, and holds it up into the healing light of consciousness. The problem of what to do about Protestantism is the problem of what will happen if the scaffolding is removed. There are those who believe that human consciousness can now carry the conflict without such a crutch, but before committing ourselves to that faith, it may be wise to ponder well the nature of conflict. One thing alone is clear and certain in religion. The religious mind must go to school and learn to think in terms of conflict. This is the only dogma which I wish to teach.

30. THE FIFTH PANEL AS THE BAROMETER OF PSYCHOLOGICAL HEALTH

The fifth is the panel of delights, and of the refined wishes and choices of a life. It is the total pattern of conscious experience where feeling and thought intermingle. This, I think, is what we mean by the experience of the soul. Perhaps only two things count in human life; the influence you leave upon other minds, and what has delighted you—lighted up your imagination. Bodies vary little, minds considerably, and souls enormously. In more than an academic sense the affairs of the lower panels may be compared to the base of a pyramid whose apex is the feeling focus of awareness, playing upon the phenomena of life like the delicate antennae of a Prometheus moth.[32] The fifth panel is not so much itself a focus of conflict as an indicator and a barometer of conflict, and an index of the general good health that is predominating in the mental affairs of a personality.

The great modern travail of the human soul has arisen from fourth panel failure to keep a mental balance in the face of what ought to have been an unparalleled harvest sown by the effort and sacrifice of generations that have gone before. Human ingenuity has produced so many devices for human delight, and the world has become crammed so full of them, that everywhere young minds are swamped and confused with too much stimulation. As a race we are like children with too many toys; like kittens drowning in cream.

Normally in the past, *people* have been the great source of human sympathy and delight; but now people have become common as dogs. There are millions of them where psychologically there were only a few. Human life has be-

[32] Called in some of the moth books, apparently through error, *the Promethea moth.*

come so cheap. There is so much of it. It grows hard to believe in the significance of anything; very hard to find the courage to face the fifth panel, and to resolve to grow into it. For it may not be worth while, and in the face of the animectomy complex it is fearfully painful to be caught serious. It is more difficult to grow a soul in the teeth of overstimulation than to be thrifty in a time of waster raids upon the integrity of the dollar, or to be loyal to a government when corruption is known to be dominant. Deep in civilized souls the voice of God still speaks. But it no longer urges men to be fruitful and further to populate the earth. *That* voice now comes from another quarter.

The conflict in the fifth panel is the struggle between discouragement and the will to keep the soul alive in the face of overstimulation. Discouragement is the death of the soul, and it lurks always in the path of an overstimulated mind. Yet everywhere young minds are pressed upon to hurry on, and there has come over the human world a great fear of inner contemplation. People turn away from the awful question they find in their own souls. It seems too vital for them, they cannot face it, the stakes are too high, and they try to escape by shouting it down, by making a noise, by keeping busy, by turning on the radio, by anything. Yet this only makes more certain the ultimate discouragement, and but postpones the evil hour for a little.

Normally the fourth panel orientational structure of the mind throws up a protection behind which the fifth panel consciousness can flower and develop, but with the collapse of these protective structures, the soul is left naked to the direct blasts of an overstimulating world. Still the intensity of the human striving toward fifth panel consciousness is such that even in these tragic periods of chaos and transition, the consequent direct exposure of the soul to the ravages of profound conflict is not in itself sufficient to extinguish the flame. Only when there is superimposed the cross strain of a general disillusionment does the flame go out.

A general disillusionment is the most tragic experience in human life. It may be defined as the realization of having built a life orientation upon a false foundation. This can come about only through the practice of lying to children, which is unquestionably the blackest of crimes. One of the most delicate tests of adult character is that of the extent to which the individual has the courage to take a child fully into his fifth panel confidence.[33] An adult who has not succeeded in bringing order into his own fourth and fifth panels of consciousness, and yet lacks the courage and basic honesty to face these matters with a child, must either build up some plausible lie about the whole business, or he must turn the child over to the tender mercies of other people, who may be even less mature or more dishonest than himself. The problem of how far to take a child into adult confidence is a delicate one. There is no other experience in life that so fully searches a soul. Children are by far the best psychoanalysts.

From the formative point of view, the most important period of a human life is very likely that immediately following the mastery of language habits. Psychologists believe that the foundations of character are laid during the early years of life. If during these years there is built in a hierarchy of delights and a participation in the feeling-awareness of things which will remain compatible with a later developing intellect, it is virtually impossible for the individual to experience a general disillusionment. But if during these early years the child has been treated as if he were going to remain *intellectually* a child, then before he can grow up he must suffer the shock of disillusionment and rebirth, when his whole

[33] In response to popular psychoanalytic influences it has become quite the rage to reveal adult bodies to childhood's ingenuous gaze, the adults always taking especial care to see that the sexual organs are fully exposed; but have you the courage to fully reveal your soul to a child, both in its doubts and in its true ecstasies?

internal world will crash about his head; he will then be fortunate indeed if in later years he does not hate his own childhood and all that was associated with it. It is this disillusioned mind with its deep hatreds and resentments of its childhood that has given Freudian psychoanalysts so unleavened an impression of the universality of the Oedipus complex and of father hatred. Yet there is actually nothing inevitable about such misfortune, except where children are reared without an eye to their intellectual future. It is an orientational, not a sex-fixational problem.

The highest courage is required for an adult to take a child into his confidence concerning orientational matters, but this is the only way, except by permanently stunting the child's intellect, that the adult can hold the later love and rapport with his child that he so deeply craves and needs. We can be careless of a child's influences in the lower panels and can often make up for it later and over-ride it, but the intimate relation between orientational outlook and the development of the soul is such that whenever a parent teaches a child a religious orientation which will lead to disillusionment, the relation between that parent and child is forever ruined. The child must suffer the dying back of the brain or go through rebirth. In either event the relation with the parent is destroyed. Always the fifth panel rests upon the fourth. The fourth panel carries the function of supporting and nourishing the soul. If it crashes, the soul crashes.

Christianity grew up under conditions which have completely changed. It was written for monarchies, and its plan of second panel control was formulated during a period of predominant pessimism and discouragement concerning human nature. This new religion came into existence near the end of a period of general orientational collapse, at a time when there was little inkling of the Promethean democratic dream of the future. Christianity carried no prophecy of a general *intellectual* development of the human personality.

Its ethic therefore was a static one, and being good rather than growing up became the central ethical criterion. Such an ethic will produce a soul in a static world, but not in a growing one, and to teach it to a child who must live in even a partial democracy is the tragic error against which modern writers have been aiming such heroic castigation. The theological mind is not as generally beloved as it might be, because it is too often associated with the disillusionment experience. Theologians, like the rest of us, seem to bungle the job of introducing children to the idea of God. Yet this is one of the most important of educational tasks, for the supreme achievement of any human intellect is surely its definition of its God.

Santa Claus changes with comparative ease from a kindly red-coated man with reindeer and white whiskers to a symbol of generosity and human good will, and the maturer a mind grows, the deeper becomes its affection for him. In the minds of parents and teachers there is from the beginning a clear realization that Santa Claus is to be a dynamic concept, and that he will grow as the mind grows. To tell a child of Santa Claus is like planting a tree. Only when God is introduced with this same general point of view dominant, however reverent and chastened the outlook, does God become a safe foundation principle for the building of a soul. There are individuals in the human world who are not afraid to talk to their children about their God in such a manner that He becomes an intimate and enduring tie between the older and the younger mind, even though the latter may in later years grow well beyond the understanding of the former.

This takes courage, and it takes thought, but hundreds of thousands of human beings who are capable of both, fail to make any real use of the most valuable concept that their heritage carries, simply because the idea has never come to them through religious channels. If religious teachers would only remember that the human soul is a thing which grows mainly from bonds of affection and common understanding between old minds and young minds, between the past and the present and the future, then the God they teach might come to stand, *even in children's minds,* for all the human soul that has existed and does exist and will exist. God can become for children, as He did for Emerson, the living reality of the Oversoul, and a time-transcending personification of these most sacred of all human bonds, as Santa Claus personifies the lesser and incidental human relationship of warm first panel generosity. It may then be that religion will be able to avert the most serious disaster that can threaten the human mind—the death of its God.

The religious mind suffers severe conflict over its definition of God. It hesitates between such a fifth panel conception as this which I have just been outlining, and some fascistic or communistic marshalling of its forces in a desperate final effort to push Prometheus back into the box and nail down the lid.[34] It is for religious people a choice between making peace with the intellectual component of their own minds, and some kind of return to fundamentalism.

Turning now finally to the practical problem of carrying the fifth panel through a period of danger, one thing is clear. If the human mind is to meet the strain of the peculiarly severe stresses that the changing conception of God has brought to bear upon it, men must find and at least temporarily utilize some strong auxiliary emotional anchorage other than the traditional theological anchorage. The latter is for the time being unsafe. It is shifting too fast. A person now young can no longer safely build the foundation of the ecstasies of his life on the old theological concepts. The soul requires an anchorage in something which can be trusted at least not to change within a single lifetime.

[34] Russia has suppressed Prometheus with communism; Germany with fascism. In either of these countries, to voice a dissenting opinion in one of the first two panels is now sufficient provocation for a violent death.

As we cast about in the world of human experience, in search of the safest rock upon which to effect a fifth panel anchorage, five general possibilities suggest themselves. These are (1) *people*; (2) *the overt contrivances and creations of people;* (3) *ideas, which are implicit creations of people;* (4) *the living earth*; and (5) *the outer natural universe.*

A well-developed fifth panel consciousness will surely have roots in all five of these human supports, but it still will need in one of them a main anchorage; some solid rock upon which to fall back in moments of severest duress, where like Antaeus in his return to mother earth, the soul can always find strength and reinvigoration. The traditional Christian anchorage has been that of a group of *ideas,* built up around the idea of God. But God has receded with the stars to such bewildering heights that now only the strongest and the weakest minds can reach Him. The great intervening majority find it necessary to seek some secondary, more immediate spiritual support. Typically, they first try *people.*

To become dependent for ultimate spiritual reality upon people is in the end invariably tragic; for the individual is then not only at the mercy of the instability and insecurity of other personalities, but he is defenseless against the eternal specter of death. Death can strike him to the very vitals. At any moment, death can lay him low, and not only once, but again and again. Such a person's only defense against death is to become dependent upon *a great many people*; that is, to go over to extraversion, and this is actually the dominant religious psychology of the day. It is the religion of the waster. The great tragedy of such a solution is that with eggs so widely scattered in many baskets, the eggs are never really available at all. The fifth panel has been scattered to the four winds, and nothing is left to lean on, but a shell of superficial human sympathies.

Of the *overt creations of people,* the most conspicuous is civilization itself. Many try to worship at the shrine of overt, material progress. It is possible to feel a certain pride, even at rare moments an ecstasy, in the material evidence of man's conquest over nature. But a skyscraper or a washing machine carries little personal warmth. Only a vividly imagining mind can make out the shadow of the human soul that lies behind these things, and such a mind to its sorrow penetrates to the illusion and the transitoriness that is also there. The same dilemma faces him who attempts to make a religion of the *idea of scientific method.* The fifth panel requires a grounding in something warm, and close to the earth. The principle of objectivity alone can supply only half of the necessary supportive trunk of human consciousness.

For strong minds there is reassurance in *the outer universe.* It is possible to *feel* the stupendous serenity and the permanence of the stars. Some people experience a twinge of this sense of power over time in earthly and available things like the Pyramids, mountains, and the sea; even in possessable things like antiques, old coins, fossils, works of art, and the like. The motivation of most adult collecting is, I think, founded upon the wish to transcend time; to reach back across generations in a warm, personal, possessive identification with something which does so transcend time.

Finally, *the living earth* can be made the main foundation of fifth panel consciousness. This carries both warmth and the magic quality of permanence. The living things of the earth, both plant and animal, are psychologically immortal. Further, they have life, and hence feeling and warmth, which constitutes a great advantage over inanimate things from out of the past. For a person who has eyes trained to see, and ears to listen, there is never a day in the year when the very air does not carry some recurrent, living reassurance. And the night is even more so, if you have kept a fraction of the imagination of a child. Have you ever heard a migrating Bartramian sandpiper on a clear August night? Or the first Southward flying Canada geese in October? Did you only hear, or did you *feel* them? Each season carries the promise of the next, and religious communion in March with the dragon flies and the Mourning Cloaks is heightened in its ecstasy by foreknowledge of the golden June beetles and of the evening-flying Sphinx moths to come. In a time of human overcrowding and overstimulation, and hence of fourth panel confusion, these carry the clearest reflection that we can see, of the *living* face of our God.

There is also religious wisdom in the barnyard, and especially in the henyard. More genuine fun can be had in an hour with the hens, and more insight into *human* nature, than in many a university classroom. Watch the hens, with human second and third panel weaknesses in mind, and if they do not overcome you with a mood of good, honest, sympathetic mirth, then good humor is not in you. To the child mind, and to the first-class adult mind, all things have a personality. Hens, insects, dogs, even chairs and similar domestic objects do *funny* things, and you can't help laughing. A psychologist (silly man) would call it anthropomorphizing, and having named it in six syllables, would of course miss the meaning of it. Yet if once you learn to enjoy the hens, they will never go back on you. They may give you a fourth panel beanstalk, upon which you can climb to your God.

An early love of birds is like casting bread upon the waters. Plants and wildflowers are close to the heart of the communicant in the living earth faith, though they are not quite alive enough to carry the personality and individuality of the animal world. In the insect world and in the world of night life, particularly in the romance of the great night moths, lie some of the soundest foundations for the human soul. Toads and frogs and snakes and turtles are among the best friends of human beings who would grow a soul. To learn to love these personalities, and to identify the necessarily more transitory *human* loves of a life with them, is to develop the fifth panel of consciousness, which is the soul.

There will still be tragedy in the death of your mother and your father and your friends, but they will all live again, very close to your side, through the day and in the stillness of the night, if together with them you have loved and laughed at these living creatures who still are here. I do not wish to preach a dogma in this book, but the suggestion of grounding a childhood religious orientation upon kindness and *Einfühlung* with the lesser creatures of the earth, may be worthy of thoughtful contemplation in a world too full of people. Two generations ago this kind of religious education was almost universal in rural America. Now, in the face of overstimulation, it is becoming difficult to find. Overstimulation is the real destroyer of the human soul.

I do not by any means wish to suggest that a nature love constitutes fifth panel maturity; nor that it can substitute for the wider and sterner mental structure that is necessary to creative religious thought. What I do wish to suggest is that such an early feeling rapport with the earth life offers one sure and readily available foundation upon which to *start* the growth of a soul. The frame and the pattern of the fifth panel are in the last analysis perhaps the only things about a personality that really count, and nothing can be so important in education as to build into the child consciousness some very solid, simple, and unchanging cornerstone which will carry and support this frame through life. To try to use an intellectualized theology for this cornerstone purpose is a tragic blunder, both because it strains the child's sense of truth and simplicity, and because it ruins the later study of theology, which ought to constitute the keenest delight of the second half of life. To attempt to muddle through with an educational philosophy lacking such a cornerstone, as we have now been doing for a generation or so, is to induce everywhere the animectomy complex and soul prudery, the cardinal symptom of which is the horror of being caught serious.

The cornerstone of a soul must be laid somewhere in the wide field of the aesthetic appreciations. The choice lies between natural and artifactual aesthetics. It may be that we make a great mistake in permitting children to be too much exposed to artifactual aesthetics ahead of their development of rich and enduring feeling-awarenesses of the natural world. The danger here, I think, is much the same as in teaching children a theology. It may not be well to impose upon children too much of the frozen in pattern of adult conventionalized thought habit; too much intellectual, artificial, and hence mutable and insecure anchorage. A developed artistic flare in a child is sometimes very soul-satisfying to the parents, particularly if they themselves have no other anchorage, but it may mean a fearful sacrifice of the child's later growth. The thing may not last; it may not provide the matrix of feeling for life which would have given the child the later courage to face the second half of life, and so would have prevented the dying back of the brain in early middle age. For a child to "express itself" when very young, in some adult-approved pattern of an art, may, like the too early adoption of a theology, spell frustration and disruption of deeper-seated and more permanent habits of feeling contact with life. It is necessary to use judgment, and to exercise human insight in these matters. We need psychologists who have grown mellow, and have emerged from the animectomy complex.

31. DIAGNOSIS AND INDICATED TREATMENT

How then shall the great sickness that is upon the human mind be diagnosed? The symptoms are only too clear. Modern man has lost the courage to face the fifth panel, and to grow a soul. The fear of being caught with a sentiment has everywhere become dominant over the old fears and over the old loves. The human soul has retracted, and the mind has fallen back to the solider safety of the biological panels, as a startled snail falls back into his shell, to reëmerge only very slowly and tentatively into the dangerous outer world.

In trouble man falls back to the basic panel cures, and over and over again he tries them all, in an endless cycle. First the economic, then the political, and now the sexual interpretation of history—each has its day, coloring the literature, the common language, the aesthetics and amusements, even the biography of its period. Each in its turn is always a new discovery, always ushered in upon a wave of fanaticism following a trough of violent opposition.[35]

As a race we are like a troop of great apes, confined in and forever trying to escape from a cage that has three main doors. 'Round and 'round the cage they troop; excited, chattering, hurried and full of business, stopping at each door in turn and setting up a high turmoil, only to forget it in a while and stampede to the next. High tariffs—low tariffs, inflation—deflation; communism—fascism, republicanism—dictatorship; repression—expression, asceticism—Freudianism; first panel, second panel, third panel. Over and over each door is tried. Again and again it leads to the same place—always to nowhere.

Now and then a straggler from the troop, usually one

[35] For an expansion of this theme and a penetrative analysis of the cycle of the "three alternating materialistic philosophies," see Mr. Gerald Heard's *The Ascent of Humanity*.

unable for some reason to keep the pace, is constrained to pause, to contemplate, and to look. If perchance he looks *up* and perceives that the cage is open at the top, before he is too old to climb, he will ere long drop lightly to the ground outside, and then he will either starve, or grow a soul and roam in the Forest of Arden for the remainder of his days. There is but one thing he cannot do. He can never return to the cage, for to grow a soul is to burn that bridge.

At the more educated levels of life people have lost touch with their own souls. Stated in psychological language, a general dissociation has come about in the human mind between lower panel consciousness and higher panel consciousness. The resulting strains, and the final tragic sense of futility in individual minds, constitute what we have jokingly called the animectomy complex. The diagnosis of the modern sickness is, then: *Dissociation of the fifth panel.*

The treatment, of course, must consist in the general application of a psychology of sufficient balance and proportion to carry, not only the fifth, but *all* of the panels of consciousness in a common perspective. Where can such a psychology be found? It cannot be found, for it does not yet exist, but it may be that the materials exist from which it can be built. By combining the penetrative analytic approach to individual minds that has been the method of the confessional and more recently the method of psychoanalysis, with the experimental objectivity which academic psychology has tried to borrow from medicine and biology; and by adding to these qualifications the enthusiasm and spiritual contagiousness and rapport with the earth which have characterized the Christian minister at his best—by striving earnestly to bring these three channels of thought to a common focus, we yet may launch into the world a dynamic, five panel psychology. When such a day dawns, disillusionment, boredom, and human sophistication will begin to melt back from consciousness like a receding glacier. The dying back of the brain will become an ancestral memory, to be dug out of the vestigial remnants of awareness that some psychoanalysts call the unconscious, and finally to disappear altogether.

It must not be supposed that I have advanced the speculations and hypotheses which make up the material of this book, *as such a psychology.* This material is intended only as a preface to a five-panel psychology, and as the description of a target for it. Nor will the further elaboration of the point of view and of my own method of individual psychological analysis to be found in the companion volume following this one, constitute *a* psychology. We are only at the threshold of any comprehension at all of the human mind; and we need the support of an intense religious enthusiasm.

There is a religious sniffing of the air in many quarters. It seems probable that as a culture we are nearly ripe for determined and emotionally driven religious movements. Some of these movements are certain to take the character of reversions to the old formulae. We may be caught and destroyed in a backwash of fundamentalisms. Yet there has now accumulated in the world a very much larger increment of literate minds than has ever existed at one time before, and given one cohesive idea, this intellectual increment may already carry sufficient strength to counteract the danger of such a backwash.

The cohesive idea may lie in the emergence of an intellectually respectable religious psychology, or time-dimensional psychology. Three specific practical suggestions toward such a psychology seem to follow from the theme which has been presented in this book. 1) The religious mind is surrounded by powerful though unappreciated allies in the immortal creatures of the living earth. 2) If religion is essentially a matter of carrying emotional support to the function of orientation in time, then one primary religious concern ought to be that of enlivening and unifying the hitherto appallingly uninspired teaching of history and anthropology. If ministers will resolve to stop preaching, and will turn this energy instead to the planned and unified teaching of the drama of the human past, they may by thus coördinating with the universities save their profession, and they may even save the Protestant Church. 3) An adequate clinical or face to face psychology has now become a vital necessity to the minister. The foundations of it may lie in a five panel conception of the mind, and in further insight into the Promethean conflict.

APPENDIX

1. THE SUBJECTIVE AND THE OBJECTIVE MIND

IF A psychologist were to yield to the ever-persistent temptation to construct an elemental dichotomy of human thinking types, he might do well to found it upon the differences between objective, scientific thinking and subjective, intuitional thinking. The latter may be compared to the former as wings compare to legs. It is infinitely faster, more exciting and romantic and delightful, more fraught with rapid adventure, far less certain, and extremely dangerous. The tragedy of the legendary Icarus is directly applicable to intuitional thinking; Icarus, who with fragile, thought-created wings flew too far from the solid earth and so destroyed himself.

When a person uses *intuition*, he is simply allowing his judgment to be strongly influenced by the deeper levels of his own consciousness. He lets his mind go free, as it were, and gives attention to the course in which it travels. He allows the delicate, gossamer-like stuff of subjective comprehension to take character in his stream of consciousness, and gives it a prominent place in his system of values. A Freudian psychoanalyst would say that he is projecting his unconscious, and is rationalizing the repressed material thereby brought (in disguise) to the light.

Yet Emerson's *Oversoul* and James' *Will to Believe* represent recognition in two mature minds of an ultimately vital role to be played by this kind of thought. These two were both predominantly intuitional thinkers, Emerson all his life and James more notably in his maturer years. James found a way of balancing subjectivity with objectivity, and by giving each a purchase against the other developed both to extraordinary dimensions.

In minds in which such a balanced development has gone forward, the deeper levels are well integrated with the surface levels. Such personalities ring true clear down to the foundations of consciousness. They carry a central axis of values which runs in a straight line, and when analyzed, by whatever method, they reveal no shocking discrepancy between what has been previously accepted as the conscious will, and deeper-lying desires. An orderly mental housekeeping has been set up which does not stop at the parlor door, but extends through to the cellar. People of this sort have balanced the problem of the opposites and can therefore trust their own intuition, for the deeper levels of thought which it taps ring true to conscious values. Such persons are not always well educated, and may indeed possess little intellect, but they nevertheless can be trusted to work at subjective levels, and when they do possess unusual intellectual development they are perhaps the people who can be trusted with theology.

There are other personalities that seem upon close examination to be quite out of perspective with themselves, and to carry a profound cleavage between the consciously realized self and the great system of remoter wish that lies below the surface. The distortion is not always due to the *inward* turning of the conscious focus (introversion). It is actually quite as common to find that the habitual focus of attention has been turned disproportionately *outward*.

In a mind turned disproportionately outward, instead of the rich dwelling upon experience, and instead of the reminiscent contemplation seen in a consciousness deeply in tune with itself, there is a marked antipathy to contemplation and an increasing dependence upon social stimulation. This is the condition to which Jung originally applied the term extraversion,[1] though he himself has long since abandoned

[1] The other extreme, the inwardly turned or introverted imbalance, has been so widely popularized and journalized that there is no need of

his extravert-introvert dichotomy and has fled to the cover of more relative language.

Those persons who upon psychological analysis show the sharpest incompatibility between the surface self and the deeper self, are very frequently highly social creatures, happiest in crowds and in cities, and unhappy when alone. An overbalanced objectivity of mind is typically the cause of more profound psychological dissociation than is excessive subjectivity. The outwardly turned mind has completely lost the capacity for finding child-like delight in its own inner contemplation.[2] It has sacrificed what may in the end turn out to be the most valuable thing in life. By losing the power of contemplation, it cuts itself off from the contemplation of time, and hence from fourth and fifth panel development. Such minds in prosperity become happy wasters and celebrators. Under normal conditions they lead unhappy dissociated lives. This is one of the dangers that lie in a philosophy of excessive objectivity.

2. THE FEELING ELEMENT OF CONSCIOUSNESS, AND THE NATURE OF INTUITION

There are in general three kinds of sense organs in the body; a group which receives impressions from the external environment (distance receptors); a group receiving impressions from things in contact with the body (contact recep-

---

describing it here. The point I want to make is simply that extraversion is fully as pathological as introversion, though it is just now popular and hence very much the more common of the two mental illnesses. Many of our schools, and most of our nursery schools, are planned deliberately to "bring children out of introversion" and to push them over toward extraversion. It would be hard to imagine a stupider or more fatal error.

[2] And unfortunately it has lost it permanently. When the mind turns to an outer distortion, the process seems to be irreversible, like the "popping" of a kernal of popcorn. Children who are too introverted can be "brought out" almost at will, but once a child has become extraverted, very little can be done except leave him that way.

tors) ; and a group responding to what goes on in the internal structures of the body itself (internal receptors). All of these contribute continually to consciousness. The term *feeling* is ordinarily used to refer to consciousness characterized by domination of some blend or pattern of sensation from the internal sense organs, though the sensory response is as a rule felt *in relation* to external things, and is generally not recognized as coming from within. Students in psychology commonly are taught bizarre conceptions of feeling, the most common notion being that feeling is *merely* awareness of interoception. This is an absurdity, for consciousness is at all times complex, and is produced by the continual play of incoming sensory excitation from all main groups of receptors, with the further complication that there is probably always present some element of associative recall (memory).

The most exact statement that can safely be made concerning the biological nature of feeling, is that it is an aspect of consciousness in which organic sensations from within, coming from digestive, respiratory, circulatory, reproductive, and internal muscular and skin structure, are *dominant in the focus*, or are heard in the symphony, which is consciousness. *Feeling is consciousness in which there is a stir or change in the deep life processes of the physical being itself.* In feeling the biological centers of life are active and are *felt* to respond to the stimulating situation. We have considered the two opposed functions of the autonomic nervous system,[3] which controls the visceral structures producing most of this internal sensation. There are two correspondingly opposite, positive and negative poles to feeling, though feeling is not often entirely positive or entirely negative. Most feeling has some of both elements present, just as most behavior is both good and bad, as judged by any particular moral system.

Some of the conscious elements entering into feeling are: Sinking at the pit of the stomach (paralysis of digestive mus-

[3] P. 13.

culature); heart palpitation; thermal skin sensations from flushing; the peculiar sensation of gooseflesh, which is caused by muscular contraction in the skin, particularly up and down the spine; the sense of tension in muscles, especially in the facial muscles and in the accessory muscles of respiration; feeling of cold at the extremities, from circulatory changes (cold feet); skin sensations from perspiration and from the coolness of its evaporation; sensations of choking or of a lump in the throat, from contraction of the esophagus; a general tingling throughout the body from increased muscle tone; feeling of dryness in the mouth and throat, from cessation of salivary secretion; sensations about the eyes and nose, resulting from increased lachrymal secretion; the feeling of trembling, from interference with the stream of nervous excitation that controls muscle tonus; and the feeling of expansive aspiration, which arises in part from increased tonus of the diaphragm and of other muscles of breathing. These are merely a random sampling of the organic sensation patterns entering into feeling.

Emotion is a conscious state in which the feeling element is especially dominant, and almost always complex or confused. There are potentially as many different emotions in human consciousness as potential combinations, or blends, of feeling sensation, which is infinity.[4] Between 300 and 400 abstract nouns in the English language refer to the supposed human emotions. Yet psychologists have often tried to list and describe "the emotions," and it was an attempt to read through some of these descriptions that led James to exclaim, "I should as lief read verbal descriptions of the shapes

[4] Psychology has not yet even scratched the surface of the task of setting up an adequate objective vocabulary describing feeling and emotion. Probably it never will. So long as this is so, we must lean very heavily upon subjective, and intuitional description, though psychology at the moment has recoiled from subjective thinking, like a puppy with a burnt nose.

of the rocks on a New Hampshire farm as toil through them again."

To describe feeling comprehensively is really to describe conscious experience, which is the function of all literature at large. Here I should like to mention but three general characteristics of feeling, which seem to bear on the problem of conflict.

1. *Feeling and emotion are subject to habit formation.* For every individual there are emotional states which are fairly well patterned, are recurrent, habitual, and even become to a degree verbally definable; and there is gradation from this sharp specificity to the other end of the distribution where occur vague, ephemeral, fleeting, totally unverbalized and rare symphonies of feeling. These latter are sometimes the "rare ecstasies" that constitute the mystic experience. There can be no verbal classification of feeling which will fit two people quite alike, yet we do speak meaningfully of emotions, and there are a number of emotional patterns specific enough to be given names that carry some common meaning for different minds. The terms fear, anger, hate, love, delight, envy, horror, and a few dozen similar concepts carry sufficient common meaning to render them useful tools of communication. Yet fear in one mind is never quite the same thing as fear in another. The graphing of a clearness hierarchy of emotion makes an excellent class exercise. A student once produced such a graph for me, in which he had plotted 234 emotions.

2. Feeling and emotion are really projected references of consciousness, and the whole tenor of the language of feeling is that of reference not to what is going on in the body and actually causing the feeling, but to the outer situation with which the feeling is associated. People learn the language of emotion and come to name emotions and feelings by observing outer situations, then applying such a term as anger to a particular complex of their own feeling because of hav-

ing experienced similar feeling in a situation in which someone else was said to be angry. We name emotional life by matching outer situations, for it is these alone that supply the necessary objective purchase to support names.

It is clear then that two rather distinct elements are involved in the feeling side of consciousness. There are (1) the element of the natural sensitivity and delicacy of a mind, the native capacity for fineness of feeling; and (2) the element of habitual observant alertness to meanings[5] in the environment, with which feeling may potentially become associated. A mind combining fine feeling with high observant qualities comes to possess tremendously developed discriminative rapport with life and may *feel itself over into* a relatively great proportion of things in its world. A mind with great fifth panel development is one unusually sensitive to relationships, and is at the same time capable of unusual emotional participation in life.

This combination of fineness of feeling with close habitual observation of the world of things and people, may carry the secret of the main difference between the mind which loves solitude and hates overstimulation, and the more dependent mind that is lost without social stimulation, and loves cities. It may be that here lies the foundational difference between the reverent mind and the waster mind. The point I want especially to emphasize is that there is a very strong element of habit in this matter; that the quality of the feeling life of an adult person is closely related to the kind of aesthetic appreciation habits that were acquired in childhood. A child not exposed too much to overstimulation by other children, but spending a good proportion of his time in the company of one or more "gently and wisely mature" adults, is likely to develop such a mind himself.

3. Since feeling is a quality of consciousness, it shades off

[5] A meaning is psychologically always a relationship. An observant mind is a mind sensitive to relationships.

with consciousness to deep, remote, and distant levels that are far out in the shadows and away from the focus of clearness. *There is no boundary between conscious and unconscious feeling, but rather there are feeling attitudes so vague, elusive, and beyond the range of descriptive language that they are given in different minds a very wide variety of different interpretations.* These become the unexplained likes and dislikes of a personality, the unrealized prejudices, the sixth sense, the source of hunches and of the "feeling" of absent or departed persons, and they undoubtedly underlie much of the mental activity produced by a medium when hypnotized or in a trance. These distant levels of feeling are of quite particular importance for the student of the conflict in the religious mind, because of the fact that much of religious thinking is necessarily *intuitive.*

Intuition may be defined as the feeling of a significance, or of a meaning, at such a shadowy level of consciousness that the steps involved in arriving at the association are not traceable. Intuitional thinking is highly characteristic of sensitive and aesthetically developed minds, for it involves a mingling of feeling and intellect which is very close to the thinking of childhood. This may in fact be the characteristic that gives rise to the expression "heart of a child." Some such quality of mind at any rate is at times carried into adult life, and becomes habit. It is the habit of exploring and of systematizing the deeper fringe of consciousness, where knowing and feeling become indistinguishable.

The habit of intuitive thinking may be associated with any degree of intellectual maturity or immaturity. A mind may consist of little more than such a shadowy inner fringe, in which case we should have to speak of the heart *and mind* of a child; or an intuitive mind, may be a tremendously mature, trained, clear-thinking mind which nevertheless has carried with it all the way into adult understanding its delightful playground in the peripheral twilight shadows, where it finds perpetual refreshment, and bathes daily in the springs of emotional youth. Only such minds should write theologies or psychologies. *All of the finest human thought and feeling is carried for generations, probably for ages, in intuitional minds, long before it becomes articulate.*

The mind low in intuitional qualities is either one of poor natural sensitivity, or there is sharp dissociation between the surface consciousness and the rest of the system. If my psychological experience is typical, this sharp dissociation is less common in women than in men, though perhaps an exception should be made of women who have grown up since the war, and like male imitators of the waster, have become entangled in the mad attempt to be modern. It is probably true that the feminine mind is more likely to possess highly developed intuitional qualities than the masculine. Women's thinking is on the whole closer to their feeling. They remain wholeminded better than men do, and more often carry the heart of a child into adult life. Why this is so is open to speculation.

It may be that female physiology is actually a little closer to child physiology. The difference may be due in a measure to the more vital importance to the female of making wise choices for sexual partnership, and to her consequent closer habitual attention to the finer fifth panel qualities of another personality. Women typically watch the nuances of emotional play in other people more closely than men do, and perhaps thereby remain closer to reality, closer to truth, in their dealings with the feeling side of their own personalities. Certainly the evidence of clinical psychology reveals that at least the sort of women who talk to psychologists want and need in men a certain delicacy or fineness of feeling even more than they want strength, though they are not always fully conscious of the former need. It may be simply that they need what has recently tended to be repressed in their own natures. In Europe and America we have made a cult of the anti-intuitional intellect, referring to it almost devoutly as the objective, or rational, or *masculine* mind. When a woman tries to adopt this cult, she must either go all the way over to conspicuous objectivity and extraversion, or she is caught in a perfect devil of a jam. This is one reason, perhaps the main reason, why there are more neurotic women than men.

If well-developed intuitional play of thought represents one of the high achievements in human mental life, it is, like most high achievements, a very dangerous habit. Intuition in a mind that has not also achieved good objective perspective can lead to a capriciousness and to a childish indetermination of purpose which may render the individual a nuisance both to himself and to all who know him. It especially lays a mind open to every sort of suggestibility, and to exploitation by medicine men of many kinds. Overbalanced intuitional thinkers continually play hunches, and continually refuse to profit by experience. The average voter in a democracy lives politically at an almost purely intuitional level. It is only a step from intuition to superstition, and to the dangerous religious *doctrine of immediate experience,*[6] which is the rationalization of the fatal dogma of infallibility.

In summary the feeling element is not a mere inruption into consciousness of the softer, weaker, or "feminine" component of human life, but it is the very life-giving element of the mind. It is consciousness in which the deepest biological centers are reached and are meaningfully responsive to the outer world. A consciousness rich in feeling may also be rich in the objective detail and accuracy of its awareness, thus achieving the highest or most perfect integration between the outer and inner world. But we live in a period which has

[6] Immediate experience, recognized as intuition, becomes a useful and important religious concept. When not so recognized, it can make of religion a farce and an imposition.

produced a strong inclination to dissociate these two worlds. The old theology was founded upon a very clear perception of the importance of integration between the two worlds, and it went to heroic extremes to achieve it; but its method was to force the intellect, which represents the outer world, to adapt itself entirely to the feelings of the inner world. This actually was not an integration at all, but only a dissociation.

It was the sacrifice of Prometheus and the consequent paralysis of the mind. The brave new world that has arisen from the ashes of the old theology has made its own theology one of mortification and denial of the *feelings* in order to give the intellect free range for development. This too is a false philosophy, for the two elements of the mind must support each other, and any deliberate or involuntary influence which curtails either must in the end also stunt and destroy the other. The present intellectual or rationalistic movement places a high premium on those qualities that are associated, probably more or less rightly, with the dominantly masculine qualities of mind. This emphasis carries a peculiarly grave danger to the individual female personality, for she is thus frequently caught in the anomaly of striving toward an objectivity which is often diametrically opposed to her own best development possibilities.

There are today many thousands of unhappy college educated young men and women in America and England who if trained from childhood to develop intuitional as well as objective thinking, could have been radiantly happy and intellectually productive. They are not true to themselves in the niches of life in which they have been caught, and they therefore become a festering source of unrest and unhappiness. They constitute a manifestation of the character conflict, and they virtually support the psychoanalysts. Many of these people can be helped a little by the sort of psychoanalysis that looks upon their problem as one of misdirected or suppressed sexuality, but such an approach does not go deep enough, and fails to carry a wide enough insight into the ultimate problems of life. For most unhappy persons it would be much better to be spanked, and then to be given enlightenment on the effect of their conflict upon the fourth and fifth panels of mental life.

3. RATIONALIZATION AND THEOLOGY

To rationalize is to make a thing seem rational, or to find reasons for it. If the wisdom of some act or opinion of mine is questioned, I must justify the act; or disavow it; or face a conflict situation. Normally I will first attempt to justify it; to put it in a rational setting. I will put *reasons* behind it. They may not be the real reasons, but at least they will be good reasons. Rationalization is a case of artificially building up a defense against conflict at the expense, not at first of intellectual integrity, but rather of self-insight. The rationalizing individual too easily convinces *himself*, and this is perhaps more fatal to mental growth than outright lying. In rationalization the sense of truth is handled with a certain insidious, germinal irreverence.

In a sense rationalization may be considered a special case of compensation, as Dr. Alfred Adler often points out. It is the building up of a false sense of strength at a point where some vaguely felt weakness has existed. But yet the weakness remains, and the effort to justify the self in the face of it may come to absorb the whole mental focus of the personality until no longer can any outer ethical discrimination be made. Possibly no murder was ever committed that was not at the time justified in the mind of the murderer, and certainly no deliberate, planned crime was ever carried out without the conviction that the end justified the means.

Rationalization is the conceptual antithesis to critical thought, a term applicable to that kind of thinking in which the individual searches systematically into the implications and remoter associations of reasons advanced, not only by others but by himself as well.

Biologically the difference between these two general habits of response to conflict may be in some manner related to the degree of inhibitory domination habitually exercised by the higher centers of the forebrain over the motor pathways through the lower centers. In the one case there is the capacity to carry a conflict situation for some time at intellectual levels; in the other the balance cannot be maintained; the mind cannot tolerate conflict, but must plunge at once into quick resolution of it, throwing the weight of emotional re-enforcement all on one side. This is more accurately a process of *emotionalizing* than of rationalizing, and would have been better so named, for the adjective *rational* carries a connotation very different from that of the noun.

Emotionalizing of conflict is perhaps in the last analysis a matter of simple habit formation, and it may yield to education when educators become as familiar with the elementary principles of conflict as, say tight-rope performers are with the principles of balance. If there is a secret of mental development, it lies in learning to intellectualize, rather than to emotionalize conflict, and some day it may be easier to lay the foundations of a good mind than to learn to walk a tight-rope. In the meantime rationalization remains the unanswerable accusatory thrust by which men slay their intellectual opponents. To say that your opponent is rationalizing is almost as magically effective as calling him a mystic.

Religion is concerned ultimately with the problem of the ethical conflict, which is actually that of expanding *right* and *wrong* respectively, to *greater* and *less* understanding. The religious mind is always constrained in the end to render discriminative judgments and to evaluate wisdoms. Religious teachers are thereby subject to peculiarly poignant temptations. If you are morally sure in your own mind that the highest purposes of character development will be served by a certain teaching, though you cannot quite prove the thing to be objectively true, there is strong temptation to resort to rationalization and to reënforce the weak point with some systematic verbal logic. Theologies are born in this humble manner, from a marriage of factual weakness with moral strength.

Originating as the rationalization of a moral philosophy, a theology sometimes tends to grow like a cancer, infiltrating and obscuring the warm truth and idealism which gave it birth, finally devouring that altogether, and becoming itself the way and the goal of life. The theology is then no longer the frame of a philosophy, moral or otherwise, but is merely the rationalization of a habit system. Yet unhappily the confusing of religion with theology is almost universal, and there are still relatively few who distinguish religious thinking from a particular theology.

Deeply religious minds sometimes come to fear theologies as they fear disease, and often they find themselves arrayed in the ranks of *anti-religious* movements, when their real desire is to combat the suppression of Prometheus. Many who go down in the history of their times as great atheists are the true religious leaders of their day.

Theology may be psychologically defined as the speculative causal explanation of life, in advance of objective demonstrability of the causal factors assumed. In its origins theology is not so much the antithesis as the complement of science. That is, theology travels on ahead of science and at its best may be regarded as the advance prediction of the terrain of understanding. Yet it potentially embodies the very nemesis of human understanding and of ultimate happiness; namely the temptation to believe and teach that which most easily and quickly satisfies elemental wishes.

The point often overlooked by objective minds is that theologians do not always yield to the temptation. There are people in the world, devoted to the problems of theology, who are as self-critical, as cautious, and as fully alive to the danger of rationalization, as the maturest scientific minds. They are very much more rare, for the path to the place they reach is precipitous and beset with temptations of which the scientific mind is totally unaware. Consequently where there is one first-class theological mind in the world there are hundreds of good scientific minds. Theology begins where science ends. *At its best,* it uses the results of scientific thinking as basic data, but its own thinking is not scientific. It is creative.

If original, scientific minds are scarce and inadequately rewarded, a truly creative theological mind is extremely rare, and never rewarded; but may account itself fortunate if allowed to die a comfortable death. Science deals for the most part with fairly safe material, but the creative theologist plays continually with emotional dynamite. He penetrates to the very fountain source of the human wish itself, which underlies all gods and all of the machinations of human intelligence. He plays the Promethean game, in its most dangerous sense.

4. THREE CONCEPTS INTIMATELY RELATED TO CONFLICT

(1) *Compensation*

Sometimes when a blocked channel of expression seems to have caused unusual bafflement and damning up of energy in an individual, the conflict may be resolved through a powerful reënforcement of the blocked wish. The classical example is that of Demosthenes who, frustrated in his oratorical desires by stuttering, is said to have filled his mouth with pebbles and to have orated to the sea until his voice could be heard above the roar of the waves. That was compensation in kind. Often the story is told of the puny youth who by rigid training and self-discipline has developed the muscles of an athlete. Little men sometimes speak in loud voices; this is substitutive compensation. One of the best known of American sagas is that of the self-made man who, starting life with every sort of handicap, has lifted himself step by step by sheer will power and determination until he has at last become president of something. There is an after-dinner story concerning one of the presidents of the United States, which describes his triumphant struggle against the fearful odds of abject poverty, profound obscurity, and almost no I.Q. at all!

The idea of compensation has been used to explain the motivation of all intellectual development. Dewey makes the generalization, "We think because we have to think." That is to say, mind develops in compensation of failure of adaptation at more basic levels. The highly mental type of person is often regarded as one who is not well adapted to the simple fundamentals of life. On college campuses the fraternity boy hears that a girl is the Phi Beta Kappa type and that is usually all he wants to know about her. High-grade scholarship is so frequently a compensatory characteristic in individuals who are socially or personally unattractive, that quite a large proportion of American college students turn away from it as abnormal or off color. This gives rise to an atmosphere in many colleges which discourages and inhibits women in particular from developing their minds.

The psychologists who, following Adler, find in compensation a general key to comprehension of the mind, seem to be supported by the findings of organic pathology. Virchow's famous law, "No hypertrophy without lesion," means simply that wherever overdevelopment has taken place in an organ of the body, it is a compensatory consequence of some injury or strain. Dr. Adler's theory of personality rests simply upon the application of this hypothesis to psychological, as well as to physiological hypertrophy. He thus finds all personality development traceable to some blockage of the will to social power, and for him the compensation concept supports and vindicates a heavily overbalanced second panel social philosophy.

The compensation idea has taken root in popular language through the popularizing of psychoanalytic concepts, and many educated people now go about regarding themselves as overcompensated introverts when they behave in an uninhibited manner, or as suffering from an uncompensated inferiority complex when chastened or inhibitory attitudes are dominant. When the little fellow struts and sticks out his chest or makes a loud noise, he is compensating. Women have learned to compensate for their natural physical imperfections to such an extent that now you can hardly tell what a woman looks like by looking at her. A person disrespectful of words may use such a term as compensation *in place of a theology,* to account for all things. The whole personality may be "explained" as compensation for organic or social inferiority. Compensation becomes a magic vessel into which you pour all your wine. Most people have one or two such words, or at lower intellectual levels one or two proverbs, that explain everything. This is concept stretching, one of the most inviting of intellectual monkey traps.

(2) *Repression*

Since for practical purposes conflict may always be regarded in one of its dimensions as a rivalry between relatively direct, selfish, or instinctive (low) motives, and relatively indirect, socialized, or idealistic (high) motives, there are in this (ethical) dimension two ways in which *resolved* conflict may go. The selfish motive may achieve dominance and the individual will remain uncivilized in a particular matter; or the nobler motive may dominate, in which case the individual moves toward higher civilization. In either event, one of the two wishes remains disappointed, and, in psychoanalytic language, is *repressed.* It is not *whether* there shall be repression but *what* shall be repressed, the more civilized, or the more instinctive motive.

Everybody is to some extent exposed to ideals and civilizing influences. It is therefore theoretically as plausible to think of an uncivilized person as one in whom this vast world of ennobling influence is carried as repressed material in the remote levels of consciousness, as to consider that a highly civilized person carries a similar teeming world of repressed elemental selfish desires in his deeper levels.

By postulating an absolute unconscious, which in the Freudian sense is simply a storehouse of all that has been repressed, the psychologist can make it produce whatever he wishes, like pulling rabbits out of a hat. What is found "repressed" in the "unconscious" depends altogether upon the orientational bias of the father confessor, or of the consulting psychoanalyst. Just as by postulating an absolute God, the priest can lay down any theology that lies within his intellectual grasp, and can readily adduce evidence of a universal hereditary belief in such a theology in the minds of his most untutored parishioners, so likewise can the psychoanalyst do, quite as effectively, with his absolute unconscious. The final decadent steps are first the ritual, then the holy writ, and finally the doctrine of infallibility. All of these can even now be read in the eyes of many a Freudian psychoanalytic zealot.

If you can persuade an individual to accept the postulation of an absolute, it is then easy to convince him of the validity of a set of dream symbols, of the wisdom of an oracle, or of the divine inspiration of a book. By seeming to carry perplexed minds back to something stable and absolute, the priest in whatever guise establishes for them a kind of orientation often for the first time in their lives. They have at last a perspective, some feeling of oneness with their deeper selves and they go through a conversion experience. It is assurance of certainty that they crave. In weakness man seeks a formula; only in strength does he seek understanding. There is continual pressure from the friends of psychoanalysis to make of it the Epimethean formula of salva-tion right-eous-ness. Repression becomes for these people merely the necessary element of sin in the world.

The human mind seeks formulary reassurance of an orientation, and priests have always given it. The psychoanalyst has devised the first successful system for performing this service *in the name of science*, though Herbert Spencer with his conception of necessitous evolution toward higher levels came close to achieving the same goal in a very different way. *Freud is the first modern successful priest of a strict materialism, and he has saved for useful careers many individuals who could never have been reached by any other religion. Yet psychoanalysis like other theologies tends toward extreme intolerance of all that lies outside itself, and has learned to invoke among its own disciples a curse in the name of repression quite as potent as was ever the devil to a simple, believing Christian mind.*

The Freudian religion of expressiveness and extraversion grows rapidly and well in a society suddenly so crowded in upon itself that men must make a *hasty* choice between such a religion and some stern self-disciplinary philosophy calling for a right about face from the headlong rush toward overstimulation. For this old, old religion of self-expressive materialism Freud has written a carefully and intelligently planned modern theology. It is a reaction against the Christian theology, which too violently repressed Prometheus. Freud's new theology would swing the pendulum far to the extreme left, and would in turn repress those elements which in Christian Epimethean thought have been associated with character.

In summary, repression is the cardinal sin concept of a materialistic orientational philosophy. It refers to the relegation of infantile wishes to the unconscious, where they supposedly retain a high degree of specificity, as well as a strong element of "libido," and continue to exercise a profound influence upon personality. Personality is to be made whole by becoming fully aware of these infantile wishes and by making peace with them. This theology works, with certain types of minds, and has in it the seeds of a religion which is essentially the antithesis of the Christian outlook. It may succeed in completing the process of destroying and counteracting the influence of the latter altogether. Yet from the standpoint of what we know of psychology there are two serious flaws in the Freudian theology; namely the assumption of an absolute unconscious, and the supposition that infantile wishes normally retain specific emotional significance in adult life.

In a wider and more general sense the term repression may be used to refer to any conflict resolution in which, instead of intellectualization of the conflict, there has been a hasty or premature or unwise attempt at resolution of it, by supporting too vigorously one side of the balance and opposing the other. In this premature resolution of conflict, the higher, more civilized motive is actually the one most often repressed—a point which Freudian psychoanalysts practically ignore. They seem not to have comprehended that aspiration for the stars *may* be as native and as deeply rooted in the human heart, as craving for the mud.

(3) *Dissociation*

This is a term in which the normal and the pathological grade over into each other so gently that no adequate boundary can be made out between them. There are, for example, certain incompatibilities between parlor habits and swimming-pool habits, and the individual dissociates one from the other. That is perfectly normal dissociation. But in the character of Dr. Jekyl-Mr. Hyde, Stevenson has described a dissociation of so extensive a nature that one of the two dominant patterns is a genuinely uncivilized personality, while in the other almost the perfect antithesis is seen. This is pathological dissociation. There is a cleavage in consciousness inhibiting, rather than promoting, the normal life adaptations.

The splitting off of a part of the normal associational system may take place along many cleavage lines. It may produce an unbalanced focusing of mental energy upon one idea, giving rise in pathology to paranoia. There may be *two* alternating rival systems of consciousness, as in the Dr. Jekyl-Mr. Hyde situation, so common a phenomenon in its normal ranges that seldom does a student read for the first time a description of dissociation without feeling that surely he too is a split personality; and finally, the dissociation cleavage may be a multiple one, resulting in three or more discrete personality systems. This too has perfectly normal manifestations. Many people in ordinary social contacts can serially assume with sincerity a number of mutually incompatible personalities and philosophies. Such dissociation is merely a form of adaptive behavior. It is characteristic of alert, socially adopted persons, especially of good salesmen.

But there is a curious reversal of this kind of dissociational adaptive behavior. Sometimes highly intelligent, closely observant individuals, instead of using their insight into human nature to their own social advantage and thereby behaving more *adaptively*, respond in a strikingly *unadaptive* manner, by overreacting to the hidden antagonisms and incompatibilities of their environment. These individuals appear to take upon themselves the function of compensating, or *correcting* the apparent distortions and trends that they continually observe about them. At intuitive levels such persons are reformers, combating and checking the overaggressive, encouraging and stimulating the sensitive and shy, and always antagonizing those possessing less insight than themselves. This is not an uncommon psychological pattern. I have sometimes called it the correctional personality. It is, I think, very closely related to the Promethean personality, except that its energies are focused too sensitively upon the immediate environment. The correctional personality becomes *unadaptively*[7] different in every social situation. To the outer world the person seems to lack consistency, being at one moment radical among conservatives, and a little later conservative with radicals. This is unquestionably the most universally hated person in the world.

When such personalities succeed by dint of great moral and physical strength in overcoming the terrific social handicap with which they load themselves, they sometimes become the finest educators and the kindest and wisest of administrators, for they possess great insight, and they are almost invariably kind and wise with those who are under their power. But they display a shocking want of "tact" in their relations with persons exercising power over them. In their own minds all things must fit together and make a meaningful system, and they deeply antagonize the compartmental mind, or *adaptively dissociated* mind, which seems to them impenitently to carry a theology running counter to its economics, or a sexual philosophy contradicting its theology as the case may be. The motivation of the correctional personality, so closely related to the character-phyllic mind, constitutes a promising field of analytic study. There is present in these minds a factor preventing them from accepting the normal dissociations of social life; an intense anti-dissociational factor.

We have several times crossed the trail of the terms *extraversion* and *introversion*. The former seems to refer to a condition in which a mind has, in turning the focus of attention resolutely outward, cut itself off or dissociated its active

[7] Unadaptively, from the standpoint of its own happiness and survival; from the standpoint of the outer social good, the reaction may be an adaptive one.

consciousness from its own deeper levels. Such a mind floats on the surface of things and requires continual buoying up by social stimulation. The introvert has similarly turned away from outer stimulation, and has thereby dissociated the real outer world from his consciousness. Christian theology encouraged introversion and the counter-reaction to introversion has produced the ghastly spectacle of overstimulation that is modern urban life. What the reaction to *that* may be, one dare not speculate.

Set in Benedictine Book type.
Format by A. W. Rushmore.
Manufactured by the Haddon Craftsmen, Inc.
Published by HARPER & BROTHERS
New York and London.

INDEX

no